An Index and Guide to Audubon's
BIRDS OF AMERICA

John James Audubon (1785–1851) by John Syme, 1826.
Courtesy of The White House Collection, Washington, D.C.

An Index and Guide to Audubon's BIRDS OF AMERICA

by Susanne M. Low

A Study of the
Double-Elephant Folio of
John James Audubon's
Birds of America,
as Engraved by
William H. Lizars and
Robert Havell.

The American Museum of Natural History
Abbeville Press • Publishers • New York

For Francis Hine Low
with love and appreciation
for his support

Editorial director: Walton Rawls
Editor: Amy Handy
Designer: Stephanie Bart-Horvath

Library of Congress Cataloging-in-Publication Data

Low, Susanne M.
  An index and guide to Audubon's Birds of America.

  Bibliography: p.
  1. Audubon, John James, 1785–1851. Birds of America—
Indexes. I. Title.
QL674.A913L69   1988   598.2973   87-35147
ISBN 0-89659-817-9

CONTENTS

PART ONE

INTRODUCTORY NOTES

John James Audubon was born April 26, 1785, in Santo Domingo (now Haiti) and died January 27, 1851, at Minnie's Land, his estate on the Hudson River just north of what were then the limits of New York City. He was the son of a French naval officer, Jean Audubon, and his mistress, Jeanne Rabine, who died shortly after his birth. When he was six his father took him home to France where he was lovingly raised by his father's tolerant wife.

In 1803 he went to the United States and in 1808 he married Lucy Bakewell. They had two sons, Victor Gifford, born 1809, and John Woodhouse, born 1812. Two daughters died in infancy.

In 1820, after unsuccessful attempts to succeed in business, Audubon settled down to his life's ambition, to paint every bird in the "United States and its Territories," as he defined his own boundaries. Although he did not succeed in capturing every bird, the enormity of what he accomplished is staggering in its size and beauty. Audubon's plan was to have engravings made from his paintings, which he would sell on a subscription basis. His first engraver was W.H. Lizars of Edinburgh, Scotland, who in 1826 and 1827 engraved the first ten plates from which prints were pulled. Then there was a strike in Lizars's studio, and Audubon turned to Robert Havell, Senior, of London. Havell felt he was too old to undertake such a vast project, and so in June 1827 the work was entrusted to his son, Robert Havell, Junior, although the father did work on some of the early plates. After the senior Havell's death in 1832, his son dropped the junior from his name. Havell finished the job in June 1838.

The completed work is known as "The Double Elephant Folio of *The Birds of America*" by John James Audubon. The term "Double Elephant" refers to the large size of the paper. Each print is an engraving printed in black on white paper and then hand-colored by Havell's staff of watercolorists. Today some of the Folios exist in their entirety, but many have been broken up and the prints sold separately. There are a few prints that were never colored; they remain just as they came off the copperplate. The plates were etched, not engraved, but in these notes the term "engraving" is used in a loose sense, as it was in the eighteenth and nineteenth centuries when it covered all the intaglio processes, such as etching, engraving in its strict sense, and aquatint.

Audubon made 433 paintings for *Birds of America*, the majority of which are in watercolor, but pastel, pencil, oil, egg tempera, and ink were also used. For such an enormous project with constant pressure of time it was essential that Audubon have assistants who would help him with backgrounds. Joseph Roberts Mason, a gifted young teenager, joined Audubin in 1820 for a trip down the Mississippi River and stayed with him in Louisiana until the summer of 1822. George Lehman, who was Swiss, worked for Audubon in the east in 1829 and again on the trip to Florida in 1831 and 1832. Maria Martin, the Reverend John Bachman's sister-in-law, met Audubon in Charleston in 1831 and from then on sent him delicate drawings of flowers and insects that he incorporated into his paintings. In addition to these three, Audubon received help from his son, John Woodhouse Audubon, and from his engraver, Robert Havell. Havell did a great deal of the work as Audubon often sent him incomplete paintings with instructions about how he wished them to be finished. Efforts to identify where and when Audubon made his paintings and in just which ones the backgrounds were painted by his assistants are largely speculative.

The New-York Historical Society owns all the original paintings with the exception of the two that are lost: the Blue-gray Gnatcatcher that was painted for Plate LXXXIV and the Black-throated Blue Warbler that was painted for Plate CLV. (Do not confuse the latter with another painting of the Black-throated Blue Warbler, O.P. 426, which was painted for Plate CXLVIII.) The Society assigned a number to each original painting, and hereafter each will be referred to as O.P. plus the number.

From these 433 paintings, 435 plates were made. There are two more plates than paintings because on two occasions Havell made two plates from the birds in one painting. O.P. 186 was split into Plates CCCXCIII and CCCXCV, and O.P. 327 was split into Plates CCCXCIX and CCCCXIV.

The prints were issued in 87 sets of 5 each, each set to have one large plate, one medium, and three small, of which one would be a previously undescribed species. Each print is marked with its number in Roman numerals (a few variants in Arabic) and its set number in Arabic numerals. The first 352 plates depict one species each with the exception of Plate CXLI, which depicts two. Plate CCCLIII shows three species and from then on there are more and more multispecied plates. One plate has ten birds representing five species. Audubon was feeling the pressure to get the job done, and putting several species in one painting moved him more quickly to completion.

Havell finished the first hundred copperplates late in 1830, the second hundred early in 1834, the third hundred early in 1836, and the last hundred and thirty-five in the spring of 1838.

It is impossible to say how many complete Double Elephant Folios were produced, but a fair estimate would be between 175 and 200. In addition there were incomplete sets, sometimes caused by subscribers cancelling their subscription part way through. Furthermore, there were odds and ends; extra prints struck off by Havell that the Audubons gave away as gifts, for example. One could order the complete set from Havell bound in four volumes or unbound, leaving the purchaser free to have it bound as he wished.

Audubon's portrayal of birds in natural positions in their native habitats was an important breakaway from the stiff drawings of stuffed birds that until then had illustrated ornithological works. Audubon was determined to paint each bird life-size. In the case of the larger species this took some doing. For example, note the way the head and neck of the Roseate Spoonbill (Plate CCCXXI) are bent down in a feeding position, a clever way to fit this large bird onto the paper.

This work is solely concerned with Audubon's original paintings for *Birds of America* and the plates engraved from these paintings, the whole known as "The Double Elephant Folio." The primary concern is the birds. Not considered are the Royal Octavo Edition (also called miniature), published in book form with text, for which John T. Bowen was the lithographer, or the Bien Chromolithographs that were commissioned by John Woodhouse Audubon after Audubon's death.

Recently some excellent copies of the Double Elephant Folio have been made by the photo offset process. These copies are so perfect, from their size to the line that reads "Engraved, Printed, & Coloured by R. Havell," that only an expert eye can tell them from the originals. One can tell an engraving from a photo offset by feel, by close inspection with a magnifying glass, which shows the little colored dots that reveal color offset, or by inspection of the watermark, which in the case of original Lizars and Havells is always Whatman. A caveat goes with the latter method as it is possible the watermark might be sliced away when a print is trimmed. It is regrettable that many of these copies have no identification to aid an unwary buyer not sophisticated enough to demand a close inspection.

In 1985 the American Museum of Natural History had prints struck from six original Havell plates. The work was done by Editions Alecto, Ltd., London, by a process called *à la poupée*, one Havell probably would have used had Audubon been able to afford it. In *à la poupée* (so called because the paint dauber is shaped like a little doll) the plates are inked in color rather than in black. Because so much of the color is laid on in the printing, the work of the watercolorists is greatly reduced and what they do add is clearer and more luminous, as the slightly muddy effect caused by painting over black is eliminated. These prints are considered to be even finer than Havell's. Happily they are clearly identified by a stamp on the back.

TRACKING PAINTING, PLATE, AND BIRD

Keeping track of painting, plate, and bird is confusing and complicated, for which there are several basic reasons:

1. Differences between original painting and resulting plate

Havell was a fine artist in his own right and Audubon gave him a very free hand. Audubon often sent paintings of birds with no background, trusting Havell to supply one, which he did very well. If Havell did not like the way Audubon had arranged the birds, he would rearrange them for a more pleasing effect. If he thought there were too many birds in a painting he would put some of them in other plates that he felt could be filled out. For the most confusing of these situations, charts of original paintings can be found in Part III.

2. The nomenclature of the birds

The names of birds in Audubon's time were often different from those used today. Known today by one approved name, a species in Audubon's day could have been known by several different names, depending on the locale and the disparate views of various ornithologists. Audubon's genius was as a portrayer of birds, but as a formal ornithologist he had his limitations. The group in Philadelphia who revered Wilson and resented Audubon's appearance on the scene gave him an unwarranted bad time, but their criticism of his rather cavalier attitude in naming what he thought were new species without paying enough attention to published data was somewhat justified. However, to give Audubon his due, it must be noted that ornithology was in its infancy then, and there was only fragmentary knowledge of the different forms within a species. Audubon himself was the discoverer of many new species, but he could be fooled into claiming a bird as a new species when it was actually a female, immature, or color morph of one already known. Nevertheless, of the ninety birds Audubon considered new to science, thirty-seven proved to be valid new forms recognized to this day, twenty-five of them full species, and the rest subspecies. Of these, fourteen of the species and many of the subspecies are portrayed in *Birds of America.* Considering that until Audubon went to England he worked in a virtual vacuum, with hardly any literature and no fellow ornithologists to consult, his is a remarkable record. Audubon sometimes wrote what he thought was the name of the bird directly on the painting. If he was in error, as he could be, the error might or might not be caught before the legend was engraved for the plate. As to modern nomenclature, advances in the knowledge of what constitutes a genus and a species have been rapid in recent years, causing bewildering changes in birds' names, often to the despair of bird-watchers.

The authority used here is the most recent checklist of the American Ornithologists' Union, 1983. If a bird is commonly known by a name other than that approved by the A.O.U., it is listed with a cross-reference. For example:

Baltimore Oriole   *see* Northern Oriole
Whistling Swan   *see* Tundra Swan

Today the correct way to write out the name of a species is as follows:

Barn Swallow,	*Hirundo*	*rustica*	Linnaeus
[Common Name]	[Genus, italicized and capitalized]	[species, italicized but not capitalized]	[describer]

If the genus in which the describer placed the bird has been changed, the describer's name is placed in parentheses: (Linnaeus). In less formal references, the describer's name is often eliminated. Do not confuse the describer with the discoverer. John Doe might spot a new bird in the United States in the eighteenth century, collect it, and send it to Linnaeus in Sweden. If Linnaeus agreed that it was indeed a new species he would name it, classify it, and publish his findings. Thus John Doe is the discoverer but Linnaeus is the describer.

As mentioned above, ornithology was in its infancy in Audubon's day and the rules of nomenclature were not as widely known nor always agreed upon. In this work when the name on the plate or on the original painting is mentioned, it is written just as found even though it may seem to be an error or a misspelling by present day standards. On O.P. 183 (for Plate CCCLXIX), for example, Audubon wrote Robbin, not Robin. When Audubon wrote the name of a bird, he sometimes capitalized the species and sometimes did not, and he sometimes named the describer and sometimes did not. The scientific name of the bird on the legend of the plate was usually engraved all in capital letters; thus when the name of a bird on the plate legend is referred to in this work, the scientific name will be written in capital letters.

So it can be seen that one species in *Birds of America* can be associated with a myriad of names: its current name, other names by which it has been known, the name on the plate legend, other names on the plate legends of variants, different names for one species when it appears in more than one plate, and the name Audubon wrote on the painting.

3. Variants

Sometimes after a plate had been engraved and prints pulled, Audubon would decide that the legend was in error. The legend would then be reengraved and more prints pulled. This could happen two, three, and, in one case, five times. These different pulls are called variants. One finds variants among the earlier plates where the plate number is in Arabic rather than the customary Roman numerals. Variants are listed under plate numbers in Part II. Although the author has seen most of the variants listed here, there are some known only from the writings of others. In the majority of these the differences are so minute that one suspects they may not be variants at all but simply the result of typographical errors in the text. Rather than not include them, they are listed with the caveat "unconfirmed." The author knows of 145 plates that have one or more variants, some of which also have an unconfirmed variant. In addition there are another 37 plates each of which has an unconfirmed variant. It is very possible there are more variants that have not yet come to light.

LEGENDS

Most legends are below the picture and have the information about the birds in the center, although in some of the early plates they may be left, right, or even above. Most commonly there is an English name, a scientific name, sometimes a describer's name, and sometimes numbers to indicate males, females, and immatures. In some cases there is information about the flora or a line such as "View of Baltimore." On the left is the credit line to Audubon and may read "Drawn from Nature by J.J. Audubon, F.R.S. F.L.S." or "Drawn from Nature & Published by John J. Audubon, F.R.S. F.L.S." F.R.S. stands for Fellow of the Royal Society and F.L.S. for Fellow of the Linnaean Society. One also sees other letters representing different societies to which Audubon was elected. On the right is the credit line to Havell, and it usually reads "Engraved, Printed & Coloured by R. Havell," sometimes followed by a date and sometimes by "London." As noted before, the 435 plates were issued in 87 sets of 5 each. The set number, always in Arabic numerals, is placed in the upper-left corner of the plate. The plate number, in Roman numerals (except for a few in Arabic by mistake), is in the upper right. Not all legends are exactly as described above, especially not the first ten. Because of the complexities of the transfer of these ten plates from Lizars to Havell, details of their legends are in Part II, and in "The First Ten Plates" in Part I.

NUMBER OF SPECIES

There are 457 species depicted in *Birds of America* plus one hybrid and five so-called birds of mystery that may be hybrids or mutations. Other sources may give different totals; this disparity is due to the changes in nomenclature made from time to time by the American

Ornithologists' Union. For example, Audubon's Warbler and the Myrtle Warbler, long considered to be two species, are now one, the Yellow-rumped Warbler.

FOREIGN BIRDS

In Audubon's prospectus for *Birds of America* the lead reads "Birds of America from drawings made during a residence of upwards of twenty-five years in the United States and its territories." When Audubon arrived in this country in 1803 there were seventeen states and by the time *Birds of America* was finished in 1838 there were twenty-seven. In the intervening years all the rest of what would be the continental forty-eight states was a vast hodge-podge that was constantly changing. Parts were territories, some of it was under foreign flags, and much of it was unknown wilderness. Audubon roamed all over the eastern part of this area collecting and painting. For the western parts he relied on skins that were sent to him or that he bought. He made a collecting trip by sea from Maine to Labrador with stops at Newfoundland, Nova Scotia, and New Brunswick, and an unproductive trip along the Gulf coast to Texas. These, then, are the lands from which came the birds in *Birds of America*.

There are, however, instances of birds that were not native to this area and that should not have been included. They are as follows:

Black-Throated Magpie-Jay. Plate xcvi. Mexico.
Audubon believed that the skins from which he painted these birds had been collected on the Columbia River, but this is not true.

Black-throated Mango. Plate clxxxiv. Panama and South America.
The skins of these birds were given to Audubon, but the reputed localities of where they had been collected were undoubtedly incorrect.

Great Crested Grebe. Plate ccxcii. Old world species.
Audubon painted this bird from preserved specimens in London in the mistaken belief that he had seen the bird in Ohio.

Light-mantled Albatross. Plate ccccvii. Subantarctic islands.
Audubon was told the skin of this bird had been collected on the Columbia River but it had not. One can only surmise that the skin reached the West Coast on a ship that had been in the Antarctic.

Crested Bobwhite. Plate ccccxxiii. Central America–northern South America.
Audubon drew this bird from a specimen in the Zoological Society of London.

Little Owl. Plate ccccxxxii. Europe.
Audubon erroneously believed his skin of this bird had been collected in Nova Scotia. It is strictly European.

In addition to the birds listed above, the inclusion of the following species is questionable:

Common Greenshank. Plate CCLXIX. Eurasia.
Audubon's report of a Florida sighting is regarded by the A.O.U. as questionable.

Hooded Siskin. Plate CCCXCIV. South America.
Audubon collected this bird in Kentucky but it is regarded as an escape.

Trudeau's Tern. Plate CCCCIX. Chile and Argentina.
Audubon believed his skin of this bird had been collected in New Jersey, but the A.O.U. regards this as highly questionable.

EXTINCT BIRDS

Carolina Parakeet. Plate XXVI.
Passenger Pigeon. Plate LXII.
Labrador Duck. Plate CCCXXXII.
Great Auk. Plate CCCXLI.

BIRDS NEAR EXTINCTION

Ivory-billed Woodpecker. Plate LXVI.
Bachman's Warbler. Plate CLXXXV.
Eskimo Curlew. Plate CCVIII.
Whooping Crane. Plate CCXXVI.
California Condor. Plate CCCCXXVI.

BIRDS OF MYSTERY

(Probably hybrids or mutations.)
Cuvier's Kinglet. Plate LV.
Carbonated Warbler. Plate LX.
Townsend's Bunting. Plate CCCC.
Blue Mountain Warbler. Plate CCCCXXXIV.
Small-headed Flycatcher. Plate CCCCXXXIV.

MISNUMBERING

There are only three instances of a plate's being misnumbered, an incredibly small figure when one considers the size of the project.

1. The plate of Wilson's Phalarope was wrongly engraved CCLVI. It should have been CCLIV. The true CCLVI is the Reddish Egret.

2. Although most plates of the Tree Swallow are correctly engraved XCVIII, there is a variant engraved 100. The true C is the Marsh Hen, with a variant marked 98.

3. Although most plates of Leach's Storm-Petrel are correctly labeled CCLX, there is a variant labeled CCXL. The true CCXL is the Roseate Tern.

SAME BIRD IN TWO PLATES

There are two instances where the same painting of a bird appears in two different plates.

1. The flying Bluebird at the top of Plate CXIII was added by Havell to Plate XXXVI, which depicts two Cooper's Hawks.

2. The Wilson's Plover on the right in Plate CCIX was added by Havell to the two Purple Sandpipers in Plate CCLXXXIV.

BIRDS AUDUBON DID NOT PAINT

Audubon painted for *Birds of America* every bird a capable bird-watcher might see in the eastern United States, with the exception of the Alder Flycatcher, the Lesser Scaup, the Long-billed Dowitcher, the Caspian Tern, the Smooth-billed Ani, the Yellow-bellied Flycatcher, the Mourning Warbler, the Northern Rough-winged Swallow, the Swainson's Thrush, and the Gray-cheeked Thrush. In addition he missed the Cory's Shearwater and the Sooty Shearwater, which require off-shore observation; the Black-whiskered Vireo and the Snail Kite, restricted to areas of southern Florida; the Brewer's Blackbird, which probably had not worked its way east as it has now; and the Mottled Duck, a Florida bird not described until 1874. He did not note the Heath Hen, the name by which the eastern population (now extinct) of the Greater Prairie-Chicken was known, but he did portray the western bird in Plate CLXXXVI.

Audubon never went far west, and for birds of that area he relied on skins sent to him by correspondents or on skins he purchased. Although this method produced some good results it did not begin to cover the western avian population. Notably lacking are birds of the southwest. Think of how he might have portrayed the Greater Roadrunner, *Geococcyx californianus* (Lesson), or a Pyrrhuloxia, *Cardinalis sinuatus* Bonaparte.

It is also important to remember that many birds taken for granted today were not here in Audubon's time, such as the introduced Cattle Egret, *Bubulcus ibis* (Linnaeus) and the Ring-necked Pheasant, *Phasianus colchicus* Linnaeus.

THE COMPOSITE PLATES

As the publication of *Birds of America* was drawing to a close, Audubon, with McGillivray's help, issued a small volume, *Synopsis of Birds of America,* in which the birds were listed in systematic order. Audubon and two close friends, Dr. Benjamin Phillips of London and Edward Harris of New Jersey, decided to have their copies of *Birds of America* arranged in this systematic order, rather than by plate number as was usually the custom.

By this time Audubon's ornithological knowledge was greatly improved, and so he decided to order the thirteen composite plates that he felt would correct past mistakes and come nearer to his wish to depict male, female, and immature of each species on the same plate, although the latter was not accomplished in every case.

The Hooded Warblers are a good case in point. Plate CX portrays a pair of birds he correctly identified as Hooded Warblers, but he did not recognize the bird in Plate IX as an immature of the same species; thinking he had discovered a new species he named it Selby's Flycatcher. Now, the error recognized, he ordered new prints of Plate

CX into which the immature in Plate IX was incorporated. The original legend and number of the major Plate CX were unchanged, which might seem curious unless one is aware that these thirteen plates were specifically for the Audubon–Phillips–Harris copies; Audubon did not feel that with their knowledge they needed to be instructed by a legend change. In addition the specifics were in the *Synopsis*.

In working on these composites Havell did no further engraving on the plate. He simply stopped out a space on the major plate to make room for the overprinting of the bird from the minor plate. In two cases two birds were added. Havell then brought it all together by drawing and coloring directly on the print the addition of leaves, branches, and sometimes background.

Six prints were pulled from each of the thirteen. The three best examples were inserted into the Audubon–Phillips–Harris copies, each laid directly behind the original print of the same number. The remaining thirty-nine went into Havell's stockpile. A few have been found here and there in copies of *Birds of America* and it may be that there are more unrecognized, but the three copies—Audubon's, Phillips's, and Harris's—are the only ones that had all thirteen.

The Audubon and Phillips copies are safe in the United States. There is no trace of the Harris copy. Incomplete evidence suggests it was broken up.

Following is a list of the thirteen. The current name of the species is listed with the name on the legend following in parentheses if different.

Plate XII originally depicted two male and one female Northern Orioles (Baltimore Oriole). A female Northern Oriole (Baltimore Oriole) from Plate CCCCXXXIII was added at upper left.

Plate XXIII originally depicted a pair of Common Yellowthroats (Yellow-breasted Warbler or Maryland Yellow Throat). The male Common Yellowthroat (Roscoe's Yellow-throat) from Plate XXIV was added at center right.

Plate CVII originally depicted two Gray Jays (Canada Jay). An immature Gray Jay (Canada Jay) from Plate CCCCXIX was added at upper left.

Plate CX originally depicted a pair of Hooded Warblers. The immature Hooded Warbler (Selby's Flycatcher) from Plate IX was added at bottom right.

Plate CXXXV originally depicted one male Blackburnian Warbler. A female Blackburnian Warbler from Plate CCCXCIX was added at upper right of center.

Plate CXL originally depicted a pair of Pine Warblers (Pine Creeping Warbler). An immature Pine Warbler (Vigor's Warbler or Vigor's Vireo) from Plate XXX was added just above center.

Plate CCIX originally depicted two Wilson's Plovers in breeding plumage. A Wilson's Plover (not named in legend) from Plate CCLXXXIV was added at lower right.

Plate CCXXX originally depicted two Sanderlings (Ruddy Plover or Sanderling) in winter plumage. One Sanderling (no common name but scientific name *Tringa arenaria*) in summer plumage from Plate CCLXXXV was added at lower left.

Plate CCCLIV originally depicted two male Western Tanagers (Louisiana Tanager) and a pair of Scarlet Tanagers. The female Western Tanager (Louisiana Tanager) from Plate CCCC was added at center left.

Plate CCCLXIX originally depicted a male Sage Thrasher (Mountain Mocking bird) and a pair of Varied Thrushes. A female Varied Thrush from Plate CCCCXXXIII was added lower right.

Plate CCCLXXIII originally depicted an Evening Grosbeak and two male and one female Black-headed Grosbeaks (Spotted Grosbeak). A female and young male Evening Grosbeak from Plate CCCCXXIV were added, male at upper left and female at upper right.

Plate CCCLXXXVIII originally depicted a male Tricolored Blackbird (Nuttall's Starling), a female, immature, and the head of a Yellow-headed Blackbird (Yellow-headed Troopial), and a male Northern Oriole (Bullock's Oriole). A pair of Northern Orioles (Bullock's Oriole) from Plate CCCCXXXIII was added, male at upper left and female at lower left.

Plate CCCXCVIII originally depicted a Lazuli Bunting (Lazuli Finch), a Clay-colored Sparrow (Clay-coloured Finch), and a pair of Dark-eyed Juncos (Oregon Snow Finch). A Lazuli Bunting (Lazuli Finch) from Plate CCCCXXIV was added at upper right.

A quick check to spot a composite:		
Plate No.	No. of birds in original	No. of birds in composite
XLII	3	4
XXIII	2	3
CVII	2	3
CX	2	3
CXXXV	1	2
CXL	2	3
CCIX	2	3
CCXXX	2	3
CCCLIV	4	5
CCCLXIX	3	4
CCCLXXIII	4	6
CCCLXXXVIII	5	7
CCCXCVIII	4	5

ORNITHOLOGICAL TERMS

To assist readers unfamiliar with ornithological terms, these definitions may prove helpful.

Accidental:
Used to describe a species's appearance in an area where there are one or possibly two records and little chance of its recurring.

Casual:
Used to describe a species's appearance in an area where there are two or more records and a fair possibility of its recurring.

Scientific name (in Latin and/or Greek):
Birds are of the class Aves, which is further divided into orders, families, genera, and species. Only the genus and species are given in a bird's scientific name.

Species:
A population in the wild, whose individuals breed with one another and produce viable, fertile offspring.

Subspecies:
A subdivision of a species that is morphologically slightly different from other subspecies within the species. These subspecies when brought together can breed and produce viable, fertile young.

SIZE AND WATERMARKS

The original folio of *Birds of America* is known as the Double Elephant Folio, the name being taken from the size of the paper. The Oxford English Dictionary defines "elephant" as a size of drawing and cartridge paper 28" x 23" and "double elephant" as a similar paper 40" x 26 1/2". (Note that "double elephant" is not twice the size of "elephant.") The paper Havell used was 39 1/2" x 29 1/2" and, while not exactly the double elephant size as defined in the Oxford English Dictionary, was close enough to be described as such. Audubon in his prospectus announcing *Birds of America* said in the particulars, "The size of the Work will be double Elephant Folio and printed on the finest drawing paper."

In the late eighteenth century James Whatman was a well-known papermaker. By Audubon's time Whatman was gone from the scene. A family called Hollingsworth had part of the old Whatman company with rights to the watermark J Whatman/Turkey Mill, and a man called Balston had part with rights to the watermark J Whatman. The two firms were leading paper makers and great rivals. Not only did Havell use their paper exclusively for *Birds of America* but Audubon also used it for his watercolors.

The paper watermarked J Whatman/1827 (to 1838) was of a heavier weight, with the watermark located fairly close to the center of the paper. The paper watermarked J Whatman/Turkey Mill was lighter, with the watermark located very close to the edge of the paper. Some believe the heavier paper produced prints that held their brilliance while those of the lighter softened with age.

A watermark has a figurative design, while a countermark contains just the name or initials of the papermaker sometimes with a date; so strictly speaking both Whatman papers are countermarked, but it seems simpler here to go with familiar usage of the term watermark.

Prints were pulled from the plates as the orders came in. Thus one can see prints of the Wild Turkey (I) with watermark dates as early as 1828 and as late as 1834. It is tempting to date the pulling of all the prints by the watermark date on the paper, but this may not always be an accurate criterion. Imagine a scene in Havell's studio in 1832: Havell is pulling prints on paper watermarked 1832; he gets to the bottom of the pile and finds a few sheets of paper left over from 1828, which he then uses. As a general rule, however, the watermark date is a fairly good indication of the date the print was pulled.

In regard to Audubon's statement that the finest paper was to be used, there is some doubt. Whatman paper was very fine indeed, but some feel that Havell did not purchase the top of the line, as there are examples of better Whatman paper from the 1830s that do not have the tendency to fox as does the paper that Havell used. If this is true, as it well may be, it was probably due to an effort to keep costs down. Money was always in short supply during the making of *Birds of America*.

The areas on the paper actually occupied by the plates differ. Over eighty of the largest and most impressive plates, such as the Osprey, take up almost the entire sheet. Over a third are about 19" x 12", the most common size. The remainder are various sizes between these two, with a few slightly smaller. Some are greater in height than width and some are the reverse.

When folios were first broken up and the plates sold separately, the prints were often trimmed down to a suitable border. No one dreamed in those days how valuable Audubons would become, and not enough care was taken. Trimming was done carelessly, and legends, plate numbers, and set numbers were often partially or wholly cut off. Often cut off too was the watermark, especially in the case of paper watermarked J Whatman/Turkey Mill where the watermark was close to the edge of the paper. The print itself in some instances was glued onto cardboard that was not acid free, with disastrous results. Happily, conservators can rescue many of these, but time is of the essence and work should commence immediately.

VALUE

The original price of the Double Elephant Folio of the *Birds of America* was £182.14 in England and $1000 in the United States. This averaged out to $2.30 a print. In 1973 a Folio sold for $246,000, in 1977 one went for $396,000, and in February 1984 one was sold in London for £1,100,000, which at that time was $1,540,000 or an average of $3,540 a print.

It is a tragedy to see these folios broken up, but the economic fact is that the seller can realize a great deal more money by selling the prints individually. The rise in the value of the prints in the past fifteen years has been meteoric. The Snowy Heron (CCXLII) was valued in 1970 at $2,200 and sold in 1983 for $25,300. In the same period the Canvasback (CCCI) went from $2,500 to $18,700 and the Wild Turkey (I) from $3,500 to $35,200. In 1980 an incomplete set of 345 prints sold for $1,308,670. Recent major auctions from 1982 to 1987 realized from over a million and a half dollars to over a million and three-quarters.

For a great many years the Wild Turkey (I) was considered the most valuable, but it now shares honors with others. In the 1982 sale the three highest prices were $35,200 for the Wild Turkey (I), $33,000 for the Trumpeter Swan (CCCCVI), and $28,600 for the Great Blue Heron (CCXI). In the 1983 sale the tops were $45,100 for the Trumpeter Swan (CCCCVI), $41,800 for the Great Blue Heron (CCXI), and $35,200 for the American Flamingo (CCCCXXXI). In the 1985 sale the tops were $30,800 for the Great Blue Heron (CCXI), $29,700 for the American White Pelican (CCCXI), and $28,600 for the American Flamingo (CCCCXXXI). In the 1987 sale honors went to the Trumpeter Swan (CCCCVI) at $48,400, the Common American Swan (CCCCXI) at $46,200, and the Great Blue Heron (CCXI) and the American Flamingo (CCCCXXXI) both at $41,800. It is curious that the interest in swans generated by the high price paid for the Trumpeter Swan in 1983 drove the Common American Swan so far up from a previous high of $24,200. Sixteen others have brought over $20,000 each: Roseate Spoonbill, Great White Heron, Mallard, Snowy Heron, Snowy Owl, Canada Goose, Great American Hen, Carolina Parrot, Eider Duck, Louisiana Heron, Long-billed Curlew, Northern Bob White, Whooping Crane, Wood Stork, Osprey, and Iceland or Jer Falcon. The rest went from these highs to a low of $660.

Many factors determine what a print will bring, particularly in the excitement of a high-powered auction. The condition of the print is of vital importance. Personal preference, size, historical association, and beauty all play a part. Some prints are more beautifully colored than others due to the varying degrees of competence among the colorists in Havell's studio. Probably the strongest factor is the competitiveness of the bidders. It was these last two points that drove the Trumpeter Swan (CCCCVI) up to the astonishing price of $45,100 in the 1983 sale.

Auctions produce curious results. The author's favorite, the Osprey (LXXXI), is surely one of the most beautiful of all the plates, yet it has never brought more than $22,000. It is an interesting exercise to study the Trumpeter Swan side by side with the Osprey and puzzle why the former brought over twice as much as the latter.

Some galleries report that buyers tend to shy away from plates in which there is any hint of cruelty, such as the Peregrine Falcons feeding on dead ducks in Plate XVI or the Golden Eagle flying off with a Snowshoe Hare in Plate CLXXXI, which routinely bring only only about $4,500. Perhaps the Osprey's talons digging into the flesh of the Weakfish adversely affects some. On the other hand, the Red-tailed Hawk attacking a covey of Bobwhites in Plate LXXVI recently went for $20,350 even though it is a rather savage depiction.

Historical association, such as the early nineteenth-century view of Charleston in the background of the Long-billed Curlew (CCXXXI), enhances a print's value. Yet the three prints of the Bald Eagle—our national bird—have each brought only a modest sum. One can speculate endlessly about why some prints bring more than others.

HAVELL'S TECHNIQUE

Of all the author's research into *Birds of America*, the matter of Havell's technique has proved to be the most interesting.

The term "engraving," in its loosest sense, can be a catchall for any process whereby a print is pulled from an incised metal plate. The proper term is "intaglio," which covers many different processes: engraving (in its strict sense), etching, aquatint, mezzotint, drypoint, and others. Only engraving, etching, and aquatint concern us here.

To create an engraving, the artist incises the image directly onto a metal plate, preferably copper, with a tool called a burin. The plate is then inked, wiped clean so only the ink in the incised lines remains, and the paper pressed to the plate to receive a transfer of the image.

To create an etching, the artist covers the plate with a ground composed of wax and resinous substances and then draws on this ground with a sharp tool down to, but not into, the plate. When the plate is dipped into an acid bath, the acid bites into the lines on the plate exposed by the artist. The plate is then cleaned, inked, wiped so only the ink in the etched lines remains, and the paper pressed to the plate to receive the image.

Aquatinting is a form of etching, but the term is misleading because the process has nothing to do with water or tinting. The term comes from the nitric acid (aquaforties) which is used to bite the plate. Some believe that the term arose because the results of aquatinting are reminiscent of the brushed-in shadings of watercolors (aquarelles), but in all probability the first explanation is correct. Lizars did not use aquatint on the first ten plates, and much of the retouching that Havell did to these plates was the addition of this process.

To create an aquatint, the metal plate is covered with a rosin dust, which is then heated so that it bubbles and then hardens into a congestion of minute particles of rosin, each one surrounded by the exposed metal, the whole making a porous surface. The area not to be aquatinted is stopped out, and the plate is then immersed in an acid bath where the acid eats away at the exposed surface of the plate. The artist then removes the plate, stops out more areas with varnish, and returns the plate to the bath where the acid bites deeper into the remaining exposed surface. This can be done as many times as the artist wishes. When a print is pulled from such a plate it will have subtle shadings from palest gray to black.

When aquatint is used in conjuction with other processes, it is done last. The rosin-dust ground is transparent, so the artist can see what has been done and thus be guided.

The prints of the Double Elephant Folio are customarily referred to as engravings primarily because of the line below the print that reads "Engraved, printed, and coloured by R. Havell." In the eighteenth and nineteenth centuries the word "engraving" was used in its loosest sense and covered a number of the intaglio processes already described. All evidence points to the fact that etching was Havell's primary process, with the secondary addition of aquatint. Possibly he occasionally engraved a line when it suited a particular detail.

Two pieces of research back this up. One well-qualified print expert made an intensive study of a copy of the Double Elephant Folio and came to the conclusion that the plates were indeed etched, adding that "etched lines are characteristically blunt-ended and rather squiggly compared to the taper-ended and rather more curved engraved lines." The other opinion comes from the firm in London that recently published prints pulled from six original Havell plates. They report that without question the plates were etched with the addition of aquatint. They mention in particular that the "v" shape of an engraved line is very distinctive and that there was no evidence of engraving on these plates. So we have two authoritative opinions in agreement; one from the evidence on the prints and the other from the evidence on the six original plates.

Before starting work on a clean plate, the image must somehow be put on the plate to guide the artist. There are several methods, but it is not known which one Havell used. It is thought that he must have traced directly off Audubon's paintings so carefully that no trace of the operation shows. It is possible that he then followed a method in which the tracing paper is dampened, laid face down on the plate (thus taking care of the reverse), and paper and plate run through the press. The damp paper is then peeled off, leaving the graphite of the tracing pencil on the plate. All of this is pure speculation; no one knows for certain what method he used.

Havell employed a special man who engraved the letters of the legends, the plate numbers, and the set numbers. He did beautiful work, as one can see, but Audubon complained regularly about his errors.

After the plates were inked in black and plates and paper sent through the press, the prints were turned over to the colorists, who were supplied with the finest watercolors, some breathtaking in their beauty and brilliance such as the blue in the ruff of the Ruffed Grouse. Occasionaly Audubon would complain about a slightly muddy effect caused by painting over the black lines, which would not have occurred had he been able to afford the *à la poupée* process whereby the plate is inked in color.

It would not have been possible for Havell to complete 425 plates by himself between 1827 and 1838: there simply wasn't enough time. So we must assume that he had assistants, but the quality of the work also allows us to assume that he kept a close watch over any plate he did not do entirely himself.

When Havell emigrated to America in 1839 he had all 435 copper plates shipped over and consigned to "Mr. Hall's store" in New York. Many were ruined in an 1845 fire. The surviving 350 were then stored on the Audubon estate until 1871 when Lucy Audubon, desperate for money, sold them for scrap metal to the Ansonia Brass and Copper Co. Thanks to the alertness of a young boy, about a quarter were saved from the melting pot at the last minute. Mr. William E. Dodge, the president of the company, took an interest in the plates and gave them to individuals and such institutions as the American Museum of Natural History and the Smithsonian. A letter in the archives of the Smithsonian Institution, dated April 23, 1884, from Mr. Dodge to Spencer Fullerton Baird, Secretary of the Institution, states that before giving the plates away Mr. Dodge had them cleaned, made perfectly flat, faced with nickel to preserve them, and the engraved lines filled in with gold bronze. About 85 survive today.

THE FIRST TEN PLATES

Plates I through x were engraved, printed, and colored by William H. Lizars of Edinburgh. They were marked in the legend, "Engraved by W.H. Lizars, Edinr." The author has never seen prints of Plate VII or

Plate x so marked without the addition of a Havell credit line. Some do, perhaps, exist, or it is possible that Lizars never pulled prints from these plates.

Before Lizars could commence work on the third number, Plates xi to xv, the colorists in his studio went on strike and all work ceased. Audubon had grown unhappy about the quality of the colorists' work, so the strike was fortuitous in that it brought matters to a head, forcing him to make the change that led him to the Havells of London. Robert Havell, Sr., felt he was too old for such a vast project so the work was entrusted to his son, Robert Havell, Jr., although the elder Havell worked on some of the early plates.

Audubon owned the Lizars plates, which he turned over to Havell who used them to make more prints The Havells also colored prints Lizars had pulled but not finished. Some of the prints Havell pulled were from the plates just as Lizars left them, but others were from the plates after Havell had "retouched" them. Lizars did not use aquatint, and the "retouching" Havell did was to add this process that produced subtle shading. There is a widely held belief that Havell, Jr., added aquatint to all ten of Lizars's plates, but in fact he only did so to Plates I, II, VI, and VII. In later variants of Plates II, III, IV, V, and X Lizars's name was left off the legend entirely. It was not a very gracious thing to do and justifiably Lizars was highly annoyed.

There are two to five variants of each of the first ten plates on which one can find one or more of the following lines: "Engraved by W. H. Lizars, Edinr."; "Retouched by R. Havell Junr."; "Coloured by R. Havell, Sr."; "Engraved, Printed & Coloured by R. Havell Junr."

Two plates need special comment:

Plate III, Prothonotary Warbler. There is an often told story that when Audubon was considering Havell, Havell engraved Plate III as a sample of his work even though Lizars had done it, and that Audubon was so pleased with it he hired Havell on the spot. The closest inspection of a Lizars III next to a Havell III gives no indication that two plates were involved. Both come from the Lizars plate. So the old story seems to be a legend that has been repeated and embroidered over the years with no evidence to back it. In the many, many books in which this story is repeated, Plate III is always the one mentioned except for one book that says it was the Baltimore Oriole, Plate XII. This version could very well be true.

Plate VI, Hen Turkey. Variant 3 is marked "Engraved by W.H. Lizars" with no mention of Havell, but in this variant it is clear that Havell had added aquatint and the snail in the corner to the plate before the prints were made. It would seem that the "Retouched by R. Havell Junr." was left off the legend by mistake, an error that was corrected in the later variant 4.

It is interesting to compare Lizars's work with Havell's. Lizars was a competent and well-respected engraver, but in his plates bird and background tend to be all of one tone and the work is a bit fussy. Havell's plates seem to glow by contrast, the birds stand out, and there is a beautiful clarity of line.

PERSONS WHOSE NAMES APPEAR IN THE NOMENCLATURE OF *BIRDS OF AMERICA*.

Audubon, John James, 1785–1851. Audubon considered himself to be the describer of many of the species in *Birds of America*. However many of these species turned out to have been previously described by others. Nonetheless, Audubon is today the accredited describer of fourteen of the species in *Birds of America*. Two birds have borne Audubon's name but there is only one today.
1. Audubon's Shearwater, *Puffinus lherminieri* Lesson (Plate CCXCIX)
2. For many years the warbler in Plate CCCXCV was known as Audubon's Warbler but today it and the Myrtle Warbler are one species, the Yellow-rumped Warbler, *Dendroica coronata* (Linnaeus).

Bachman, The Reverend John, 1790–1874. Pastor of St. John's Lutheran Church, Charleston, S.C. Audubon met Bachman in Charleston in 1831. Bachman, interested in the natural sciences, took a shine to Audubon and they became great friends. Two of Bachman's daughters married Audubon's sons, although they died young and the boys married again. Bachman's sister-in-law Maria Martin (later his second wife) painted flora and insects for Audubon. Bachman co-authored the *Quadrupeds of North America* with Audubon. Audubon named two species for Bachman, the Bachman's Sparrow in Plate CLXV and the Bachman's Warbler in Plate CLXXXV. He also named one of the oystercatchers in Plate CCCCXXVII, for Bachman, thinking it to be a new species, but here he was wrong.

Bartram, William, 1739–1823. Son of the famous botanist John Bartram, and a famed naturalist in his own right. Bartram lived in Philadelphia, but he died the year before Audubon arrived there to meet many of the city's scientific community. It is a great pity these two great explorers of America's wilderness never met. Two species in *Birds of America* were named for Bartram but in both cases the name did not survive. The Bartram's Vireo in Plate CCCCXXXIV is a Red-eyed Vireo; the Bartram Sandpiper in Plate CCCIII is an Upland Sandpiper.

Bewick, Thomas, 1753–1828. Famed British engraver on wood and author of classics on British fauna. Audubon visited Bewick in Newcastle in 1827. Bewick was impressed by Audubon, befriended him, and secured for him eight subscribers to *Birds of America*. Audubon named the Bewick's Wren, Plate XVIII, in his honor.

Bonaparte, Charles Lucien Jules Laurents, Prince of Canino and Musigano, 1803–1857. Son of Napoleon's brother, Lucien. He married his first cousin, Princess Zenaide, daughter of Napoleon's brother, Joseph. He lived in the United States from 1824 to 1833, and as an eminent ornithologist was a member of the Philadelphia scientific community. He wrote the four volume *American Ornithology*. Audubon and Bonaparte had a very patchy off-and-on-again relationship. Audubon was difficult and Bonaparte had an unattractive habit of claiming as his own ornithological information he had elicited from others. There was a fearful row over a hawk Audubon claimed as a new species and named the Stanley Hawk (see Lord Stanley). This species had previously been named for Cooper (see William Cooper) and described by Bonaparte. Audubon was wrong and today the bird is the Cooper's Hawk, Plates CXLI and XXXVI. Audubon was very bitter about Bonaparte's including information Audubon had given him in a paper he published in 1837 without giving Audubon any acknowledgment or thanks. At one point Audubon almost asked Bonaparte to collaborate on *Birds of America*, as he felt he needed his scientific expertise, but dropped the idea when Bonaparte made it clear that he, a prince, was above collaborating with Audubon, a commoner. Audubon credited Bonaparte with being the describer of over thirty species in *Birds of America*, but only nine of these are credited to him today. Audubon did not recognize that the young female warbler in Plate V was a Canada Warbler and erroneously thinking he had a new species named it for Bonaparte. The gull in Plate CCCXXIV was named for Bonaparte.

Bonaparte, Princess Zenaide Charlotte Julie. Eldest daughter of Napoleon's brother, Joseph, who was King of Spain from 1808 to 1813. She married her cousin, Charles (see above) in 1822. The Zenaida Dove, Plate CLXII, was named in her honor.

Brandt, Johann Friederich, 1802–1879. German zoologist, paleontologist, and geographist. He spent fifty years in Russia and was the describer of Brandt's Cormorant, Plate CCCCXII.

Brewer, Thomas Mayo, 1814–1880. Boston physician who gave up medicine to be an editorial writer and book publisher. An enthusiastic ornithologist and oologist, he exchanged information with Audubon. Audubon thought he had a new species of duck, which he first called Bemaculated then changed to Brewer's to honor his friend. Audubon worried about this bird and finally identified it correctly as a hybrid, Mallard x Gadwall—Plate CCCXXXVIII. Brewer's Blackbird and Brewer's Sparrow, neither in *Birds of America*, also honor Brewer.

Bullock, William, 1775– ? English traveler, naturalist, and entrepreneur. He did extensive natural history research in Mexico. The Bullock's Oriole, Plates CCCLXXXVIII and CCCCXXXIII, which used to be a separate species, was named for him. Today the Bullock's Oriole and the Baltimore Oriole are conspecific under the name Northern Oriole, *Icterus galbula* (Linnaeus).

Children, John George, 1777–1852. Secretary of London Royal Society, librarian at the British Museum, editor of scientific journals. Audubon met Children in London. Children and Lord Stanley put Audubon up for membership in the London Royal Society. Children became a close friend of Audubon's and assisted him in his dealing with Havell. Audubon thought the species in Plate XXXV was new and named it for Children but the birds turned out to be Yellow Warblers.

Clark, William, 1770–1838. Co-leader of the Lewis and Clark expedition of 1803. Audubon met William Clark and his brother, Gen. George Rogers Clark, when all three lived in Louisville, Kentucky.

Two of the species discovered on the 1803 expediton were named for the expedition's leaders: the Clark's Nutcracker, Plate CCCLXII, and Lewis' Woodpecker, Plate CCCCXVI.

Cooper, William, 1798– ? Ornithologist and member of the New York Lyceum. Audubon met Cooper in New York. At first cool, Cooper warmed to Audubon. Then came the famous row over the hawk, which had already been named for Cooper and described by Bonaparte. Audubon insisted it was a new species, called it Stanley Hawk, and painted it for Plates CXLI and XXXVI. Audubon was wrong and today the bird is the Cooper's Hawk. Audubon credited Cooper as the describer of two species in *Birds of America* but only one holds good today.

Cuvier, Baron George L.C.F.D., 1769–1832. Revered scientist of France. Cuvier was extremely hostile to any form of evolutionary teaching, which was one reason why the doctrine of evolution was so slow in establishing itself in France. Audubon visited Cuvier at the Jardin des Plantes and was courteously received. Audubon had already named a bird for Cuvier, Cuvier's Kinglet, Plate LV. This is a bird of mystery as no other like it has ever been seen.

Gould, John, 1804–1881. Famed British portrayer of birds. When the Audubons were living on Wimpole Street, London, the Goulds called on them. Mrs. Gould was an accomplished lithographer and did Gould's birds. Audubon was jealous of Gould's fame and financial success. Gould loaned Audubon the House Finch that Audubon portrayed in Plate CCCCXXIV and the Large-billed Puffins he portrayed in Plate CCXCIII. Audubon credited Gould as the describer of one species in *Birds of America* but the credit belongs to another today.

Harlan, Dr. Richard, 1796–1843. Quaker doctor and zoologist of Philadelphia. Harlan befriended Audubon and stood up for him against the Philadelphia scientific community. Audubon discovered a new hawk and named it Black Warrior, *Falco harlani*. The name Black Warrior didn't last but the "*harlani*" did and for many years it was called Harlan's Hawk, but today it has been reclassified as a subspecies of the Red Tail Hawk.

Harris, Edward. Gentleman farmer and naturalist of Moorestown, New Jersey. Harris was a true friend to Audubon, often advancing him money. He accompanied Audubon on two expeditions, to the Texas coast in 1837 and up the Missouri in 1843, a trip about which he wrote a book. The Harris' Hawk in Plate CCCXCII was named for him as was the Harris' Sparrow, not depicted in *Birds of America*.

Havell, Robert, Jr., 1793–1878. The engraver of *Birds of America*. Audubon did not recognize the Forster's Tern in Plate CCCCIX, and thinking he had a new species he named it for Havell. It is very sad that Audubon did not name a truly new species for Havell and thus perpetuate the name of this man who by his magnificent engravings contributed so much to *Birds of America*. The correct pronunciation of Havell is debatable. The late Mrs. Herman Wunderlich, the highly respected expert on early American art, always insisted that it was pronounced as in "shovel." Samplings of Havells in the current London telephone directory found some who pronounce their name as in "paddle" and some as in "la belle." One occasionally hears it as in "haven," but current usage favors it as in "la belle."

Henslow, The Reverend John Steven, 1796–1861. Professor at Cambridge University, England. In 1831 Audubon advised Cambridge that vol. I of their subscription to *Birds of America* was ready. In an aside to Henslow, he asked for his help in getting payment. It was Henslow who was responsible for getting his pupil Darwin on the *Beagle*. Audubon named Henslow's Sparrow, Plate LXX, in his honor.

Leach, William Elford, 1791–1836. English authority on crustacea; worked in the British Museum. Leach's Storm-Petrel was named in his honor, Plate CCLX.

LeConte, Major John, 1818–1891. Bright young naturalist. One report says Audubon met him in Savannah, Georgia, in 1831 and another says St. Augustine, Florida, in 1832. Perhaps both are true. Audubon discovered and described a sparrow he named for LeConte. He did not paint this bird for *Birds of America* but did include it in the 1844 Octavo Edition. Even though Le Conte's name does not appear in *Birds of America*, it seems a word about him is appropriate.

Lewis, Meriwether, 1774–1809. Co-leader of the Lewis and Clark expedition of 1803. See Clark, William.

Lincoln, Thomas. A young friend of Audubon's. Lincoln shot and gave to Audubon a new species, which Audubon described and named for him. He first called it "Tom's Finch," later "Lincoln's Finch," and then "Lincoln's Pinewood Finch." It is now Lincoln's Sparrow, Plate CXCIII.

MacGillivray, William, 1796–1852. Professor at Edinburgh University, Scotland. He was Darwin's companion on collecting walks on the east coast of Scotland just prior to Darwin's voyage on the *Beagle*. While writing his *Ornithological Biography* that described the birds in *Birds of America*, Audubon was acutely conscious of his limitations. His English was poor, his education limited, and his formal ornithological knowledge spotty. His wife, Lucy, smoothed out his English but he was in great need of someone to help with the scientific details. With the greatest good fortune he was able to hire MacGillivray. Although MacGillivray bristled a bit because he felt Audubon did not appreciate how much he contributed, in the end Audubon gave handsome acknowledgment. Audubon did not recognize the species in Plate CCCLV as a Seaside Sparrow and, thinking it a new species, he named it for MacGillivray. When Audubon painted the birds in Plate CCCXCIX he thought they were Mourning Warblers and had Havell so label the plate. Later he decided he was wrong and in fact had a new species. He named it MacGillivray's Warbler, a name good to this day.

Nuttall, Thomas, 1786–1859, and John Kirk Townsend. Nuttall, a

Boston naturalist, and Townsend, a Philadelphia pharmacist and scientist, went on the Wyeth expedition to the Columbia River. After some difficult negotiations Audubon purchased a large number of the bird skins they brought back. At first enthusiastic about his purchase, he later cooled due to the poor condition of some of the skins and the carelessness with which the accompanying field notes had been written. Nevertheless many of these skins were models for portrayals in *Birds of America*. Audubon is the describer of two species he named in Nuttall's honor: the Yellow-billed Magpie, *Pica nuttalli* (Audubon) in Plate CCCLXII, and the Common Poorwill, *Phalaenoptilus nuttalli* (Audubon), not in *Birds of America*. In addition, Audubon is the describer of the Tricolored Blackbird in Plate CCCLXXXVIII, which he called Nuttall's Starling. The species Plate CLXXV that Audubon called Nuttall's lesser-marsh Wren is a Sedge Wren. Nuttall's Woodpecker is not in *Birds of America*.

Ord, George, 1781–1866. Member of the Philadelphia Academy of Science. After Alexander Wilson's death Ord completed his great work. As did many others in the Philadelphia scientific community, Ord considered Audubon to be a threat to Wilson's supremacy. He carried his dislike to extremes and developed a maniacal hatred for Audubon. When he stumbled upon the fact that Charles Waterton of England also harbored a bitter dislike for Audubon, he teamed up with him and the two men made a life's work of persecuting Audubon. Ord is the credited describer of four species in *Birds of America*.

Rathbone, Mrs. William, and her sons, Richard and William, Jr. Audubon met the Rathbones in England in 1826. They became great friends and supporters of Audubon. They were a prominent family with a large house in Liverpool and another, Green Bank, in the country, and were in a position to be of enormous help to Audubon. Audubon did not recognize the females in Plate LXV as Yellow Warblers and thinking erroneously that he had a new species named it for the Rathbones.

Roscoe, William, 1753–1831. English member of Parliament, distinguished poet, author, botanist, and foremost historian of his day. He met Audubon through the Rathbones and befriended him. Audubon did not recognize the bird in Plate XXIV as a Common Yellowthroat; thinking it a new species he called it Roscoe's Yellow-throat.

Sabine, Joseph, 1770–1837. English naturalist, horticulturist, and one of the founders of the Linnaean Society. He was the describer of Sabine's Gull, Plate CCLXXXV.

Say, Thomas, 1787–1834. Eminent Philadelphia naturalist. He was a great-grandson of John Bartram, the famous botanist, and thus nephew of William Bartram, who encouraged him. He was a founder of the Philadelphia Academy of Natural History. Because of his work *American Entomology*, he is known as the father of entomology in America. In 1825 he joined Owen's utopian community in New Harmony, Indiana. Audubon shipped insects to Say from his various travels. Bonaparte named the Say's Phoebe, Plate CCCLIX, in his honor.

Selby, Prideaux J., 1788–1867. Eminent British naturalist and ornithological painter with whom Audubon had a prickly relationship. Audubon did not recognize the immature bird in Plate IX as a Hooded Warbler and thinking he had a new species named it Selby's Flycatcher. Lizars, who engraved the first ten plates in *Birds of America*, was the engraver of Selby's paintings.

Smith, Gideon B., 1793–1867. American enthusiast of silkworm culture, editor of agricultural magazines, and breeder of racehorses. He acted as agent for his friend Audubon in marketing the Royal Octavo Edition of *Birds of America*. Swainson named the Smith's Longspur, Plate CCCC, in his honor.

Stanley, Lord, later fourteenth Earl of Derby, 1799–1869. President of the Zoological Society of London. Stanley and Children nominated Audubon to the Royal Society. He knew and liked Audubon and admired his work. He hinted to Audubon that he might hire him to paint the fauna on his country estate but gave the job to Edward Lear. Audubon named what he thought to be a new species of hawk in honor of Stanley but the bird had already been named for Cooper and described by Bonaparte. It caused great controversy and created a fearful row. Audubon was wrong and to this day the bird is Cooper's Hawk, Plates CXLI and XXXVI.

Swainson, William, 1789–1855. English zoologist and highly regarded artist. He wrote a very complimentary article about Audubon for the *London Magazine*. He accompanied Audubon to Paris where they paid a call on Cuvier. Their early friendship cooled due to Audubon's tendency to self-aggrandizement and his brushing off Swainson when it suited him, all of which irritated Swainson. Two species in *Birds of America* honor Swainson: Swainson's Hawk, Plate CCCLXXII (named by Bonaparte), and Swainson's Warbler, Plate CXCVIII (named by Audubon).

Temminck, Conrad J. Respected British zoologist who unfortunately had nothing but scorn for Audubon's work. Audubon credited Temminck as the describer of fourteen species in *Birds of America* but of these only four hold good today.

Townsend, John Kirk, 1809–1851. See Nuttall and Townsend.

Traill, Dr. Thomas Stewart, 1781–1862. English zoologist, professor, writer for the Encyclopaedia Brittanica. Traill was a great friend of Audubon's and was helpful in promoting *Birds of America*. Audubon named Traill's Flycatcher in Plate XLV in his honor. At one time the Willow Flycatcher and the Alder Flycatcher were subspecies of Traill's Flycatcher, but they are now each a species in their own right and the name Traill's Flycatcher is no more. However, Traill persists in the scientific name of the Willow Flycatcher, *Empidonax traillii*.

Trudeau, Dr. James, 1817–1887. Trudeau gave Audubon a bird he claimed to have shot in New Jersey, saying he had seen more in Long Island, New York. Audubon, considering it a new species, called it

Trudeau's Tern and painted it for Plate ccccix. The A.O.U. says this bird is native to Argentina and Chile and doubts its appearance in New Jersey and Long Island. Trudeau was a physician, surgeon, artillery officer, painter, and sculptor. John Woodhouse Audubon painted his portrait in Osage costume.

Vigors, Nicholas Aylward, 1787–1840. Secretary of the Zoological Society of London. He was a powerful, contentious, unpredictable man; at first he was friendly with Audubon but later fell out with him. Audubon did not recognize the species in Plate xxx as a Pine Warbler and thinking he had a new species named it for Vigors. Audubon became very bitter about Vigors and undoubtedly regretted having named a bird for him. Vigors is the credited describer of two species in *Birds of America*.

Wilson, Alexander, 1766–1813. One of the great fathers of American ornithology. Wilson arrived in Louisville in 1810 with a letter of introduction to Audubon, who had a store there at the time. Wilson was traveling in search of subscribers to his great ornithological work on American birds. He showed samples of his works to Audubon and Audubon showed him some of his paintings, which surprised Wilson. After a stay of three or four days during which time Audubon took him birding, Wilson went on his way. After Wilson's death the Philadelphia scientific community revered his memory, and it was their fear that Audubon might be a challenge to Wilson's supremacy that caused so much trouble. Audubon credited Wilson as the describer of forty-nine species in *Birds of America*, of which twenty-five hold good today. Birds in *Birds of America* associated with Wilson are Wilson's Phalarope, Plate cclvi (mislabeled ccliv); Wilson's Plover, Plate ccix; Wilson's Warbler, Plate cxxiv; Common Snipe, Plate ccxliii, which for many years was known as Wilson's Snipe; and Wilson's Storm-Petrel, Plate cclxx.

Tribute to Robert Havell, Jr.

Havell was much more than the engraver of *Birds of America*. He was a genius, having invented techniques that gave subtle shadings to his work that put him head and shoulders above his peers and even those who came later. He was a fine artist in his own right, with a discerning eye for composition. To really understand how much he contributed to *Birds of America* one must compare Audubon's original paintings to Havell's finished plates. While in no way denigrating Audubon, whose greatness is unquestioned, Havell should be regarded as far more than the "Engraved, Printed, & Coloured by R. Havell" that is on the legends of the plates, and recognition should be given to the technical and artistic expertise of this splendid man whose steadfast attention to the work at hand made possible *Birds of America*.

PART TWO

INFORMATION BY PLATE

For Each Plate

Plate number, original painting (O.P.) number, number of species in
  plate, size in inches (height before width)
A block about each species including
  Current name
  Other names by which it has been and is known
  Name on plate with variants if any
  Name on painting if there and if legible
  History
  Other plates in which same species appears
  Description of painting and plate including location of birds. When
  necessary, referral is made to the appropriate chart of original
  painting in Part III.

Notes
The transfer of the first ten plates from Lizars to Havell made for a
complicated series of events. Please refer to "The First Ten Plates" in
Part I and detailed notes under the plate numbers that follow.

Unless otherwise noted in the text accompanying each plate, it may
be assumed that the species in question can be observed in Audubon's
territory, most of what became the contintental forty-eight states plus
the areas where he collected and painted during his trip to Labrador,
which included Nova Scotia, New Brunswick, and Newfoundland. For
those wishing exact distribution, please refer to the A.O.U. checklist or
a current bird guide.

Audubon executed these paintings expressly to be engraved and not as
finished paintings, although some of them were. He sometimes wrote
the name of the bird directly on the painting and also wrote directions
to Havell, such as the dimensions of the bird.

Unless other media are mentioned it may be assumed the painting
was done in watercolor.

When the New-York Historical Society numbered the original
paintings, it did so in arbitrary fashion.

Although this work is not concerned with the flora depicted, when
mention is made it is as described in the New-York Historical Society's
1966 volumes. The reader is cautioned that there have been changes in
horticultural nomenclature since 1966.

Note that often the man Audubon gave as the describer differs from
the credited describer in the bird's currently approved name. It was
probably true that the man Audubon named had described the bird, but
research proved that the bird had earlier been described by another
person. It is the earliest describer who gets the credit.

Variants that have not been seen by the author and are known only
from the writings of others are listed as unconfirmed and are marked
with an asterisk.

Measurements are roughly accurate, but are not necessarily exact.

I

Plate I, O.P. 1, One Species, 38 1/8 x 25 1/2
Current name: Wild Turkey, *Meleagris gallopavo* Linnaeus
Name on plate: three variants
   1. Great American Cock Male—Vulgo (Wild Turkey—)
MALEAGRIS GALLOPAVO
Engraved by W.H. Lizars Edinr. (*without aquatint*)
   2. Great American Cock Male—Vulgo (Wild Turkey—)
MALEAGRIS GALLOPAVO
Engraved by W.H. Lizars Edinr.
Retouched by R. Havell Junr. London 1829. (*with aquatint*)
   3. Wild Turkey. MELEAGRIS GALLOPAVO. Linn, Male
Engraved by W.H. Lizars Edinr.
Retouched by R. Havell Junr. (*with aquatint*)
   Also in VI
Painting and plate alike and depict bird in stand of cane.

II

Plate II, O.P. 22, One Species, 20 7/8 x 26 3/8
Current name: Yellow-billed Cuckoo, *Coccyzus americanus*
(Linnaeus)
Name on plate: five variants
   1. Black-billed Cuckoo, COCCYZUS
ERYTHOPHTHALMUS.
Engraved by W.H. Lizars Edinr. (*without aquatint*)
(bird misidentified in legend)
   2. Yellow-billed Cuckoo. COCCYZUS
CAROLINENSIS.
Engraved by W.H. Lizars Edinr. (*without aquatint*)
   3. Yellow-billed Cuckoo COCCYZUS CAROLINENSIS
Engraved by W.H. Lizars Edinr.
Retouched by R. Havell Junr., London 1829 (*with aquatint*)
   4. Yellow-billed Cuckoo, COCCYZUS AMERICANUS.
Bonap,
Engraved by W.H. Lizars Edinr.
Retouched by R. Havell Junr. London 1829. (*with aquatint*)
   5. Yellow-billed Cuckoo, COCCYZUS AMERICANUS.
Bonap,
Engraved, Printed and Coloured by R. Havell Junr. (*with
aquatint*)
(Lizars's name should not have been left off legend.)
Painting and plate alike and depict two birds in a fruited
paw paw tree. The bird on the right is catching a Tiger
Swallowtail butterfly.

III

Plate III, O.P. 93, One Species, 20 1/2 x 12 1/2
Current name: Prothonotary Warbler, *Protonotaria citrea*
(Boddaert)
Name on plate: two variants
   1. Prothonotary Warbler. DACNIS
PROTONOTARIUS.
Engraved by W.H. Lizars Edinr. (*without aquatint*)
   2. Prothonotary Warbler. SYLVIA PROTONOTARIUS.
Lath.
Engraved, Printed & Coloured, by R. Havell Junr. (*without
aquatint*)
(Lizars's name should not have been left off legend)
History: It is not true, as legend has it, that Havell
engraved his own plate for III. Both variants come from
Lizars's plate. See "The First Ten Plates" in Part I.
Painting and plate depict two birds in a cane-vine.

Plate IV, O.P. 143, One Species, 20 3/8 x 12 1/2
Current name: Purple Finch, *Carpodacus purpureus*
(Gmelin)
Name on plate: three variants
    1. Purple Finch. FRINGILLA PURPUREA.
Engraved by W.H. Lizars Edinr.
    2. Purple Finch. FRINGILLA PURPUREA.
Engraved by W.H. Lizars Edinr. *(without aquatint)*
(Only difference between 1 & 2 is flora identification)
    3. Purple Finch FRINGILLA PURPUREA. Gmel,
Engraved, Printed & Coloured, by R. Havell, Junr.
(without aquatint)
(Lizars's name should not have been left off legend.)
Painting and plate depict two males, above, and a female,
below, in branches of a red larch.

IV

Plate V, O.P. 6, One Species, 20 1/2 x 12 1/2
Current name: Canada Warbler, *Wilsonia canadensis*
(Linnaeus)
Name on plate: two variants
    1. Bonaparte Fly Catcher. MUSCICAPA
BONAPARTII.
Engraved by W.H. Lizars Edinr. *(without aquatint)*
    2. Bonaparte's Flycatcher, MUSCICAPA
BONAPARTII, Aud,
Engraved, Printed & Coloured, by R. Havell Junr. *(without
aquatint)*
(Lizars's name should not have been left off legend.)
Name on painting: Cypress Swamp Fly Catcher,
Muscicapa
History: Audubon correctly identified the birds in Plate
CIII as Canada Warblers but he thought this young bird a
new species. He called it Cypress Swamp Fly Catcher
then changed it to honor Bonaparte, an eminent ornithologist with whom Audubon had a bristly relationship.
    Also in CIII
Painting and plate depict a young female on a branch of
Southern Magnolia.

V

Plate VI, O.P. 5, One Species, 25 5/8 x 38 1/4
Current name: Wild Turkey, *Meleagris gallopavo* Linnaeus
Name on plate: four variants
    1. Great American Hen & Young.Vulgo, Female Wild
Turkey.—MELEAGRIS GALLOPAVO
Engraved by W.H. Lizars Edinr. *(without aquatint)*
    2. Great American Hen & Young Vulgo Female Wild
Turkey MELEAGRIS GALLOPAVO
Engraved by W.H. Lizars Edinr.
Retouched by R. Havell Junr. London 1829
Coloured by R. Havell Senr. *(with aquatint)*
(snail in lower right corner),
    3. Wild Turkey, MELEAGRIS GALLOPAVO. Linn
Female and Young
Engraved by W. H. Lizars. *(with aquatint)*
(snail in lower right corner)
("Retouched by R. Havell Junr." left off by mistake)
    4. Wild Turkey, MELEAGRIS GALLOPAVO. Linn
Female and Young
Engraved by W.H. Lizars
Retouched by R. Havell, Junr. *(with aquatint)*

VI

VII

VIII

IX

(snail in lower right corner)
Also in I
Painting depicts hen and chicks on floor of a dark forest.
The hen is pastel, the chicks watercolor, the habitat oil.

Plate VII, O.P. 104, One Species, 26 3/8 x 20 3/4
Current name: Common Grackle, *Quiscalus quiscula*
(Linnaeus)
Other names: At one time the Purple Grackle and the
Bronzed Grackle were considered two species but now are
one, the Common Grackle.
Name on plate: three variants
  1. Purple Grackle QUISCALUS VERSICOLOR.
Engraved by W.H. Lizars Edinr.
Printed & Coloured by R. Havell Senr. *(without aquatint)*
  2. Purple Grackle, QUISCALUS VERSICOLOR
Engraved by W.H. Lizars Edinr.
Retouched by R. Havell Junr. London 1829 *(with aquatint)*
Printed, & Coloured by R. Havell Senr.
  3. Purple Grakle or Common Crow Blackbird,
QUISCALUS VERSICOLOR. Vieill.
Engraved by W.H. Lizars Edinr.
Retouched by R. Havell Junr. London 1829. *(with aquatint)*
Painting and plate depict female, above, and male, below.

Plate VIII, O.P. 337, One Species, 20 1/2 x 12 3/4
Current name: White-throated Sparrow, *Zonotrichia
albicollis* (Gmelin)
Name on plate: two variants
  1. White throated Sparrow FRINGILLA
PENNSYLVANICA. Lath,
Engraved by W.H. Lizars Edinr. *(without aquatint)*
  2. White Throated Sparrow FRINGILLA
PENSYLVANICA.
Engraved by W.H. Lizars Edinr.
Printed & Coloured by R. Havell, Senr. *(without
aquatint)*
Painting and plate depict male, below, and either an
immature or a female, above, in a branch of dogwood.

Plate IX, O.P. 391, One Species, 20 3/4 x 12 7/8
Current name: Hooded Warbler, *Wilsonia citrina*
(Boddaert)
Name on plate: two variants
  1. Selby's Flycatcher, MUSCICAPA SELBII. Aud,
     Engraved by W.H. Lizars Edinr. *(without aquatint)*
  2. Selby's Fly Catcher MUSCICAPA SELBII.
Engraved by W.H. Lizars Edinr.
Printed & Coloured by R. Havell. Senr. *(without aquatint)*
Name on painting: Louisiana Fly Catcher, Muscicapa
ludoviciana
History: Although Audubon correctly identified the birds
in Plate CX as Hooded Warblers he did not recognize the
immature bird here as such; thinking he had a new species
he named it for Prideaux J. Selby, a British ornithologist
with whom Audubon had a touchy relationship.
Also in CX
Painting and plate depict the immature bird on a stalk of
pheasant's eye.

Plate X, O.P. 58, One Species, 12 3/4 x 20 1/2
Current name: Water Pipit, *Anthus spinoletta* (Linnaeus)
Name on plate: two variants
1. Brown Lark ANTHUS AQUATICUS.
Engraved by W.H. Lizars Edinr.
Printed and Coloured by R. Havell. Senr. (*without aquatint*)
2. Brown Titlark, ANTHUS SPINOLETTA. Bonap,
Engraved, Printed, & Coloured, by R. Havell. (*without aquatint*)
(Lizars's name should not have been left off legend.)
Also in LXXX
Painting and plate depict a male, left, and a female, right, looking up at an insect and standing on a clump with toadstools.

X

Plate XI, O.P. 228, One Species, 38 1/4 x 25 5/8
Current name: Bald Eagle, *Haliaeetus leucocephalus* (Linnaeus)
Name on plate: two variants
1. The Bird of Washington or Great American Sea Eagle FALCO WASHINGTONIENSIS (marked 11)
2. Bird of Washington FALCO WASHINGTONII, Aud.
Name on painting: Sea Eagle, Falco ossifragus
History: When Audubon painted this bird he considered it a new species. By the time he wrote his Ornithological Biography he was aware the dark-headed bird was the immature of the white-headed Bald Eagle.
Also in XXXI and CXXVI
Painting (in pencil, watercolor, pastel, and ink) and plate depict one bird standing on a rock with no other background. In the painting there is extensive writing on the rock including "Sea Eagle, Falco Ossifragus."

XI

Plate XII, O.P. 96, One Species, 26 x 23 3/4
Current name: Northern Oriole, *Icterus galbula* (Linnaeus)
Other names: The Baltimore group and The Bullock's group, once considered as two species, are now one, the Northern Oriole.
Name on plate: two variants
1. Baltimore Oriole ICTERUS BALTIMORE. Daud.
2. Baltimore Oriole ICTERUS BALTIMORE. Daud. (marked 12)
Also in CCCLXXXVIII (Bullock's) and CCCCXXXIII (Bullock's and Baltimore)
Painting and plate depict two males, right, and a female clinging to her nest.
SEE COMPOSITE PLATES IN PART I

XII

XIII

XIV

XV

Plate XIII, O.P. 290, One Species, 19 3/8 x 12 1/4
Current name: Dark-eyed Junco, *Junco hyemalis* (Linnaeus)
Other names: The Slate-colored Junco and the Oregon Junco were long considered two species but they are now grouped within one species, the Dark-eyed Junco.
Name on plate: two variants
1. Snow Bird FRINGILLA HYEMALIS, Linn.
2. Snow Bird FRINGILLA NIVALIS (marked 13)
Also in CCCXCVIII (Oregon group)
Painting and plate depict a female, above, and a male, below, in a cotton-gum tree.

Plate XIV, O.P. 260, One Species, 19 5/8 x 12 1/2
Current name: Prairie Warbler, *Dendroica discolor* (Vieillot)
Name on plate: two variants
1. Prairie Warbler SYLVIA DISCOLOR. Vieill.
2. Prairie Warbler SYLVIA DISCOLOR. Vieill (marked 14)
Name on painting: Prairie Warbler, Sylvia Minuta
Painting and plate depict a female, above, and a male, below, in sedge.

Plate XV, O.P. 10, One Species, 19 1/4 x 12 1/4
Current name: Northern Parula, *Parula americana* (Linnaeus)
Other names: also called Parula Warbler and Northern Parula Warbler
Name on plate: Blue Yellow-backed Warbler SYLVIA AMERICANA. Lath
(* Blue Yellow-back Warbler SYLVIA AMERICANA)
Name on painting: Blue Yellow Back Warbler, Sylvia pussilla
Painting and plate depict a male, above, and a female, below, on a red iris.

Plate XVI, O.P. 315, One Species, 25 5/8 x 38 1/4
Current name: Peregrine Falcon, *Falco peregrinus* Tunstall
Other names: once called Duck Hawk
Name on plate: two variants
    1. Great-footed Hawk FALCO PEREGRINUS.
Gmel.
    2. Great-footed Hawk FALCO PEREGRINUS.
Gmel. (marked 16)
Painting and plate depict a female, right, and a male,
left, feeding on a dead Green-winged Teal. For the
painting Audubon cut out a pastel of the female he had
drawn previously and pasted it onto his paper. He then
painted the male and completed the background in
watercolor.

XVI

Plate XVII, O.P. 160, One Species, 26 3/4 x 20 3/4
Current name: Mourning Dove, *Zenaida macroura*
(Linnaeus)
Name on plate: two variants
    1. Carolina Pigeon, or Turtle Dove COLUMBA
CAROLINENSIS (marked 17)
    2. Carolina Turtle Dove COLUMBA CAROLINENSIS
Linn.
Painting and plate depict two pairs of birds in a silky
camellia, also called Virginia-Stewartia.

Plate XVIII, O.P. 240, One Species, 19 5/8 x 12 1/8
Current name: Bewick's Wren, *Thryomanes bewickii*
(Audubon)
Name on plate: two variants
    1. Bewick's Wren TROGLODYTES BEWICKII. Aud.
    2. Bewick's Long-tailed Wren TROGLODYTES
BEWICKII (marked 18)
Name on painting: Bewick's long-tailed Wren—Long
Tailed Creeper. Certhia.
History: Audubon was the discoverer and describer of this
species which he named for his friend Thomas Bewick, a
famed English engraver on wood and writer of classics on
British birds and animals. Bewick received Audubon with
enthusiasm and in three days he secured eight subscribers
to *Birds of America* and put him up for membership in two
learned societies. What Audubon wrote on the painting is
curious. It is probable that the second and third lines were
written first and then the top line added later.
Painting and plate depict one male in a winged elm.

XVII

XVIII

Plate XIX, O.P. 200, One Species, 19 3/4 x 12 1/2
Current name: Louisiana Waterthrush, *Seiurus motacilla* (Vieillot)
Name on plate: two variants
  1. Louisiana Water Thrush TURDUS LUDOVICIANUS. Aud.
  2. Louisiana Water Thrush TURDUS AQUATICUS (marked 19)
Name on painting: Louisiana Watter Thrush, Turdus Ludovicianus
Painting and plate depict one bird in a fruited jack-in-the-pulpit.

Plate XX, O.P. 320, One Species, 19 1/2 x 12 1/4
Current name: Blue-winged Warbler, *Vermivora pinus* (Linnaeus)
Name on plate: two variants
  1. Blue-winged Yellow Warbler SYLVIA SOLITARIA. Wils.
  2. Blue Winged Yellow Warbler DACNIS SOLITARIA (marked 20)
(* Blue-winged Yellow Warbler DACNIS SOLITARIA)
Painting and plate depict a male, below, and a female, above, in a hibiscus bush.

XIX

Plate XXI, O.P. 44, One Species, 33 1/4 x 23 5/8
Current name: Northern Mockingbird, *Mimus polyglottos* (Linnaeus)
Other names: commonly called Mockingbird
Name on plate: two variants
  1. Mocking Bird TURDUS POLYGLOTTUS. Linn.
  2. Mocking Bird TURDUS POLYGLOTTUS. Linn. (marked 21)
Painting and plate depict two pairs of Mockingbirds defending a nest from a timber rattlesnake, the whole entwined in a jessamine vine. Audubon was severely attacked by critics who claimed rattlesnakes never climb trees and do not have fangs that curl outwards at their tips. These criticisms have much validity. The fangs of a rattlesnake do not recurve as depicted in this plate. The artist has not only greatly exaggerated the size of the teeth but has misplaced their position in the snake's mouth. Threatening the birds with open mouth is highly improbable. Rattlesnakes do climb trees, but such occasions are rare and not their usual habit.

XX

XXI

Plate XXII, O.P. 86, One Species, 25 1/2 x 20 1/2
Current name: Purple Martin, *Progne subis* (Linnaeus)
Name on plate: two variants
  1. Purple Martin HIRUNDO PURPUREA, Linn.
  2. Purple Martin HIRUNDO PURPUREA, Linn.
(marked 22)
Painting and plate alike and depict two males, left, and
two females, right, around hollowed out gourds the birds
are using for nests. There is a human touch in this scene
since someone has hollowed out the gourds and hung them
in the tree.

Plate XXIII, O.P. 407, One Species, 19 3/8 x 12 1/8
Current name: Common Yellowthroat, *Geothlypis trichas*
(Linnaeus)
Other names: commonly called Yellowthroat
Name on plate: two variants
  1. Yellow-breasted Warbler SYLVIA TRICHAS, Lath.
  2. Maryland Yellow Throat SYLVIA TRICHAS
(marked 23)
History: See history notes in Plate XXIV
Also in XXIV
Painting and plate depict a male, above, and a female,
below, in what may be a withe-rod or a sheepberry.
SEE COMPOSITE PLATES IN PART I.

XXII

Plate XXIV, O.P. 294, One Species, 19 5/8 x 12 1/4
Current name: Common Yellowthroat, *Geothlypis trichas*
(Linnaeus)
Other names: commonly called Yellowthroat
Name on plate: two variants
  1. Roscoe's Yellow-throat SYLVIA ROSCO. Aud.
  2. Roscoe's Yellow-throat SYLVIA ROSCO. Aud.
(marked 24)
Name on painting: Louisiana Yellow Throat, Sylvia
History: Although Audubon had painted this species in
April 1821, when he painted this bird the following
September he did not recognize it as the same species. He
thought it a new species, which he first called Louisiana
Yellow Throat but then changed the name to honor the
English historian William Roscoe. Roscoe was a neighbor
of Audubon's great friends the Rathbones, and he was very
kind to Audubon. Audubon's misidentification of this bird
was probably due to fall or immature plumage.
  Also in XXIII
Painting and plate depict one male bird on a limb of the
water oak.

XXIII

XXIV

XXV

XXVI

XXVII

Plate XXV, O.P. 256, One Species, 19 3/8 x 12 1/8
Current name: Song Sparrow, *Melospiza melodia* (Wilson)
Name on plate: two variants
   1. Song Sparrow FRINGILLA MELODIA
   2. Song Sparrow FRINGILLA MELODIA (marked 25)
Name on painting: Song Sparrow, Fringilla Melodia
   Also in CCCXC
Painting and plate depict two birds in what may be a tree-huckleberry.

Plate XXVI, O.P. 223, One Species, 33 1/4 x 24
Current name: Carolina Parakeet, *Conuropsis carolinensis* (Linnaeus)
Name on plate: two variants
   1. Carolina Parrot PSITACUS CAROLINENSIS, Linn.
   2. Carolina Parrot PSITACUS CAROLINENSIS, Linn. (marked 26)
Name on painting: Carolina Parrot, Psitacus carolinensis
History: The Carolina Parakeet was once plentiful, but the last one died in the Cincinnati Zoological Garden in 1914. Of the seven birds depicted, six have the yellow head of an adult but the second bird from the bottom has the green head of an immature. Audubon implied in his notes that this bird was a different "variety," by which he may have meant "species."
Painting and plate depict seven birds feeding in a cocklebur.

Plate XXVII, O.P. 267, One Species, 25 3/8 x 21 3/4
Current name: Red-headed Woodpecker, *Melanerpes erythrocephalus* (Linnaeus)
Name on plate: two variants
   1. Red headed Woodpecker PICUS ERYTHROCEPHALUS, Linn.
   2. Red headed Woodpecker PICUS ERYTHROCEPHALUS, Linn. (marked 27)
Painting and plate depict two parents feeding three young, two of whom are clinging to a dead tree trunk and the third peeping out of the nesting hole.

Plate XXVIII, O.P. 313, One Species, 19 1/2 x 12 1/4
Current name: Solitary Vireo, *Vireo solitarius* (Wilson)
Name on plate: two variants
   1. Solitary Flycatcher or Vireo VIREO SOLITARIUS,
Vieill.
   2. VIREO SOLITARIUS—Solitary Vireo (marked 28)
Name on painting: Solitary Flycatcher, Muscicapa
Solitaria
Painting and plate depict two birds in cane.

XXVIII

Plate XXIX, O.P. 20, One Species, 19 5/8 x 12 3/8
Current name: Rufous-sided Towhee, *Pipilo
erythrophthalmus* (Linnaeus)
Other names: commonly called Towhee
Name on plate: three variants
   1. Towee Bunting, FRINGILLA ERYTHROPHTHALMA
(marked 29)
   2. Towhe bunting, FRINGILLA
ERYTHROPHTHALMA, Linn,
   3. Towhe Bunting, FRINGILLA
ERYTHROPHTHALMA, Linn,
History: It is curious that although Audubon correctly
named the birds depicted here, when it came to the same
species in Plate CCCXCIV he called the birds there Arctic
Ground Finch.
   Also in CCCXCIV
Painting and plate depict a male, above, and a female,
below, in a blackberry bush.

XXIX

Plate XXX, O.P. 23, One Species, 19 1/2 x 12 1/4
Current name: Pine Warbler, *Dendroica pinus* (Wilson)
Name on plate: two variants
   1. Vigor's Warbler SYLVIA VIGORSII. Aud.
   2. Vigors Vireo, VIREO VIGORSII (marked 30)
Name on painting: [smudge] Warbler, Sylvia
History: Audubon painted this bird twice, for Plates XXX
and CXL. In the case of Plate XXX he thought the bird
was a new species and named it for Nicholas Vigors, a
volatile, whimsical, selfish figure in London's
ornithological world. It was a curious choice as Audubon
did not think highly of Vigors.
   Also in CXL
Painting and plate depict one bird in a spiderwort.

XXX

XXXI

XXXII

XXXIII

Plate XXXI, O.P. 2, One Species, 25 5/8 x 38 1/4
Current name: Bald Eagle, *Haliaeetus leucocephalus*
(Linnaeus)
Name on plate: two variants
 1. White headed Eagle FALCO LEUCOCEPHALUS.
Linn.
 2. White headed Eagle FALCO LEUCOCEPHALUS.
Linn. (marked 31)
(* White-headed Eagle FALCO LEUCOCEPHALUS)
Name on painting: White-headed Eagle, Falco
leucocephalus
History: Although Audubon was confused about the young
Bald Eagle he painted for Plate XI, he had the species
correct in the birds he painted here (an adult) and for
Plate CXXVI (an immature).
 Also in XI and CXXVI
Painting and plate depict one adult bird on a rock feeding
on a catfish with mountains in distance. Audubon was
dissatisfied with an earlier painting he had done in
which the eagle was feeding on a Canada Goose, so he
painted a copy in which he replaced the goose with a
catfish.

Plate XXXII, O.P. 15, One Species, 18 3/4 x 26 3/8
Current name: Black-billed Cuckoo, *Coccyzus
erythropthalmus* (Wilson)
Name on plate: two variants
 1. Black-billed Cuckoo COCCYZUS
ERYTHROPHTHALMUS. Bonap.
 2. Black-billed Cuckoo COCCYZUS
ERYTHROPHTHALMUS. Bonap. (marked 32)
History: One of the variants of Plate II, which depicts the
Yellow-billed Cuckoo, was mismarked Black-billed
Cuckoo
Painting and plate depict two birds in a magnolia tree
pursuing a fly.

Plate XXXIII, O.P. 214, One Species, 19 3/8 x 12 1/4
Current name: American Goldfinch, *Carduelis tristis*
(Linnaeus)
Other names: commonly called Goldfinch
Name on plate: two variants
 1. American Goldfinch FRINGILLA TRISTIS. Linn.
 2. Yellow Bird or American Goldfinch CARDUELIS
AMERICANA (marked 33)
Painting and plate depict a male, above, and a female,
below, on bull thistles.

Plate XXXIV, O.P. 379, One Species, 19 5/8 x 12 1/4
Current name: Worm-eating Warbler, *Helmitheros vermivorus* (Gmelin)
Name on plate: two variants
   1. Worm eating Warbler SYLVIA VERMIVORA. Lath
   2. Worm-eating Warbler DACNIS VERMIVORA (marked 34)
Painting and plate depict two birds in pokeweed.

Plate XXXV, O.P. 263, One Species, 19 1/2 x 12 1/4
Current name: Yellow Warbler, *Dendroica petechia* (Linnaeus)
Name on plate: three variants
   1. Children's Warbler SYLVIA CHILDRENI (marked 35)
   2. Children's Warbler SYLVIA CHILDRENI. Aud.
   3. Children's Warbler SYLVIA CHILDRENII, Aud.
Name on painting: Louisiana Warbler, Sylvia Ludowiciana, Sylvia Childreni
History: Although Audubon correctly identified the male bird in Plate XCV as a Yellow Warbler he did not realize the females and young in this plate and Plate LXV were the same species. In both cases he thought he had a new species which he called respectively Children's and Rathbone's Warblers. John George Children was a distinguished Englishman, librarian at the British Museum, editor of two scientific journals, and a stalwart friend to Audubon.
  Also in LXV and XCV
Painting and plate depict a female, below, and a young, above, in a coffee-wood.

XXXIV

Plate XXXVI, O.P. 194, One Species, 38 1/4 x 25 5/8
Current name: Cooper's Hawk, *Accipiter cooperii* (Bonaparte)
Name on plate: two variants
   1. Stanley Hawk FALCO STANLEII, Aud.
   2. Stanley Hawk. ASTUR STANLEII (marked 36)
History: Audubon named this bird for Lord Stanley, who later became the fourteenth Earl of Derby. He was a noted sportsman, parliamentarian, and translator of the *Iliad*. He greatly befriended Audubon and almost asked him to paint his collection of fauna, but in the end he gave the job to Edward Lear. Audubon's naming of this bird for Lord Stanley caused controversey and bitterness as the bird had already been named for William Cooper of the New York Lyceum by Charles Lucien Bonaparte.
  Also in CXLI
Painting depicts one young bird on a branch and another young flying above. In the plate, Havell added a Bluebird flying off upper right. Havell used the same Bluebird that is at the top of Plate CXIII. This is one of only two instances of the same painting of a bird appearing twice in *Birds of America*; the other is the Wilson's Plover in Plates CCIX and CCLXXXIV.

XXXV

XXXVI

XXXVII

Plate XXXVII, O.P. 264, One Species, 25 7/8 x 20 3/4
Current name: Northern Flicker, *Colaptes auratus* (Linnaeus)
Other names: formerly called Common Flicker. The Yellow-shafted, the Red-shafted, and the Gilded Flickers, once thought separate species, are now grouped in one species, the Northern Flicker.
Name on plate: two variants
　　1. Golden-winged Woodpecker PICUS AURATUS Linn.
　　2. Gold-winged Woodpecker PICUS AURATUS (marked 37)
Name on painting: Gold-winged Woodpecker, Picus auratus
Also in Plate CCCCXVI (Red-shafted)
Painting and plate depict two quarreling females, top, plus three males, all on a dead tree trunk. In the painting Audubon began with the two females in watercolor and pastel. He then attached a five-inch piece of paper to the bottom and added a male, the head of a male, and another head of a male upper left, all in watercolor.

XXXVIII

Plate XXXVIII, O.P. 90, One Species, 19 1/2 x 12 1/4
Current name: Kentucky Warbler, *Oporornis formosus* (Wilson)
Name on plate: two variants
　　1. Kentucky Warbler SYLVIA FORMOSA
　　2. Kentucky Warbler SYLVIA FORMOSA (marked 38)
Name on painting: Kentucky Warbler, Sylvia formoda
Painting and plate depict a male, left, on an umbrella tree and a female, right, on a stem.

Plate XXXIX, O.P. 298, One Species, 19 1/2 x 12 1/4
Current name: Tufted Titmouse, *Parus bicolor* Linnaeus
Name on plate: two variants
　　1. Crested Titmouse PARUS BICOLOR. Linn. (marked 39)
　　2. Crested Titmouse PARUS BICOLOR, Linn.
Name on painting: Crested Titmouse, Parus bicolor
Painting and plate depict a male, above, and a female, below, in a branch of white pine.

XXXIX

Plate XL, O.P. 365, One Species, 19 3/8 x 12 1/8
Current name: American Redstart, *Setophaga ruticilla*
(Linnaeus)
Other names: usually called Redstart
Name on plate: two variants
   1. American Redstart MUSCICAPA RUTICILLA
   2. American Redstart MUSCICAPA RUTICILLA
(marked 40)
Name on painting: American Redstart, Muscicapa
ruticilla
Painting depicts the male attacking a wasp that is part of
the colony living in the large wasp's nest shown attached
to a hornbeam branch. The female is separate with no
branch to perch on. In the plate a branch was provided for
the female.

XL

Plate XLI, O.P. 227, One Species, 25 5/8 x 38 1/4
Current name: Ruffed Grouse, *Bonasa umbellus* (Linnaeus)
Name on plate: two variants
   1. Ruffed Grouse TETRAO UMBELLUS, Linn.
   2. Ruffed Grouse TETRAO UMBELLUS, Linn. (marked
41)
Name on painting: Ruffed Grous, Vulgo Pheasant, Tetrao
umbellus
Painting and plate depict two males, top, and a female,
below, feeding on the blue-black berries of moonseed. For
the painting Audubon used oil for the moss-covered stump
and watercolor for the rest.

XLI

Plate XLII, O.P. 131, One Species, 26 x 20 7/8
Current name: Orchard Oriole, *Icterus spurius* (Linnaeus)
Name on plate: two variants
   1. Orchard Oriole ICTERUS SPURIUS
   2. Orchard Oriole ICTERUS SPURIUS (marked 42)
Name on painting: Orchard Oriole, Icterus spurius
Painting and plate depict two males, top and bottom, two
immatures, top right and behind nest, and a female,
middle right; all five birds around a nest in a honey locust.

XLII

XLIII

XLIV

XLV

Plate XLIII, O.P. 9, One Species, 19 5/8 x 12 1/4
Current name: Cedar Waxwing, *Bombycilla cedrorum*
Vieillot
Name on plate: two variants
   1. Cedar Bird BOMBYCILLA CAROLINENSIS
   2. Cedar Bird BOMBYCILLA CAROLINENSIS
(marked 43)
Name on painting: Cedar Bird, Bombycilla Carolinensis
Painting and plate depict a female, above, and a male,
below, in a branch of red cedar.

Plate XLIV, O.P. 269, One Species, 19 5/8 x 12 /14
Current name: Summer Tanager, *Piranga rubra* (Linnaeus)
  Name on plate: two variants
   1. Summer Red Bird TANAGRA AESTIVA (marked 44)
   2. Summer Red Bird TANAGRA AESTIVA
Name on painting: Summer Red Bird, Tanagra Aestiva
Painting and plate depict a male, top, a female, center,
and a young, bottom, in a muscadine vine. The painting is
largely in watercolor but there is some pastel on the center
bird.

Plate XLV, O.P. 382, One Species, 19 1/2 x 12 1/4
Current name: Willow Flycatcher, *Empidonax traillii*
(Audubon)
Other names: The Willow Flycatcher and the Alder
Flycatcher, once considered races of Traill's Flycatcher,
are now separate species and the name Traill's Flycatcher
is discarded.
Name on plate: two variants
   1. Traill's Fly-catcher MUSCICAPA TRAILLI
   2. Traill's Fly-Catcher MUSCICAPA TRAILLI
(marked 45)
Name on painting: Traill's Flycatcher Muscicapa trailli
Muscicapa palustris
History: Audubon was the discoverer and describer of this
bird, which he named for his friend Dr. Thomas Stewart
Traill, English professor and writer for the Encyclopaedia
Britannica.
Painting and plate depict one bird atop a sweet gum.
There is a tiny drawing of the bird's bill at lower left in
the painting that is not in the plate.

Plate XLVI, O.P. 188, One Species, 38 1/4 x 25 5/8
Current name: Barred Owl, *Strix varia* Barton
Name on plate: two variants
  1. Barred Owl STRIX NEBULOSA
  2. Barred Owl STRIX NEBULOSA (marked 46)
Name on painting: Barred Owl, Strix nebulosa
Painting depicts one male on a thick branch. In his notes
Audubon said he had painted the bird facing a squirrel,
but for some reason he did not put the squirrel directly into
the painting; instead he made a separate painting of it,
which was then incorporated into the plate.

XLVI

Plate XLVII, O.P. 237, One Species, 25 7/8 x 20 3/4
Current name: Ruby-throated Hummingbird, *Archilochus colubris* (Linnaeus)
Name on plate: two variants
  1. Ruby-throated Humming Bird TROCHILUS
COLUBRIS (marked 47)
  2. Ruby-Throated Humming Bird TROCHILUS
COLUBRIS. Linn.
(marked XLVII)
Name on painting: Ruby throated Humming-bird,
Trochilus Colubris
Painting and plate depict ten birds in a trumpet-flower
vine.

Plate XLVIII, O.P. 415, One Species, 19 3/4 x 12 1/4
Current name: Cerulean Warbler, *Dendroica cerulea* (Wilson)
Name on plate: two variants
  1. Cerulean Warbler SYLVIA AZUREA (marked 48)
  2. Azure Warbler SYLVIA AZUREA. Steph.
Name on painting: Cerulean Warbler, Sylvia azurea
History: Apparently in Audubon's day there was confusion
as to whether the common name of this bird was Cerulean
or Azure; today it is Cerulean.
  Also in XLIX
Painting depicts a male bird in a branch of Dahoon. It is
clear from the writing on the painting that Audubon
wished a female to be added to his composition and there
is a "2" where he wished it to be. In the plate Havell did
indeed add the female flying in pursuit of an insect.
Havell was not able to obtain a painting of a female by
Audubon, so unfortunately he used one of Wilson's instead.

XLVII

XLVIII

XLIX

L

LI

Plate XLIX, O.P. 233, One Species, 19 5/8 x 12 1/4
Current name: Cerulean Warbler, *Dendroica cerulea*
(Wilson)
Name on plate: two variants
   1. Blue-green Warbler SYLVIA RARA. Wils.
   2. Blue-green Warbler SYLVIA RARA. Wils. (marked
49)
Name on painting: Blue Green Warbler, Sylvia Rara
History: Neither Audubon nor Wilson recognized the
female bird as a Cerulean (Azure). Wilson had previously
named it. Audubon commented on how strongly this bird
resembled the young of the Cerulean and were it not for
the form of the bill and some of its habits he would be
tempted to regard it as a variety of Cerulean.
Nonetheless, what he had was a Cerulean.
   Also in XLVIII
Painting depicts a female in a stalk of French mulberry,
the top third of which is not painted, just outlined in
pencil. In the plate the plant is complete.

Plate L, O.P. 421, One Species, 19 1/2 x 12 1/4
Current name: Magnolia Warbler, *Dendroica magnolia*
(Wilson)
Name on plate: two variants
   1. Swainson's Warbler SYLVICOLA SWAINSONIA
(marked 50)
     (bird misidentified)
   2. Black & Yellow Warbler SYLVIA MACULOSA.
Lath.
Name on painting: Swainson's Warbler, Sylvicola
Swainsonia
(Audubon misidentified the bird)
History: The whole situation regarding this painting and
plate was a comedy of errors. Audubon wrote that he drew
this immature bird, which he called Black and Yellow
Warbler, for inclusion with the two male Magnolias in
Plate CXXIII, but Havell misunderstood and made a
separate plate of it. Then Audubon wrote Swainson's
Warbler on the painting, which was a mistake evidently
made in haste. He did paint the Swainson's, which is in
Plate CXCVIII.
   Also in CXXIII
Painting and plate depict one immature bird in a branch of
swamp white oak.

Plate LI, O.P. 76, One Species, 38 1/8 x 25 1/2
Current name: Red-tailed Hawk, *Buteo jamaicensis*
(Gmelin)
Name on plate: two variants
   1. Red-tailed Hawk FALCO BOREALIS, Gmel.
   2. Red Tailed Hawk FALCO BOREALIS (marked 51)
   Also in LXXXVI
Painting depicts a male attacking a female in an attempt
to wrest away the rabbit she holds in her talons. The
rabbit's fur is drawn in ink. The plate is the same except
for the addition of mountains in the distance.

Plate LII, O.P. 196, One Species, 26 x 20 5/8
Current name: Chuck-will's-widow, *Caprimulgus carolinensis* Gmelin
Name on plate: two variants
   1. Chuck-will's Widow CAPRIMULGUS CAROLINENSIS. Briss.
   2. Chuck Will's Widow CAPRIMULGUS CAROLINENSIS (marked 52)
Name on painting: Chuck Wills widow, Caprimulgus Carolinensis
Spanish Whippoor Will common name
Painting depicts a male, above, and a female, below, on dead tree limbs showing aggression at a snake twining along upper limb. Audubon wrote that this was the harmless harlequin snake but it is actually the deadly coral snake. The plate is the same except for the addition of a vine.

LII

Plate LIII, O.P. 357, One Species, 19 3/8 x 12 1/8
Current name: Painted Bunting, *Passerina ciris* (Linnaeus)
Name on plate: two variants
   1. Painted Bunting FRINGILLA CIRIS (marked 53)
   2. Painted Finch FRINGILLA CIRIS, Temm.
Name on painting: Painted Buntings, Fringilla Emberiza Ciris
Painting and plate depict a female, top, two females, bottom, and two immatures, center, all in a chickasaw plum tree.

Plate LIV, O.P. 373, One Species, 19 1/2 x 12 1/4
Current name: Bobolink, *Dolichonyx oryzivorus* (Linnaeus)
Other names: still often called Rice Bird
Name on plate: three variants
   1. Rice Bunting (marked 54)
   2. Rice Bird
   3. Rice Bird ICTERUS AGRIPENNIS. Ch. Bonap.
(* Rice Bunting ICTERUS AGRIPENNIS)
Name on painting: Rice Bird, Icterus agripennis
Painting and plate depict a male, above, and a female, below, in a red maple.

LIII

LIV

LV

Plate LV, O.P. 207, One Species, 19 1/2 x 12 1/8
Current name: Cuvier's Kinglet, *Regulus cuvieri* Audubon
Name on plate: two variants
    1. Cuviers Regulus REGULUS CUVIERII
    2. Cuvier's Wren REGULUS CUVIERI (marked 55)
Name on painting: Cuvier's Wren, Regulus Cuvierii
History: Audubon said he painted this bird from one he collected in Pennsylvania. He considered it to be a new species and named it for Baron Cuvier. No bird like this one has since been seen.
Painting and plate depict a male bird in a branch of mountain laurel.

Plate LVI, O.P. 249, One Species, 38 1/8 x 25 1/2
Current name: Red-shouldered Hawk, *Buteo lineatus* (Gmelin)
Name on plate: two variants
    1. Red-shouldered Hawk FALCO LINEATUS. Gmel.
    2. Red-shouldered Hawk FALCO LINEATUS. Gmel. (marked 56)
Name on painting: Red-shouldered Hawk, Falco lineatus
  Also in LXXI and LXXVI
Painting and plate depict a female, above, and a male, below, in what is probably a white oak.

LVI

Plate LVII, O.P. 225, One Species, 26 x 20 5/8
Current name: Loggerhead Shrike, *Lanius ludovicianus* Linnaeus
Name on plate: two variants
    1. Loggerhead Shrike LANIUS LUDOVICIANUS. Linn.
    2. Loggerhead Shrike LANIUS CAROLINENSIS (marked 57)
Name on painting: Loggerhead Shrike, Lanius Carolinensis
Painting and plate depict two birds at the top of a dead tree around which twines a hagbrier.

LVII

Plate LVIII, O.P. 344, One Species, 19 3/8 x 12 1/8
Current name: Hermit Thrush, *Catharus guttatus* (Pallas)
Name on plate: three variants
1. Hermit Thrush TURDUS MINOR, Gmel.
2. Hermit Thrush TURDUS SOLITARIUS
3. Hermit Thrush TURDUS SOLITARIUS (marked 58)
Name on painting: Hermit Thrush, Turdus solitarius. Wilson.
Tawny Thrush
  Also in CCCCXIX
Painting and plate depict a male, top, and a female, bottom, in a branch of what is probably a bearberry.

LVIII

Plate LIX, O.P. 369, One Species, 19 1/2 x 12 1/4
Current name: Chestnut-sided Warbler, *Dendroica pensylvanica* (Linnaeus)
Name on plate: two variants
1. Chestnut-sided Warbler SYLVIA ICTEROCEPHALA. Lath.
2. Chestnut Sided Warbler (marked 59)
Name on painting: Chestnut-Sided Warbler, Sylvia icterocephala
Painting and plate depict a female, upper right, and a male, lower left, in a moth mullein. Audubon wrote the name of the bird at the bottom of the painting. He then added a six-inch strip of paper to make the painting longer and wrote the name again at the new bottom.

Plate LX, O.P. 348, One Species, 19 1/2 x 12 1/4
Current name: Carbonated Warbler, *Sylvia carbonata* Audubon
Name on plate: two variants
1. Carbonated Warbler SYLVIA CARBONATA
2. Carbonated Warbler SYLVIA CARBONATA (marked 60)
Name on painting: Carbonated Warbler, Sylvia carbonata
History: Audubon said he drew these birds from two he shot in Kentucky. He never again saw a bird like it and neither has anyone else. The A.O.U. considers the bird hypothetical. Sir William Jardine, in his revised edition of *Wilson's Ornithology*, 1832, considered the bird to be a young Cape May Warbler.
Painting and plate depict two young males in what is probably a juneberry.

LIX

LX

LXI

Plate LXI, O.P. 412, One Species, 38 1/8 x 25 1/2
Current name: Great Horned Owl, *Bubo virginianus*
(Gmelin)
Name on plate: two variants
1. Great Horned Owl STRIX VIRGINIANA. Gmel.
2. Great horned Owl STRIX VIRGINIANA (marked 61)

Name on painting: Great horned-Owl, Strix Virgiana
Painting and plate depict a female, left, and a male,
right, on dead lichen-covered branches. The male was
painted separately in pencil, pastel, and watercolor, then
cut out and pasted onto the paper next to his mate, who is
done in watercolor.

Plate LXII, O.P. 36, One Species, 26 x 20 7/8
Current name: Passenger Pigeon, *Ectopistes migratorius*
(Linnaeus)
Name on plate: two variants
1. Passenger Pigeon COLUMBA MIGRATORIA. Linn.
2. Passenger Pigeon COLUMBA MIGRATORIA. Linn.
(marked 62)
Name on painting: Passenger Pigeon, Columba migratoria
History: The last Passenger Pigeon died in the Cincinnati
Zoo in 1914. It was once so plentiful that Audubon reported
seeing flocks passing a point for days, so thick they
darkened the sky.
Painting and plate depict a female, above, and a male,
below, on branches.

Plate LXIII, O.P. 77, One Species, 19 3/8 x 12 1/4
Current name: White-eyed Vireo, *Vireo griseus*
(Boddaert)
Name on plate: two variants
1. White eyed Flycatcher VIREO
NOVEBORACENSIS. Ch. Bonap.
2. White Eye Flycatcher VIREO NOVEBORACENSIS
(marked 63)
Name on painting: White Eyed Flycatcher, Vireo
noveboracensis
Painting and plate depict one male pursuing an insect
while in a chinaberry branch.

LXII

LXIII

Plate LXIV, O.P. 331, One Species, 19 3/8 x 12 1/4
Current name: Swamp Sparrow, *Melospiza georgiana*
(Latham)
Name on plate: two variants
   1. Swamp Sparrow SPIZA PALUSTRIS (marked 64)
   2. Swamp Sparrow FRINGILLA PALUSTRIS. Wils.
Name on painting: Swamp Sparrow, Spiza palustris
History: Audubon wrote on the painting, "Drawn from
Nature by Lucy Audubon. Mr. Havell will please have
Lucy Audubon's name on the plate instead of mine." The
painting is surely by Audubon; Lucy Audubon may have
assisted with some of the leaves and Audubon wished to
thank her by having her name on the legend instead of
his. The legend on the plate is as Audubon wished and
reads, "Drawn from Nature by Lucy Audubon."
Painting and plate depict one male on a mandrake.

LXIV

Plate LXV, O.P. 383, One Species, 19 1/4 x 12 1/8
Current name: Yellow Warbler, *Dendroica petechia*
(Linnaeus)
Name on plate: two variants
   1. Rathbone Warbler SYLVIA RATHBONIA
   2. Rathbone's Warbler SYLVIA RATHBONI (marked
65)
Name on painting: Rathbone's Warbler, Sylvia Rathboni
History: Although Audubon correctly identified the male
adult Yellow Warbler in Plate XCV, he did not recognize
the females and young in this plate and Plate XXXV. In
each case he thought he had a new species, which he
called Children's and Rathbone's Warblers. He named
the birds in this plate after the Rathbone family. Mrs.
William Rathbone, the matriarch of the family, had a
salon in her Liverpool town house and at Green Bank in
the country where eminent and learned men of England and
France came. She and her two sons were Audubon's
greatest supporters in England.
Painting and plate depict two females in a trumpet
flower. For the painting Audubon pasted onto the upper
right hand corner a previously executed drawing of
trumpet flowers. He then completed the vine and painted
on the two birds.

LXV

Plate LXVI, O.P. 181, One Species, 38 1/4 x 25 5/8
Current name: Ivory-billed Woodpecker, *Campephilus
principalis* (Linnaeus)
Name on plate: two variants
   1. Ivory-billed Woodpecker PICUS PRINCIPALIS.
Linn.
   2. Ivory-billed Woodpecker PICUS PRINCIPALIS.
Linn. (marked 66)
Name on painting: Ivory-billed Woodpecker, Picus
principalis
History: Recent U.S. sightings are unconfirmed and the
species is feared extinct here. However, in 1986 four birds
were observed in Cuba; although a different subspecies
from the American, it is essentially the same bird. This
sighting aroused great joy in the ornithological world.
Painting and plate depict a male, left, and two females,
right, on a dead tree. The painting has a bad stain, one of
the few instances of damage to the paintings.

LXVI

LXVII

LXVIII

LXIX

Plate LXVII, O.P. 324, One Species, 25 7/8 x 20 3/4
Current name: Red-winged Blackbird, *Agelaius phoeniceus* (Linnaeus)
Name on plate: two variants
   1. Red winged Starling or Marsh Blackbird ICTERUS PHOENICEUS. Daud.
   2. Red-winged Starling ICTERUS PHOENICEUS (marked 67)
Name on painting: Red-winged Starling, Icterus phoeniceus
   Also in Plate CCCCXX
Painting and plate depict an adult male, top, a young male, left center, an adult female, right center, and a younger bird at bottom, all in branches of a swamp maple.

Plate LXVIII, O.P. 133, One Species, 19 1/2 x 12 1/4
Current name: Cliff Swallow, *Hirundo pyrrhonota* Vieillot
Name on plate: two variants
   1. Republican or Cliff Swallow HIRUNDO FULVA. Vieill.
   2. Republican or Cliff Swallow HIRUNDO FULVA. Vieill. (marked 68)
Name on painting: Republican Cliff Swallow, Hirundo fulva
Painting and plate depict a female, top, and a male, bottom, perched on nests which are clinging to a cliffside. A baby peeps out from one of the nests and an egg lies exposed nearby. For the painting, the cliffside was done separately, cut out and pasted onto the paper, and the rest painted over it.

Plate LXIX, O.P. 103, One Species, 19 1/2 x 12 1/4
Current name: Bay-breasted Warbler, *Dendroica castanea* (Wilson)
Name on plate: two variants
   1. Bay-breasted Warbler SYLVIA CASTANEA. Wils.
   2. Bay-breasted Warbler SYLVIA CASTANEA. Wils. (marked 69)
Name on painting: Bay breasted Warbler, Sylvia castanea
   Also in LXXXVIII
Painting and plate depict a male, top, and female, bottom, in an upland cotton plant. The painting is in watercolor with pastel added over the breasts of the birds.

Plate LXX, O.P. 89, One Species, 19 1/2 x 12 1/4
Current name: Henslow's Sparrow, *Ammodramus henslowii* (Audubon)
Name on plate: two variants
  1. Henslow's Bunting EMBERIZA HENSLOWII
  2. Henslow's Bunting AMMODRAMUS HENSLOWII
(marked 70)
Name on painting: Henslow's Bunting, Ammodramus Henslowii
History: Audubon was the discoverer and describer of this species. He named the bird for Professor Henslow of Cambridge University, whose influence got his favorite pupil, Charles Darwin, on the *Beagle*.
Painting depicts one bird on a little rock amid various plants, including worm grass and verbena. In the lower left corner there is a drawing showing the shape of the bird's tail as seen from above. The plate is the same except the sketch of the tail was eliminated.

LXX

Plate LXXI, O.P. 42, One Species, 25 1/2 x 38 1/8
Current name: Red-shouldered Hawk, *Buteo lineatus* (Gmelin)
Name on plate: two variants
  1. Winter Hawk FALCO HYEMALIS. Gmel.
  2. Winter Hawk CIRCUS HYEMALIS (marked 71)
Name on painting: Winter Hawk, Circus hyemalis
  Also in LVI and LXXVI
Painting and plate depict one bird seizing a frog in a watery marsh. The habitat in the painting was done mostly in oil.

LXXI

Plate LXXII, O.P. 45, One Species, 20 3/4 x 27 1/8
Current name: American Swallow-tailed Kite, *Elanoides forficatus* (Linnaeus)
Other names: commonly called Swallow-tailed Kite
Name on plate: two variants
  1. Swallow-tailed Hawk FALCO FURCATUS. Linn.
  2. Swallow-tailed Hawk FALCO FURCATUS. Linn.
(marked 72)
Name on painting: Swallow-tailed Hawk, Falco furcatus
Painting and plate depict one bird in flight holding a garter snake.

LXXII

LXXIII

LXXIV

LXXV

Plate LXXIII, O.P. 279, One Species, 19 1/2 x 12 1/4
Current name: Wood Thrush, *Hylocichla mustelina*
(Gmelin)
Name on plate: two variants
   1. Wood Thrush TURDUS MUSTELINUS. Gmel.
   2. Wood Thrush TURDUS MUSTELINUS. Gmel.
(marked 73)
Name on painting: Wood Thrush, Turdus mustelinus
Painting and plate depict a male, above, and a female,
below, in a branch of dogwood.

Plate LXXIV, O.P. 316, One Species, 19 5/8 x 12 1/4
Current name: Indigo Bunting, *Passerina cyanea* (Linnaeus)
Name on plate: two variants
   1. Indigo Bird FRINGILLA CYANEA. Wils.
   2. Indigo-bird FRINGILLA CYANEA (marked 74)
Name on painting: Indigo-bird, Fringilla cyanea
Painting depicts two immature birds, top, an adult male,
center, and a female, bottom. The three upper birds are in
a wild sarsaparilla and the lower one is on a heavy tree
branch. There is a spider at the lower left. The plate is
the same but for the elimination of the spider.

Plate LXXV, O.P. 156, One Species, 19 1/2 x 12 1/4
Current name: Merlin, *Falco columbarius* Linnaeus
Other names: long called Pigeon Hawk
Name on plate: two variants
   1. Le Petit Caporal FALCO TEMERARIUS
   2. Le Petit Caporal FALCO TEMERARIUS (marked 75)
Name on painting: Le petit Caporal, Falco temerarius
History: Although Audubon correctly identified this
species in Plate XCII, he was convinced that this male
was different. He remarked in his *Ornithological
Biography* that the bird appeared to be closely allied to
the European Hobby. He called it Le Petit Caporal, the
affectionate name by which Napoleon was known to his
soldiers. He said if he had found a new eagle he would
have called it Napoleon's or Bonaparte's but that Le Petit
Caporal seemed more appropriate to this little hawk, a
quite endearing remark.
   Also in XCII
Painting and plate depict one adult male on the stump of a
tree that is entwined with smilax. The painting is done in
pencil and pastel.

Plate LXXVI, O.P. 95, One Species, 25 5/8 x 38 1/4
Current name: Northern Bobwhite, *Colinus virginianus*
(Linnaeus)
Other names: formerly Bobwhite, formerly Common
Bobwhite; commonly called Quail. In certain parts of the
rural countryside these birds are called Partridge.
Name on plate: two variants
   1. Virginian Partridge PERDIX VIRGINIANA. Lath.
   2. Virginian Partridge PERDIX VIRGINIANA. Lath.
(marked 76)
Name on painting: Virginian Partridge Perdix Virginiana
Painting and plate depict a covey of eighteen birds being
attacked by a Red-shouldered Hawk, which is not
identified in the plate legend. There are males with
white throats, females with yellow throats, and young.
The habitat is up in the hills. For the painting Audubon
used oil for the foreground and pastel and watercolor for
the rest.

LXXVI

Plate LXXVII, O.P. 257, One Species, 25 7/8 x 20 3/4
Current name: Belted Kingfisher, *Ceryle alcyon*
(Linnaeus)
Other names: usually called Kingfisher
Name on plate: Two variants
   1. Belted Kingfisher ALCEDO ALCYON. Linn.
   2. Belted Kingfisher ALCEDO ALCYON. Linn.
(marked 77)
Name on painting: Belted Kingfisher, Alcedo alcion
Painting and plate depict two males, upper left, and a
female, lower right, ingesting a fish. The background in
the plate is clearer and more defined.

Plate LXXVIII, O.P. 113, One Species, 19 3/8 x 12 1/8
Current name: Carolina Wren, *Thryothorus ludovicianus*
(Latham)
Name on plate: two variants
   1. Great Carolina Wren TROGLODYTES
LUDOVICIANUS. Bona.
   2. Great Carolina Wren TROGLODYTES
LUDOVICIANUS. Bona. (marked 78)
Name on painting: Great Carolina Wren, Troglodytes
ludovicianus
Painting and plate depict a male, above, and a female,
below, on a branch of scarlet buckeye.

LXXVII

LXXVIII

Plate LXXIX, O.P. 100, One Species, 19 1/2 x 12 1/4
Current name: Eastern Kingbird, *Tyrannus tyrannus*
(Linnaeus)
Other names: usually called Kingbird
Name on plate: two variants
  1. Tyrant Fly catcher MUSCICAPA TYRANNUS.
Briss.
  2. Tyrant Flycatcher MUSCICAPA TYRANNUS
(marked 79)
Name on painting: Tyrant Flycatcher, Muscicapa tyrannus
Painting and plate depict a female, top, and a male,
bottom, on a branch of a cottonwood tree; the male is
eating a bee.

LXXIX

Plate LXXX, O.P. 212, One Species, 12 1/8 x 19 3/8
Current name: Water Pipit, *Anthus spinoletta* (Linnaeus)
Name on plate: two variants
  1. [No English name] ANTHUS HYPOGAEUS (marked
80)
  2. Prairie Titlark ANTHUS PIPIENS
History: Audubon thought this was a new species and
named it Prairie Titlark. He later decided the bird was
the same species as the Water Pipits in Plate X, which he
called Brown Titlarks.
  Also in X
Painting and plate depict an adult bird perched on some
rocks amid moss phlox.

LXXX

Plate LXXXI, O.P. 84, One Species, 38 1/4 x 25 5/8
Current name: Osprey, *Pandion haliaetus* (Linnaeus)
Name on plate: two variants
  1. Fish Hawk or Osprey FALCO HALIAETUS
  2. Fish Hawk FALCO HALIAETUS (marked 81)
Name on painting: Fish Hawk, Falco haliaetus
Painting and plate depict one bird flying with a large
weakfish in its talons and no background. In the plate sea
and cliffs were added in the distance. There is more color
in the plate.

LXXXI

Plate LXXXII, O.P. 218, One Species, 25 3/4 x 20 3/4
Current name: Whip-poor-will, *Caprimulgus vociferus*
Wilson
Name on plate: two variants
   1. Whip-poor-will CAPRIMULGUS VOCIFERUS.
Wils.
   2. Whip-poor-will CAPRIMULGUS VOCIFERUS.
Wils. (marked 82)
Name on painting: Caprimulgus vociferus, Whip-poor-
will
Painting and plate depict a male, above, and two females,
below, in a black or red oak with two butterflies.

LXXXII

Plate LXXXIII, O.P. 4, One Species, 19 1/2 x 12 1/4
Current name: House Wren, *Troglodytes aedon* Vieillot
Name on plate: two variants
   1. House Wren TROGLODYTES AEDON. Vieill.
   2. House Wren TROGLODYTES AEDON. Vieill.
(marked 83)
Name on painting: House Wren, Troglodytes (?) edon
History: Audubon correctly identified the birds in this
plate, but when it came to the bird in Plate CLXXIX he
was convinced he had a new species because he thought he
detected a difference in song. He called the bird Wood
Wren, but it too is a House Wren.
   Also in CLXXIX
Painting depicts two baby birds peering out from their
nest, which is in an old hat, while a third baby clings to
the hat's far side. A female is offering them a spider and
a male is perched on top of the hat. The plate is the same
except that the hat is jammed into a branch.

LXXXIII

Plate LXXXIV, O.P. lost, One Species, 19 1/2 x 12 1/4
Current name: Blue-gray Gnatcatcher, *Polioptila caerulea*
(Linnaeus)
Name on plate: two variants
   1. Blue Grey Flycatcher SYLVIA COERULA (marked
84)
   2. Blue-grey Flycatcher MUSCICAPA COERULEA
(* Blue-grey Flycatcher SYLVIA COERULA)
History: The painting for this plate is one of the two that
are lost.
Plate shows two birds in branches of a black walnut.

LXXXIV

Plate LXXXV, O.P. 14, One Species, 19 3/8 x 12 1/4
Current name: Yellow-throated Warbler, *Dendroica dominica* (Linnaeus)
Name on plate: two variants
    1. Yellow Throat Warbler SYLVIA PENSILIS (marked 85)
    2. Yellow Throated Warbler SYLVIA PENSILIS, Lath.
    ....(* Yellow-throat Warbler SYLVIA PENSILIS)
Name on painting: Yellow Throat Warbler, Sylvia Flavicollis pensilis
Painting and plate depict a male bird on a twig of a chinquapin tree.

LXXXV

Plate LXXXVI, O.P. 174, One Species, 38 1/8 x 25 1/2
Current name: Red-tailed Hawk, *Buteo jamaicensis* (Gmelin)
Other names: The hawks in this plate are Harlan's, which used to be a separate species but is now included in the Red-tailed.
Name on plate: two variants
    1. Black Warrior FALCO HARLANI
    2. Black Warrior FALCO HARIANI (marked 86)
Name on painting: Black Warrior, Falco Harlani
History: Audubon found this bird in Louisiana and believed it to be a new species. Although he gave it the common name of Black Warrior, he honored his friend Dr. Richard Harlan in the scientific name. The name Black Warrior didn't stick and the bird became known as Harlan's Hawk.
    Also in LI
Painting depicts a male, above, and a female, below, perched on separate branches. Plate is the same except the upper branch comes from a trunk that extends down on the right.

LXXXVI

Plate LXXXVII, O.P. 13, One Species, 25 3/4 x 20 1/2
Current name: Scrub Jay, *Aphelocoma coerulescens* (Bosc)
Other names: The A.O.U. names four groups within this species. The birds in this plate are of the *coerulescens* group.
Name on plate: two variants
    1. Florida Jay GARRULUS FLORIDANUS (marked 87)
    2. Florida Jay CORVUS FLORIDANUS. Bartram.
Name on painting: Florida Jay, Garrulus Floridanus
History: Audubon painted the birds in this plate from eastern specimens and the bird in Plate CCCLXII from a western specimen.
    Also in CCCLXII
Painting and plate depict two birds in a persimmon tree.

LXXXVII

Plate LXXXVIII, O.P. 364, One Species, 19 3/8 x 12 1/4
Current name: Bay-breasted Warbler, *Dendroica castanea*
(Wilson)
Name on plate: two variants
   1. Autumnal Warbler SYLVIA AUTUMNALIS. Wils.
   2. Autumnal Warbler SYLVIA AUTUMNALIS. Wils.
(marked 88)
Name on painting: Autumnal Warbler, Sylvia autumnalis
   Also in LXIX
Painting and plate depict a young female, above, and a
young male, below, in a branch of a canoe birch.

LXXXVIII

Plate LXXXIX, O.P. 63, One Species, 19 3/8 x 12 1/4
Current name: Nashville Warbler, *Vermivora ruficapilla*
(Wilson)
Name on plate: two variants
   1. Nashville Warbler SYLVIA RUBRICAPILLA.
Wils.
   2. Nashville Warbler SYLVIA RUBRICAPILLA.
Wils. (marked 89)
Name on painting: Nashville Warbler, Sylvia
rubricapilla
Painting depicts a female, above, and a male, below, in a
black alder. The legs of the female are incomplete in the
painting but are finished in the plate.

LXXXIX

Plate XC, O.P. 57, One Species, 19 1/2 x 12 1/4
Current name: Black-and-white Warbler, *Mniotilta varia*
(Linnaeus)
Name on plate: two variants
   1. Black & White Creeper CERTHIA VARIA. Wils.
   2. Black and White Creeper SYLVIA VARIA (marked
90)
Painting and plate depict a male bird in a branch of black
larch with a small drawing of the bird's foot at the lower
left.

XC

XCI

XCII

XCIII

Plate XCI, O.P. 259, One Species, 38 1/8 x 25 1/2
Current name: Broad-winged Hawk, *Buteo platypterus*
(Vieillot)
Name on plate: two variants
   1. Broad-winged Hawk FALCO PENNSYLVANICUS.
Wils.
   2. Broad-winged Hawk FALCO PENNSYLVANICUS.
Wils. (marked 91)
Name on painting: Broad-winged Hawk, Falco
Pennsylvanicus
Painting and plate depict a male, above, and a young
female, below, in a pignut tree.

Plate XCII, O.P. 30, One Species, 25 3/8 x 20 3/8
Current name: Merlin, *Falco columbarius* Linnaeus
Other names: long called Pigeon Hawk
Name on plate: three variants
   1. Pigeon Hawk FALCO COLUMBARIUS. Linn.
   2. Pigeon Hawk FALCO COLUMBARIUS
   3. Pigeon Hawk FALCO COLUMBARIUS (marked 92)
Name on painting: Pigeon Hawk, Falco columbarius
History: Audubon knew well the identity of the species in
this plate, but when it came to the male in Plate LXXV he
thought he had a new species, which he called Le Petit
Caporal.
  Also in LXXV
Painting depicts a young male, above, and a young female,
below, on a bare branch. In the plate, leaves were added
to the lower part of the branch.

Plate XCIII, O.P. 33, One Species, 19 1/4 x 12 1/4
Current name: Seaside Sparrow, *Ammodramus maritimus*
(Wilson)
Other names: The A.O.U. says there are three groups
within this species: *maritimus*, *nigrescens*, and *mirabilis*.
As the birds from which this painting was made were in
New Jersey, it may be presumed they are of the *maritimus*
group.
Name on plate: two variants
   1. Sea-side Finch FRINGILLA MARITIMA. Wils.
   2. Sea-side Finch FRINGILLA MARITIMA. Wils.
(marked 93)
Name on painting: Sea Side Finch, Fringilla maritima
  Also in CCCLV
Painting and plate depict two birds in a wild rose.

Plate XCIV, O.P. 217, One Species, 19 1/2 x 12 1/4
Current name: Vesper Sparrow, *Pooecetes gramineus*
(Gmelin)
Name on plate: two variants
   1. Grass Finch, or Bay-winged Bunting FRINGILLA
GRAMINEA, Gmel.
   2. Bay-winged Bunting FRINGILLA GRAMINEA
(marked 94)
Name on painting: Bay-winged Bunting, Fringilla
graminea
Painting and plate depict one bird in front of a prickly
pear.

XCIV

Plate XCV, O.P. 147, One Species, 19 3/8 x 12 1/4
Current name: Yellow Warbler, *Dendroica petechia*
(Linnaeus)
Name on plate: two variants
   1. Blue-eyed yellow Warbler SYLVIA AESTIVA
(marked 95)
   2. Yellow-poll Warbler SYLVIA AESTIVA. Gmel.
      (* Blue-eyed Yellow Warbler SYLVIA AESTIVA)
Name on painting: Blue-eyed yellow Warbler, Sylvia
aestiva
History: Audubon correctly identified the male here as a
Yellow Warbler but when it came to the females and
young in Plates XXXV and LXV he did not; in both cases
thought he had a new species, which he called
Rathbone's and Children's Warblers.
   Also in XXXV and LXV
Painting and plate depict a male in a wisteria.

XCV

Plate XCVI, O.P. 53, One Species, 38 1/8 x 25 1/2
Current name: Black-throated Magpie-Jay, *Calocitta
colliei* (Vigors)
Other names: There are two species, Black-throated and
White-throated. The birds here clearly have black
throats. However, there are those who consider the two
to be conspecific, in which case the bird is called Magpie
Jay.
Name on plate: two variants
   1. Columbia Jay GARRULUS ULTRAMARINUS
(marked 96)
   2. Columbia Jay CORVUS BULLOCKII
   History: The skins from which Audubon painted these
birds were given to him by a correspondent who said they
had been collected on the Columbia River, Oregon. This
was not true; the species is Mexican. The only sighting of
this species in the United States was at an Arizona feeder
and this was undoubtedly an escape.
Painting and plate depict two birds in a dead tree
entwined with poison ivy.

XCVI

XCVII

Plate XCVII, O.P. 26, One Species, 25 3/8 x 20 3/4
Current name: Eastern Screech-Owl, *Otus asio* (Linnaeus)
Other names: Formerly one species, this bird has now been divided into several, including Eastern and Western; usually called Screech-Owl.
Name on plate: two variants
1. Mottled Owl STRIX ASIO (marked 97)
2. Little Screech Owl STRIX ASIO, Linn.
Name on painting: Mottled Owl, Strix asio
History: As indicated by the writing on the painting, Audubon thought the gray bird at top an adult and the red-brown birds at bottom young ones. Apparently he did not know of the color phases in this species. All these birds are actually adults. One can be sure they are Eastern as the Western does not have the red-brown phase. Painting and plate depict two birds in red-brown color phase, below, and one bird in gray phase top, all in a scrub pine. In the painting the bottom birds were done in watercolor. The top bird, drawn in pastel separately some years before, was cut out and pasted onto the paper.

XCVIII

Plate XCVIII, O.P. 397, One Species, 19 5/8 x 12 1/4
Current name: Tree Swallow, *Tachycineta bicolor* (Vieillot)
Name on plate: two variants
1. White-bellied Swallow HIRUNDO BICOLOR
2. Green-blue or White Bellied Swallow HIRUNDO BICOLOR (marked 100)
(Confusion between the Tree Swallow and the Marsh Wren: There are two variants of the Tree Swallow, one correctly marked XCVIII and one erroneously marked 100. There are also two variants of the Marsh Wren, one correctly marked C and one erroneously marked 98.)
Name on painting: Green-blue, or White Bellied Swallow, Hirundo bicolor
Painting depicts a male, above, and a female, below, both in the air with no background. A drawing of a Tree Swallow's egg is in the lower left corner. In the plate there is a background of clouds and the egg is eliminated.

XCIX

Plate XCIX, O.P. 59, One Species, 12 1/4 x 19 5/8
Current name: Brown-headed Cowbird, *Molothrus ater* (Boddaert)
Other names: usually called Cowbird
Name on plate: two variants
1. Cow Bunting ICTERUS PECORIS (marked 99)
2. Cow-pen Bird ICTERUS PECORIS
Name on painting: Cow Bunting, Icterus pecoris
Also in CCCCXXIV
Painting and plate depict a male, right, and a female, left, on clumpy mossy ground with a variety of small plants.

Plate C, O.P. 336, One Species, 19 1/2 x 12 1/4
Current name: Marsh Wren, *Cistothorus palustris*
(Wilson)
Name on plate: two variants
   1. Marsh Wren TROGLODYTES PALUSTRIS. Ch.
Bonap.
   2. Marsh Wren TROGLODYTES PALUSTRIS (marked
98)
(Confusion between the Tree Swallow and the Marsh
Wren: There are two variants of the Tree Swallow, one
correctly marked XCVIII and one erroneously marked 100.
There are also two variants of the Marsh Wren, one
correctly marked C and one erroneously marked 98.)
Name on painting: Marsh Wren, Troglodytes palustris
Painting and plate depict a male, right, and two females,
top and left, around the nest.

C

Plate CI, O.P. 120, One Species, 38 1/8 x 25 3/8
Current name: Common Raven, *Corvus corax* Linnaeus
Other names: Northern Raven, Holarctic Raven. Usually
called Raven.
Name on plate: Raven CORVUS CORAX
Name on painting: Raven, Corvus Corax
Painting and plate depict a male bird in a branch of shag
bark hickory.

Plate CII, O.P. 70, One Species, 25 1/2 x 20 1/2
Current name: Blue Jay, *Cyanocitta cristata* (Linnaeus)
Name on plate: Blue Jay CORVUS CRISTATUS
Name on painting: Blue Jay, Corvus cristatus
Painting depicts two birds on a dead tree trunk. There is a
vine around the tree lightly indicated in ink. In the plate
the vine is a finished trumpet vine.

CI

CII

Plate CIII, O.P. 46, One Species, 19 1/4 x 12 1/8
Current name: Canada Warbler, *Wilsonia canadensis*
(Linnaeus)
Name on plate: Canada Warbler SYLVIA PARDALINA
Name on painting: Canada Flycatcher, Sylvia pardalina
History: Audubon did not correctly identify the immature
bird in Plate V as a Canada Warbler and thought he had
a new species, but he did identify this bird correctly.
    Also in V
Painting and plate depict a male, above, and a female,
below, in a laurel.

Plate CIV, O.P. 430, One Species, 19 1/2 x 12 1/4
Current name: Chipping Sparrow, *Spizella passerina*
(Bechstein)
Name on plate: Chipping Sparrow FRINGILLA
SOCIALIS
Name on painting: Chipping Sparrow, Fringilla socialis
Painting and plate depict one bird on a limb of a black
locust.

CIII

Plate CV, O.P. 352, One Species, 19 5/8 x 12 1/4
Current name: Red-breasted Nuthatch, *Sitta canadensis*
Linnaeus
Name on plate: Red-breasted Nuthatch SITTA
CANADENSIS
Name on painting: Red breasted Nuthatch, Sitta
Canadensis
Painting and plate depict a male, top, and female, bottom,
on a lichen-covered tree trunk.

CIV

CV

Plate CVI, O.P. 25, One Species, 25 5/8 x 38 1/4
Current name: Black Vulture, *Coragyps atratus* (Bechstein)

Name on plate: two variants
   1. Black Vulture or Carrion Crow CATHARTES
ATRATUS
   2. Black Vulture or Carrion Crow CATHARTES IOTA
Painting depicts two birds feeding on the head of a deer.
In the plate some low-growing flowers have been added to
the foreground.

CVI

Plate CVII, O.P. 24, One Species, 26 x 20 3/4
Current name: Gray Jay, *Perisoreus canadensis* (Linnaeus)
Name on plate: Canada Jay CORVUS CANADENSIS,
Linn.
History: These birds are eastern Gray Jays which are
paler than the western Gray Jay in Plate CCCCXIX.
Also in CCCCXIX
Painting and plate depict two birds in a branch of white
oak to which a hornet's nest is attached.
SEE COMPOSITE PLATES IN PART I

Plate CVIII, O.P. 213, One Species, 12 1/4 x 19 1/2
Current name: Fox Sparrow, *Passerella iliaca* (Merrem)
Name on plate: Fox-coloured Sparrow FRINGILLA
ILIACA
Also in CCCCXXIV
Painting and plate depict two birds on a mound covered by
flora including partridge-berry and Christmas fern.

CVII

CVIII

CIX

CX

CXI

Plate CIX, O.P. 246, One Species, 19 5/8 x 12 3/8
Current name: Savannah Sparrow, *Passerculus sandwichensis* (Gmelin)
Name on plate: Savannah Finch FRINGILLA SAVANNA
Name on painting: Savannah Finch, Fringilla [faded]
Painting and plate depict two birds in a marshlike area with plants that include verbena and worm-grass. In the painting the lower bird is in pastel and the upper one is in watercolor.

Plate CX, O.P. 403, One Species, 19 3/8 x 12 1/4
Current name: Hooded Warbler, *Wilsonia citrina* (Boddaert)
Name on plate: Hooded Warbler SYLVIA MITRATA
Name on painting: Hooded Fly Catcher, Muscicapa Cucullata
History: Audubon correctly identified this bird but he did not recognize the immature in Plate IX and thought he had a new species, which he called Selby's Flycatcher.
   Also in IX
Painting depicts a female on a plant stem and a male perched on a short, unattached piece of branch. In the plate the branch on which the male is perched is extended and has four seed pods.
SEE COMPOSITE PLATES IN PART I

Plate CXI, O.P. 208, One Species, 38 1/4 x 25 5/8
Current name: Pileated Woodpecker, *Dryocopus pileatus* (Linnaeus)
Name on plate: Pileated Woodpecker PICUS PILEATUS. Linn.
Name on painting: Pileated Woodpecker, Picus
Painting and plate depict a female, top, a male, center, and two young, bottom, all in a dead tree entwined with a grapevine. The painting is in pencil, watercolor, ink, and egg tempera.

Plate CXII, O.P. 306, One Species, 26 x 20 7/8
Current name: Downy Woodpecker, *Picoides pubescens*
(Linnaeus)
Name on plate: Downy Woodpecker PICUS PUBESCENS
Painting depicts a male, above, and a female, below, on a
dead tree entwined with a trumpet-flower vine. The
plate shows much more of the vine.

Plate CXIII, O.P. 342, One Species, 19 1/2 x 12 3/8
Current name: Eastern Bluebird, *Sialia sialis* (Linnaeus)
Other names: usually called Bluebird
Name on plate: Blue-bird SYLVIA SIALIS
History: The male bird flying appears again in Plate
XXXVI, which depicts Cooper's Hawks. This is one of
only two instances where the same painting of a bird
appears in two plates; the other is the Wilson's Plover in
Plates CCIX and CCLXXXIV.
    Also in XXXVI (name not in plate legend)
Painting and plate depict a male, above, a female, left,
and a young bird, right, all in stalks of mullein.

Plate CXIV, O.P. 340, One Species, 19 1/2 x 12 1/4
Current name: White-crowned Sparrow, *Zonotrichia
leucophrys* (Forster)
Name on plate: White-crowned Sparrow FRINGILLA
LEUCOPHRYS
Name on painting: White Crowned Bunting A.W.
Emberiza Leucophrys
White Crowned Sparrow. A. Wilson
Painting and plate depict a male, above, and female,
below, in a grape vine.

CXII

CXIII

CXIV

CXV

Plate CXV, O.P. 381, One Species, 19 1/2 x 12 1/4
Current name: Eastern Wood-Pewee, *Contopus virens* (Linnaeus)
Name on plate: Wood Pewee MUSCICAPA VIRENS
Name on painting: Wood Pewee Flycatcher, Muscicapa Virens
Painting and plate depict a male in a branch of swamp honeysuckle.

Plate CXVI, O.P. 271, One Species, 38 1/4 x 25 5/8
Current name: Brown Thrasher, *Toxostoma rufum* (Linnaeus)
Name on plate: Ferruginous Thrush TURDUS RUFUS. Linn.
Painting and plate depict a Black Snake attacking two males, above, and two females, below, who are defending not only a nest with eggs but their lives as well. The nest is in an oak tree.

Plate CXVII, O.P. 384, One Species, 25 7/8 x 20 7/8
Current name: Mississippi Kite, *Ictinia mississippiensis* (Wilson)
Name on plate: Mississippi Kite FALCO PLUMBEUS. Gmel.
Name on painting: Mississippi Kite, Falco Mississippiensis
Painting depicts one bird on a dead branch holding a bee. Another bird, labeled female, was added in the plate but it is a mirror image of a male that Alexander Wilson had painted years before. Audubon never admitted that Wilson had painted this bird.

CXVI

CXVII

Plate CXVIII, O.P. 203, One Species, 19 3/8 x 12 1/4
Current name: Warbling Vireo, *Vireo gilvus* (Vieillot)
Name on plate: Warbling Flycatcher MUSICAPA
GILVA. Vieill.
Name on painting: Warbling Flycatcher, Vireo gilvus
Painting and plate depict two birds in a laurel magnolia.

Plate CXIX, O.P. 83, One Species, 19 1/2 x 12 1/8
Current name: Yellow-throated Vireo, *Vireo flavifrons*
Vieillot
Name on plate: Yellow-throated Vireo VIREO
FLAVIFRONS. Vieill.
Name on painting: Yellow Throated Vireo, Vireo
flavifrons
Painting and plate depict a male in a branch of hydrangea
reaching for a wasp.

Plate CXX, O.P. 319, One Species, 19 1/2 x 12 1/4
Current name: Eastern Phoebe, *Sayornis phoebe* (Latham)
Other names: usually called Phoebe
Name on plate: two variants
    1. Pewit Flycatcher MUSICAPA FUSCA. Gmel.
    2. Pewee Flycatcher MUSICAPA FUSCA. Gmel.
Painting and plate depict two birds on a branch of sea-
island cotton.

CXVIII

CXIX

CXX

CXXI

Plate CXXI, O.P. 60, One Species, 38 1/4 x 25 5/8
Current name: Snowy Owl, *Nyctea scandiaca* (Linnaeus)
Name on plate: Snowy Owl STRIX NYCTEA. Linn.
Painting and plate depict a male, top, and a female, below, in a dead tree high up on a mountain with landscape far below. It is one of only three night scenes in *Birds of America*; the others are found in Plate CLXXI, Common Barn-Owl, and in Plate CCCXI, American White Pelican. The viewer is not immediately conscious that it is night in the painting, but the night effect is enhanced in the plate.

Plate CXXII, O.P. 400, One Species, 26 x 20 7/8
Current name: Blue Grosbeak, *Guiraca caerulea* (Linnaeus)
Name on plate: two variants
   1. Blue Grosbeak FRINGILLA CORULEA. Bonap.
   2. Blue Grosbeak FRINGILLA COERULEA. Bonap.
Painting and plate depict a male, top, and an immature male, lower left, in a dogwood with a female, center, on the edge of her nest. In the painting three branches come up from a common trunk, while in the plate they come up independently.

Plate CXXIII, O.P. 136, One Species, 19 5/8 x 12 1/4
Current name: Magnolia Warbler, *Dendroica magnolia* (Wilson)
Name on plate: Black & Yellow Warbler SYLVIA MACULOSA. Lath.
Name on painting: Black & Yellow Warblers, Sylvia maculosa
History: Audubon made a separate painting of a young Magnolia Warbler that he wished to be added to this plate. Havell misunderstood and made a separate plate of the young bird.
   Also in L
Painting and plate depict two males in a raspberry bush.

CXXII

CXXIII

Plate CXXIV, O.P. 378, One Species, 19 5/8 x 12 3/8
Current name: Wilson's Warbler, *Wilsonia pusilla*
(Wilson)
Name on plate: two variants
   1. Green Black-capt Flycatcher MUSCICAPA
PUSILLA
   2. Green Black-capt Flycatcher MUSCICAPA
WILSONII
Name on painting: Green black capt Flycatcher
Painting and plate alike depict a female, above, and a
male, below, in sprigs of turtlehead.

Plate CXXV, O.P. 307, One Species, 19 5/8 x 12 3/8
Current name: Brown-headed Nuthatch, *Sitta pusilla*
Latham
Name on plate: Brown-headed Nuthatch SITTA
PUSILLA. Lath.
Painting and plate depict two birds on a tree trunk.

CXXIV

Plate CXXVI, O.P. 106, One Species, 38 1/4 x 25 5/8
Current name: Bald Eagle, *Haliaeetus leucocephalus*
(Linnaeus)
Name on plate: White-headed Eagle FALCO
LEUCOCEPHALUS. Linn.
History: Although Audubon was confused about the
identity of the immature Eagle in Plate XI, he correctly
identified the immature bird in this plate and the mature
bird in Plate XXXI.
   Also in XI and XXXI
Painting and plate depict one immature bird perched on a
branch with no other background.

CXXV

CXXVI

CXXVII

CXXVIII

CXXIX

Plate CXXVII, O.P. 311, One Species, 25 3/4 x 20 5/8
Current name: Rose-breasted Grosbeak, *Pheucticus ludovicianus* (Linnaeus)
Name on plate: Rose-breasted Grosbeak FRINGILLA LUDOVICIANA. Bonap.
Painting depicts two young males, top, and two adult males, below, in a yew. In the plate a female was added at the upper left.

Plate CXXVIII, O.P. 285, One Species, 19 5/8 x 12 3/8
Current name: Gray Catbird, *Dumetella carolinensis* (Linnaeus)
Other names: usually called Catbird
Name on plate: Cat Bird TURDUS FELIVOX. Vieill.
Painting depicts upper bird on a branch of blackberry. The lower bird is in a perching position but there is only a suggestion of a branch pencilled in. In the plate another branch of blackberry is provided for the lower bird.

Plate CXXIX, O.P. 335, One Species, 19 1/2 x 12 1/4
Current name: Great Crested Flycatcher, *Myiarchus crinitus* (Linnaeus)
Name on plate: Great Crested Flycatcher MUSCICAPA CRINITA. Linn.
Painting and plate depict two birds fighting. The lower is perched on a dead branch and the other is flying.

Plate CXXX, O.P. 273, One Species, 19 1/2 x 12 1/4
Current name: Grasshopper Sparrow, *Ammodramus savannarum* (Gmelin)
Name on plate: Yellow-winged Sparrow FRINGILLA PASSERINA. Wils.
Name on painting: Yellow Winged Sparrow, Fringilla Passerina
Painting depicts one bird on a rock partially covered with moss phlox. The bird was originally done in pastel but Audubon went over the work in watercolor. In the plate the scene is enhanced with more rocks, more phlox, and water in the foreground.

Plate CXXXI, O.P. 50, One Species, 38 1/8 x 25 5/8
Current name: American Robin, *Turdus migratorius* Linnaeus
Other names: usually called Robin
Name on plate: American Robin TURDUS MIGRATORIUS
Painting and plate depict two adults, above, and four young, below, with a nest in a branch of what is probably a chestnut oak.

CXXX

Plate CXXXII, O.P. 130, One Species, 26 x 20 3/4
Current name: Black-backed Woodpecker, *Picoides arcticus* (Swainson)
Other names: Black-backed Three-toed Woodpecker
Name on plate: Three-toed Woodpecker PICUS TRIDACTYLUS. Linn.
History: Do not confuse this Black-backed Woodpecker (sometimes called Black-backed Three-toed Woodpecker) with the Three-toed Woodpecker, *Picoides tridactylus* (sometimes called Northern Three-toed Woodpecker) that is in Plate CCCCXVII. Note that although Audubon has the common name of his day correct, he got mixed up on the scientific name.
Painting and plate depict two males, top and bottom, and a female, center, on a dead tree trunk entwined with poison ivy.

CXXXI

CXXXII

CXXXIII

CXXXIV

CXXXV

Plate CXXXIII, O.P. 197, One Species, 19 5/8 x 12 3/8
Current name: Blackpoll Warbler, *Dendroica striata*
(Forster)
Name on plate: Black-poll Warbler SYLVIA STRIATA.
Lath.
Name on painting: Black-poll Warbler, Sylvia Striata
Painting and plate depict a female, top left, and two
males, top right and bottom, in a branch of a black-gum
tree.

Plate CXXXIV, O.P. 250, One Species, 19 1/2 x 12 3/8
Current name: Blackburnian Warbler, *Dendroica fusca*
(Müller)
Name on plate: Hemlock Warbler SYLVIA PARUS. Wils.
Name on painting: Hemlock Warbler, Sylvia parus
History: Audubon correctly identified the Blackburnian
Warblers in Plates CXXXV and CCCXCIX but he was
fooled by the two females in this plate, calling them
Hemlock Warblers as had Wilson before him.
   Also in CXXXV and CCCXCIX
Painting and plate depict two females on a branch of
mountain maple.

Plate CXXXV, O.P. 404, One Species, 19 3/4 x 12 3/8
Current name: Blackburnian Warbler, *Dendroica fusca*
(Müller)
Name on plate: Blackburnian Warbler SYLVIA
BLACKBURNIAE. Lath.
Name on painting: Black burnian Warbler, Sylvia
Blackburnia
History: Audubon correctly identified the birds in this
plate and in Plate CCCXCIX as Blackburnian Warblers,
but he did not recognize the females in Plate CXXXIV as
being of the same species.
   Also in CXXXIV and CCCXCIX
Painting depicts one male on a twig in the midst of a
flowering sweet william. In the plate the twig is made
into a longer branch with two clusters of large leaves.
SEE COMPOSITE PLATES IN PART I

Plate CXXXVI, O.P. 114, One Species, 38 1/4 x 25 5/8
Current name: Eastern Meadowlark, *Sturnella magna*
(Linnaeus)
Other names: usually called Meadowlark
Name on plate: Meadow Lark STURNUS
LUDOVICIANUS. Linn.
Painting depicts two adults, top and left, with two young,
lower right, all about a nest surrounded by downy false
foxglove.

Plate CXXXVII, O.P. 243, One Species, 25 3/4 x 20 5/8
Current name: Yellow-breasted Chat, *Icteria virens*
(Linnaeus)
Name on plate: Yellow-breasted Chat ICTERIA
VIRIDIS. Bonap.
Name on painting: Yellow-breasted Chat, Icteria viridis
Painting depicts three males flying, another male
perched, and a female in a nest which is in a rose bush.
The plate is the same except that the flying male, upper
left, was eliminated.

Plate CXXXVIII, O.P. 386, One Species, 19 1/2 x 12 1/4
Current name: Connecticut Warbler, *Oporornis agilis*
(Wilson)
Name on plate: Connecticut Warbler SYLVIA AGILIS.
Wils.
Name on painting: Connecticut Warbler, Sylvia agilis
Painting and plate depict a female, top, and a male,
below, in a soapwort gentian.

CXXXVI

CXXXVII

CXXXVIII

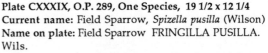

Plate CXXXIX, O.P. 289, One Species, 19 1/2 x 12 1/4
Current name: Field Sparrow, *Spizella pusilla* (Wilson)
Name on plate: Field Sparrow FRINGILLA PUSILLA.
Wils.
Name on painting: Field Sparrow, Fringilla pusilla
Painting depicts a male bird on a mound amid a growth of
grass pinks and blueberry. In the plate more shore line
and water were added on the left.

Plate CXL, O.P. 211, One Species, 19 1/2 x 12 3/8
Current name: Pine Warbler, *Dendroica pinus* (Wilson)
Name on plate: Pine Creeping Warbler SYLVIA PINUS.
Lath.
Name on painting: Pine Creeping Warbler, Sylvia Pinus
    Also in XXX
Painting and plate depict a female, above, and a male,
below, in a loblolly pine.
SEE COMPOSITE PLATES IN PART I

CXXXIX

Plate CXLI, O.P. 17, Two Species, 38 1/4 x 25 5/8
<u>Species 1</u>
Current name: Northern Goshawk, *Accipiter gentilis*
(Linnaeus)
Other names: called Goshawk
Name on plate: Goshawk FALCO PALUMBARIUS. Linn.
<u>Species 2</u>
Current name: Cooper's Hawk, *Accipiter cooperii*
(Bonaparte)
Name on plate: Stanley Hawk FALCO STANLEII. Aud.
History: Audubon thought he had a new species in this
bird and named it for Lord Stanley, later the fourteenth
Earl of Derby, noted sportsman, parliamentarian, and
translator of the Iliad. He greatly befriended Audubon
and almost employed him to paint his collection of fauna
but in the end gave the job to Edward Lear. Audubon's
claim to this bird caused bitterness and controversy as the
bird had already been named by Charles Lucien
Bonaparte for William Cooper of the New York Lyceum.
    Also in XXXVI
Painting depicts an immature Northern Goshawk at the
top, perched on a branch. Audubon cut out two earlier
paintings of an adult Northern Goshawk and an adult
Cooper's Hawk and pasted them below, Goshawk at the
left and Cooper's at the right. In the plate there is an
elaborate background of water, rocks, branches, grasses,
and distant mountains. Something went awry with this
plate and the relationship between birds and background
became distorted.

CXL

CXLI

Plate CXLII, O.P. 184, One Species, 26 x 20 5/8
Current name: American Kestrel, *Falco sparverius*
Linnaeus
Other names: formerly Kestrel, formerly Sparrow Hawk
Name on plate: American Sparrow Hawk FALCO
SPARVERIUS. Linn.
Painting and plate depict a female, top, holding a dead
sparrow, a male, below left, on a branch, and another
male flying down in pursuit of an insect.

Plate CXLIII, O.P. 356, One Species, 19 1/2 x 12 1/4
Current name: Ovenbird, *Seiurus aurocapillus* (Linnaeus)
Name on plate: Golden-crowned Thrush TURDUS
AUROCAPILLUS. Wils.
Name on painting: Golden crowned Thrush, Sylvia
aurocapilla
Painting depicts one bird on a dead branch, below, and
another, above, on a branch of bittersweet. The plate is
similar except that water was added to the foreground.

Plate CXLIV, O.P. 408, One Species, 19 5/8 x 12 3/8
Current name: Acadian Flycatcher, *Empidonax virescens*
(Vieillot)
Name on plate: Small Green Crested Flycatcher
MUSCICAPA ACADICA. Wils.
   (* Small Green-crested Flycatcher MUSCICAPA
ACADICA, Gmel.)
Name on painting: Small green crested Flycatcher,
Muscicapa acadica
Painting and plate depict a male, top, and a female under
on a branch of sassafras tree.

CXLII

CXLIII

CXLIV

CXLV

Plate CXLV, O.P. 368, One Species, 19 1/2 x 12 3/8
Current name: Palm Warbler, *Dendroica palmarum*
(Gmelin)
Name on plate: Yellow Red-poll Warbler SYLVIA
PETECHIA. Lath.
Name on painting: Yellow Red Poll Warbler, Sylvia
petechia
History: When Audubon painted these birds he did not
realize they were of the same species illustrated in Plate
CLXIII. Later, he wrote in his *Ornithological Biography*
that he had made an error and that both plates depicted
Palm Warblers, those in Plate CLXIII in full summer
plumage and those in Plate CXLV in first autumnal
plumage. The ones in this plate are probably from the
western part of the Palm Warbler's range and are of a
paler yellow.
   Also in CLXIII
Painting and plate depict a male, above, and a female,
below, in a sneezeweed. The painting is in pencil, pastel,
and watercolor.

CXLVI

Plate CXLVI, O.P. 67, One Species, 38 1/4 x 25 5/8
Current name: Fish Crow, *Corvus ossifragus* Wilson
Name on plate: Fish Crow CORVUS OSSIFRAGUS,
Wils.
Painting and plate depict two birds in a honey locust. The
lower bird is eating a crab.

Plate CXLVII, O.P. 351, One Species, 26 x 20 5/8
Current name: Common Nighthawk, *Chordeiles minor*
(Forster)
Other names: often called Nighthawk
Name on plate: Night Hawk CAPRIMULGUS
VIRGINIANUS. Briss.
Painting depicts two birds, pursuing insects, against a
branch of white oak. In the plate a female bird was
added crouching on a branch lower left.

CXLVII

Plate CXLVIII, O.P. 426, One Species, 19 5/8 x 12 1/4
Current name: Black-throated Blue Warbler, *Dendroica caerulescens* (Gmelin)
Name on plate: Pine Swamp Warbler SYLVIA SPHAGNOSA. Bonap.
Name on painting: Pine Swamp Warbler, Sylvia Sphagnosa
History: Neither Wilson nor Audubon realized these female birds were Black-throated Blues and both thought them to be a species which Wilson called the Pine Swamp Warbler. Audubon later correctly identified a male Black-throated Blue, which is in Plate CLV.
   Also in CLV
Painting and plate depict two females on a sprig of hobble-bush.

CXLVIII

Plate CXLIX, O.P. 163, One Species, 19 5/8 x 12 1/4
Current name: Sharp-tailed Sparrow, *Ammodramus caudacutus* (Gmelin)
Name on plate: Sharp-tailed Finch FRINGILLA CAUDACUTA. Wils.
Name on painting: Sharp tailed Finch, Fringilla caudacuta
Painting and plate depict two males in marsh grass with a female below in her nest. In the plate the background is more firmly delineated to show the sea in the middle distance.

Plate CL, O.P. 180, One Species, 19 1/2 x 12 1/4
Current name: Red-eyed Vireo, *Vireo olivaceus* (Linnaeus)
Name on plate: Red-eyed Vireo VIREO OLIVACEUS. Bonap.
History: Audubon recognized that this bird was a Red-eyed Vireo, but thinking that the immature in Plate CCCCXXXIV was a different species, he called it Bartram's Viroe.
   Also in CCCCXXXIV
Painting and plate depict one bird perched on a limb of honey locust reaching for a spider in its web.

CXLIX

CL

Plate CLI, O.P. 81, One Species, 25 5/8 x 38 1/4
Current name: Turkey Vulture, *Cathartes aura* (Linnaeus)
Other names: sometimes called Buzzard
Name on plate: two variants
   1. Turkey Buzzard CATHARTES ATRATUS
   2. Turkey Buzzard CATHARTES AURA
Painting depicts an adult male, above, on a short piece of branch and a young bird, below, also on a short piece of branch with no other background. In the plate the short branches lead into a tree trunk on the right. For the painting Audubon cut out a previously painted young bird and pasted it below the adult bird he had painted on the paper.

CLI

Plate CLII, O.P. 372, One Species, 26 x 20 3/4
Current name: White-breasted Nuthatch, *Sitta carolinensis* Latham
Name on plate: White-breasted Black-capped Nuthatch SITTA CAROLINENSIS. Briss.
Painting and plate depict four birds on a lichen-encrusted tree trunk. In the plate the tree trunk extends up higher and tufts of Spanish moss were added.

CLII

Plate CLIII, O.P. 127, One Species, 19 5/8 x 12 3/8
Current name: Yellow-rumped Warbler, *Dendroica coronata* (Linnaeus) (Myrtle group)
Other names: Until recently this bird, the Myrtle Warbler, and Audubon's Warbler were considered to be two species. Now they are grouped within one species, Yellow-rumped Warbler.
Name on plate: two variants
   1. Yellow-Crown Warbler SYLVIA CORONATA, Lath.
   2. Yellow rump Warbler SYLVIA CORONATA. Lath.
Name on painting: Sylvia Coronata, Yellow rump Warbler, A.W.
   Also in CCCXCV (Audubon group)
Painting, in pencil, pastel, and watercolor, depicts one male of the Myrtle group on a blue flag. In the plate this male is on the left and two young birds were added, top right and bottom right.

CLIII

Plate CLIV, O.P. 80, One Species, 19 5/8 x 12 1/2
Current name: Tennesee Warbler, *Vermivora peregrina*
(Wilson)
Name on plate: Tennessee Warbler SYLVIA PEREGRINA.
Wils.
Name on painting: Tennessee Warbler, Sylvia Peregrina
Painting and plate depict one bird in a holly.

Plate CLV, O.P. lost, One Species, 19 5/8 x 12 3/8
Current name: Black-throated Blue Warbler, *Dendroica
caerulescens* (Gmelin)
Name on plate: Black-throated Blue Warbler SYLVIA
CANADENSIS. Lath.
History: The original painting for this plate is one of the
two that are lost. Audubon recognized this bird as a
Black-throated Blue but he thought the female Black-
throated Blues in Plate CXLVIII were a different species,
the Pine Swamp Warbler of Wilson.
    Also in CXLVIII
Plate depicts a male on a stalk of columbine.

Plate CLVI, O.P. 138, One Species, 38 1/4 x 25 5/8
Current name: American Crow, *Corvus brachyrhynchos*
Brehm
Other names: Crow, Common Crow
Name on plate: American Crow CORVUS AMERICANUS
Painting and plate depict one bird on a branch of a black
walnut in which there is a hummingbird's nest.

CLIV

CLV

CLVI

CLVII

CLVIII

CLIX

Plate CLVII, O.P. 177, One Species, 25 7/8 x 20 7/8
Current name: Rusty Blackbird, *Euphagus carolinus*
(Müller)
Name on plate: Rusty Grakle QUISCALUS
FERRUGINEUS. Bonap.
Painting and plate depict two young birds, top, a male,
center, and a female, below, feeding on the berries of a
black-haw tree. In the plate the lower left branches,
which were only indicated in the painting, are completed.

Plate CLVIII, O.P. 387, One Species, 19 1/2 x 12 3/8
Current name: Chimney Swift, *Chaetura pelagica*
(Linnaeus)
Name on plate: American Swift CYPSELUS PELAGIUS.
Temm.
Painting and plate depict two birds flying. Beneath are
two drawings of nests, one labeled "front view unglued
from a chimney, " and the other labeled "nest profile
view."

Plate CLIX, O.P. 398, One Species, 19 3/8 x 12 1/4
Current name: Northern Cardinal, *Cardinalis cardinalis*
(Linnaeus)
Other names: often called Cardinal
Name on plate: Cardinal Grosbeak FRINGILLA
CARDINALIS. Bonap.
Painting depicts a male, above, on a branch of mock-
orange and a female, below, on a bare branch with a
leaflet at bottom. The plate is the same except that the
leaflet is attached to the branch on which the female is
perched.

Plate CLX, O.P. 377, One Species, 19 1/2 x 12 1/4
Current name: Carolina Chickadee, *Parus carolinensis*
Audubon
Name on plate: two variants
    1. Black-capped Titmouse PARUS ATRICAPILLUS
    2. Carolina Titmouse PARUS CAROLINENSIS
History: Audubon discovered this southern Chickadee,
which is smaller than the northern Black-capped
Chickadee in Plate CCCLIII. Audubon is credited as the
describer.
Painting and plate depict two birds in a branch of rattan-
vine or supplejack. The upper bird is pecking on a nut of
the vine.

CLX

Plate CLXI, O.P. 66, One Species, 38 1/4 x 25 5/8
Current name: Crested Caracara, *Polyborus plancus*
(Miller)
Other names: usually called Caracara. At one time this
bird was known as Audubon's Caracara, *Caracara
cheriway auduboni*. The species is divided into several
groups; this is the *plancus* group found in Florida.
Name on plate: Brasilian Caracara Eagle POLYBORUS
VULGARIS
Painting and plate depict two birds, the lower clinging to
a branch and the upper flying at the lower.

Plate CLXII, O.P. 157, One Species, 25 7/8 x 20 3/4
Current name: Zenaida Dove, *Zenaida aurita* (Temminck)
Name on plate: Zenaida dove COLUMBA ZENAIDA
    (* Zenaida Dove COLUMBA ZENAIDA)
History: In Audubon's day this bird bred in the Florida
Keys. Today it is accidental in south Florida.
Painting and plate depict two birds in a pond-apple tree.

CLXI

CLXII

CLXIII

CLXIV

Plate CLXIII, O.P. 332, One Species, 19 1/2 x 12 1/4
Current name: Palm Warbler, *Dendroica palmarum*
(Gmelin)
Name on plate: two variants
  1. Palm Warbler SYLVIA PALMARUM
  2. Yellow red poll Warbler SYLVIA PETECHIA
Name on painting: Yellow Red Poll Warbler, Sylvia
petechia
History: Audubon recognized that the birds here were
Palm Warblers, but when it came to the birds in Plate
CXLV he thought they were a new species, which he
named Yellow Red-poll Warbler. (Still, one of the
variants of this plate is called Yellow red poll.) Later in
his *Ornithological Biography* he said he had been in
error and that he now knew that both plates depicted
Palm Warblers, those in Plate CLXIII in full summer
plumage and those in Plate CXLV in first autumnal
plumage. Yet there are those who think that the birds in
Plate CXLV are of a different group within the Palm
Warbler species, one that frequents the western part of
the range and is of a paler yellow.
  Also in CXLV
Painting and plate depict a male, above, and a female,
below, in a branch of an orange tree.

Plate CLXIV, O.P. 310, One Species, 19 1/2 x 16 1/8
Current name: Veery, *Catharus fuscescens* (Stephens)
Name on plate: Tawny Thrush TURDUS WILSONII
Painting depicts one bird on a mossy mound covered with
vegetation, including a ragged orchis and a dwarf cornel.
In the plate a distant landscape of water and hills beyond
was added.

Plate CLXV, O.P. 363, One Species, 19 5/8 x 12 3/8
Current name: Bachman's Sparrow, *Aimophila aestivalis*
(Lichtenstein)
Name on plate: two variants
  1. Bachman's Finch FRINGILLA BACHMANI
  2. Bachmans Finch FRINGILLA BACHMANI
History: This species was named by Audubon for his life-
long friend the Reverend John Bachman, who discovered
the bird in South Carolina. Bachman collaborated with
Audubon on the book *Quadrupeds of North America*. Two
of Bachman's daughters married Audubon's sons, and his
sister-in-law Maria Martin (later his second) wife
painted flora for Audubon.
Painting and plate depict a male in summer plumage on a
branch of a fever-tree, a shrub of the sandy swamps of the
southern coast, now rare.

CLXV

Plate CLXVI, O.P. 49, One Species, 38 1/4 x 25 5/8
Current name: Rough-legged Hawk, *Buteo lagopus*
(Pontoppidan)
Name on plate: Rough-legged Falcon FALCO LAGOPUS
Also in CCCCXXII
Painting and plate depict one bird in a dead tree feeding
on a dead bird.

CLXVI

Plate CLXVII, O.P. 135, One Species, 20 7/8 x 25 7/8
Current name: Key West Quail-Dove, *Geotrygon chrysia*
Bonaparte
Name on plate: two variants
   1. Key-west Dove COLUMBA MONTANA
   2. Key west Pigeon COLUMBA MONTANA
History: This dove occurred in Key West prior to 1900,
then it vanished. Recently it has been recorded there
again and is now considered casual in southern Florida,
specifically the Florida Keys, Monroe County, and Palm
Beach County.
Painting and plate depict a male, left, and a female,
right, among vegetation that includes railroad-vine and
rubber-vine.

CLXVII

Plate CLXVIII, O.P. 40, One Species, 19 5/8 x 12 1/4
Current name: Fork-tailed Flycatcher, *Tyrannus savana*
Vieillot
Name on plate: Forked-tailed Flycatcher MUSCICAPA
SAVANA
History: This bird is occasionally swept north in
hurricanes. Audubon painted this bird from one he
collected in New Jersey. He recorded that he only saw
three others of this species: one brought to him dead in
Kentucky, and two others high in the air in Mississippi.
Painting and plate depict one bird perched on a branch of
loblolly bay. In the lower left corner of the painting there
is a sketch of one of the bird's primary feathers but this
was eliminated in the plate.

CLXVIII

CLXIX

CLXX

CLXXI

Plate CLXIX, O.P. 425, One Species, 19 1/2 x 12 3/8
Current name: Mangrove Cuckoo, *Coccyzus minor* (Gmelin)
Name on plate: Mangrove Cuckoo COCCYZUS SENICULUS
Name on painting: Mangrove Cuckoo
Painting and plate depict one bird on a branch of apple shrub.

Plate CLXX, O.P. 358, One Species, 19 3/4 x 12 1/4
Current name: Gray Kingbird, *Tyrannus dominicensis* (Gmelin)
Name on plate: two variants
    1. Gray Tyrant TYRANNUS GRISENS
    2. Pipiry Flycatcher MUSCICAPA DOMINICENSIS
Painting depicts one bird on a branch of the Australian corkwood. The plate is similar but the angle of the bird is slightly different and the flowers and leaves are more boldly defined.

Plate CLXXI, O.P. 110, One Species, 38 1/4 x 25 5/8
Current name: Common Barn-Owl, *Tyto alba* (Scopoli)
Other names: usually called Barn Owl
Name on plate: Barn Owl STRIX FLAMMEA
Painting depicts two birds clinging to branches. The upper bird is grasping a dead ground squirrel. There is no background. In the plate the birds are high up on a rocky mount with a night scene of a river winding through the country far below. This is one of only three night scenes in *Birds of America*; the others are found in Plate CXXI, Snowy Owl, and in Plate CCCXI, American White Pelican.

Plate CLXXII, O.P. 376, One Species, 20 7/8 x 26
Current name: Blue-headed Quail-Dove, *Starnoenas cyanocephala* (Linnaeus)
Name on plate: Blue-headed Pigeon COLUMBA CYANOCEPHALA
History: Audubon said he saw these birds in Key West. For many years there were no other sightings. However, these birds have recently been seen again in southern Florida, although the A.O.U. says these reports are most likely based on introductions or escapes.
Painting and plate depict three adult birds: one on a rock, right, another squatted down, center, and a third walking off to the left. The background shows vegetation, including grass and wild poinsettia. The flora is more defined in the plate and there is a cloud effect.

CLXXII

CLXXIII, O.P. 117, One Species, 19 1/2 x 12 1/4
Current name: Barn Swallow, *Hirundo rustica* Linnaeus
Name on plate: Barn Swallow HIRUNDO AMERICANA
Painting and plate depict a nest affixed to a board with the female in the nest and the male on the edge of it.

Plate CLXXIV, O.P. 374, One Species, 19 5/8 x 12 1/4
Current name: Olive-sided Flycatcher, *Contopus borealis* (Swainson)
Name on plate: two variants
  1. Olive-sided Flycatcher MUSCICAPA INORNATA
  2. Olive sided Flycatcher MUSCICAPA COOPERI
Painting and plate depict two birds in a balsam fir.

CLXXIII

CLXXIV

CLXXV

CLXXVI

CLXXVII

Plate CLXXV, O.P. 394, One Species, 19 1/2 x 12 1/4
Current name: Sedge Wren, *Cistothorus platensis* (Latham)
Other names: formerly Short-billed Marsh Wren
Name on plate: Nuttall's lesser-marsh Wren TROGLODYTES BREVIROSTRIS
    (* Nutall's Lesser Marsh Wren TROGLODYTES BREVIROSTRIS)
Painting and plate depict two birds perched on a nest in a clump of grass.

Plate CLXXVI, O.P. 317, One Species, 25 1/2 x 38 3/8
Current name: Spruce Grouse, *Dendragapus canadensis* (Linnaeus)
Name on plate: two variants
    1. Spotted Grous TETRAO CANADENSIS
    2. Spotted or Canada Grouse TETRAO CANADENSIS
Painting and plate depict two males, right and second from left, and two females, left and second from right, all amid vegetation that includes painted trillium and twisted-stalk.

Plate CLXXVII, O.P. 3, One Species, 25 5/8 x 20 3/4
Current name: White-crowned Pigeon, *Columba leucocephala* Linnaeus
Name on plate: three variants
    1. White-crowned Pigeon COLUMBA LEUCOCEPHALA
    2. White Headed Pigeon COLUMBA LEUCOCEPHALA
    3. White Headed Pigeon COLUMBA LEUCOCEPHALA, Linn.
Painting and plate depict a pair in a geiger-tree.

Plate CLXXVIII, O.P. 190, One Species, 19 5/8 x 12 3/8
Current name: Orange-crowned Warbler, *Vermivora celata* (Say)
Name on plate: Orange-crowned Warbler SYLVIA CELATA
Painting and plate depict two birds in a sparkleberry.

Plate CLXXIX, O.P. 427, One Species, 19 1/2 x 12 3/8
Current name: House Wren, *Troglodytes aedon* Vieillot
Name on plate: Wood Wren TROGLODYTES AMERICANA
History: Audubon correctly identified the birds he painted for Plate LXXXIII as House Wrens, but because he thought he had detected a difference in song he became convinced the bird here was a new species, which he named Wood Wren. It was not a new species but was in fact a House Wren.
   Also in LXXXIII
Painting and plate depict one bird in vegetation that includes blue-beard and bear-berry.

Plate CLXXX, O.P. 281, One Species, 19 1/2 x 12 1/4
Current name: Pine Siskin, *Carduelis pinus* (Wilson)
Name on plate: Pine Finch FRINGILLA PINUS
Painting and plate depict two birds on a branch of black larch.

CLXXVIII

CLXXIX

CLXXX

CLXXXI

CLXXXII

CLXXXIII

Plate CLXXXI, O.P. 54, One Species, 37 1/4 x 25 5/8
Current name: Golden Eagle, *Aquila chrysaetos* (Linnaeus)
Name on plate: two variants
    1. Golden Eagle FALCO CHRYSAETOS
    2. Golden Eagle AQUILA CHRYSAETOS
Name on painting: Golden Eagle, Aquila Chrysaëtos. Lin
[faded—Linn. or Linnaeus]
Painting depicts one bird taking off with a snowshoe hare in his talons. Below there is a vista of massive mountains. There is a fallen tree stretching from one rock to another, across which a man is making his way. This is believed to be a self-portrait of Audubon. The plate is the same except the man was eliminated.

Plate CLXXXII, O.P. 140, One Species, 25 7/8 x 20 7/8
Current name: Common Ground-Dove, *Columbina passerina*
(Linnaeus)
Other names: Ground Dove and, locally, Tobacco Dove
Name on plate: Ground Dove COLUMBA PASSERINA
Painting and plate depict three males, top, and a female with young, below, all in a wild orange tree.

Plate CLXXXIII, O.P. 236, One Species, 19 1/2 x 12 1/4
Current name: Golden-crowned Kinglet, *Regulus satrapa*
Lichtenstein
Name on plate: three variants
    1. Golden crested-Wren REGULUS CRISTATUS
    2. American Golden crested-Wren REGULUS
TRICOLOR
    3. Golden-Crester-Wren REGULUS CRISTATUS
    (* Golden-crester Wren REGULAS CRISTATUS,
Vieill.)
Painting and plate depict a male, below, and a female, above, on a stalk of powdery thalia.

Plate CLXXXIV, O.P. 193, One Species, 18 3/8 x 13 3/4
Current name: Black-throated Mango, *Anthracothorax nigricollis* (Vieillot)
Name on plate: two or maybe three variants
1. Mangrove Humming Bird TROCHILUS MANGO
2. Mango Humming Bird TROCHILUS MANGO
3. Mango Humming-bird TROCHILUS MANGO
History: This species is native to Central and South America. The birds depicted were painted from skins given to Audubon and the reputed localities are undoubtedly incorrect.
Painting and plate depict two females, center and lower right, and three males in a spray of trumpet-creeper.

CLXXXIV

Plate CLXXXV, O.P. 419, One Species, 20 1/2 x 14 3/4
Current name: Bachman's Warbler, *Vermivora bachmanii* (Audubon)
Name on plate: Bachman's Warbler SYLVIA BACHMANII. Aud.
History: This species was first discovered and collected by the Reverend John Bachman, pastor of St. John's Lutheran Church in Charleston, South Carolina, and a brilliant scientist. His sister-in-law Maria Martin (later his second wife) painted many of the plants and insects for the backgrounds of Audubon's paintings. Two of Bachman's daughters married Audubon's two sons. Audubon himself never saw this bird alive and knew it only from Bachman's description of its habits and the skins Bachman gave him. Audubon named the bird to honor his great friend with whom he had a long and fruitful collaboration. This is our rarest woodland warbler and it may be extinct.
Painting and plate depict a male, above, and a female, below, in a branch of the Franklinia tree.

CLXXXV

Plate CLXXXVI, O.P. 55, One Species, 25 1/2 x 37 1/4
Current name: Greater Prairie-Chicken, *Tympanuchus cupido* (Linnaeus)
Name on plate: Pinnated Grous TETRAO CUPIDO.Lin.
Painting and plate depict two males, top and right, and a female, lower left. The males are fighting over the female. There is a detailed background of meadow, trees, and hills in the distance, and a tiger lily in the right foreground.

CLXXXVI

CLXXXVII

Plate CLXXXVII, O.P. 231, One Species, 26 x 20 7/8
Current name: Boat-tailed Grackle, *Quiscalus major*
Vieillot
Name on plate: Boat-tailed Grackle QUISCALUS
MAJOR. Vieill.
Painting and plate depict a male, below, and a female,
above, on a branch of live oak adorned with Spanish moss.

Plate CLXXXVIII, O.P. 303, One Species, 19 1/2 x 12 1/4
Current name: American Tree Sparrow, *Spizella arborea*
(Wilson)
Other names: usually called Tree Sparrow
Name on plate: Tree Sparrow FRINGILLA
CANADENSIS. Lath
Painting and plate depict two adult birds in a branch of
barberry bush.

Plate CLXXXIX, O.P. 201, One Species, 19 1/2 x 12 3/8
Current name: Snow Bunting, *Plectrophenax nivalis*
(Linnaeus)
Name on plate: Snow Bunting EMBERIZA NIVALIS.
Linn.
Painting and plate depict an adult bird flying, another
adult bird perched on a grass-covered tussock, and a young
bird under the edge of the tussock. The background is
water and mountains.

CLXXXVIII

CLXXXIX

Plate CXC, O.P. 395, One Species, 19 5/8 x 12 3/8
Current name: Yellow-bellied Sapsucker, *Sphyrapicus varius* (Linnaeus)
Name on plate: Yellow-bellied Woodpecker PICUS VARIUS. Linn.
History: Note that the birds at the bottom of Plate CCCCXVI are sometimes identified as Yellow-bellied Sapsuckers. However, the A.O.U. now considers this western population to be a separate species, the Red-breasted Sapsucker.
Painting and plate depict a male, above, and a female, below, in a mock orange.

CXC

Plate CXCI, O.P. 375, One Species, 25 5/8 x 38 1/4
Current name: Willow Ptarmigan, *Lagopus lagopus* (Linnaeus)
Name on plate: two variants
   1. Willow Grous or Large Ptarmigan TETRAO SALICETI
   2. Willow Grous TETRAO SALICETI, Temm.
   (* Willow Grouse or Large Ptarmigan, TETRAO SALICETI, Temm.)
Painting and plate depict a male, left, and a female with seven chicks, right, amid vegetation that includes beach-pea, roseroot, and Labrador-tea.

CXCI

Plate CXCII, O.P. 173, One Species, 26 x 20 3/4
Current name: Northern Shrike, *Lanius excubitor* Linnaeus
Name on plate: two variants
   1. Great American Shrike or Butcher Bird LANIUS SEPTENTRIONALIS
   2. Great cinereous Shrike or Butcher Bird LANIUS EXCUBITOR
Painting depicts three adults, top, and a young bird, bottom, all in a parsley-haw. The adult third from the top is starting to feed on a dead Horned Lark that has been impaled on a thorn. The plate is the same except for the addition of an insect, for which the second bird from the top is reaching. The Shrikes are noted for impaling their prey.

CXCII

CXCIII

Plate CXCIII, O.P. 167, One Species, 19 1/2 x 12 1/2
Current name: Lincoln's Sparrow, *Melospiza lincolnii* (Audubon)
Name on plate: Lincoln Finch FRINGILLA LINCOLNII
History: Audubon named this species Tom's Finch for Thomas Lincoln, the young man who shot this new species for him. He later changed the name to Lincoln Finch and much later changed it again to Lincoln's Pinewood Finch. Painting and plate depict two birds: the lower on a low mound and the upper on a branch of bog-laurel, all in a habitat that also includes dwarf cornel and cloudberry.

Plate CXCIV, O.P. 27, One Species, 19 1/2 x 12 3/8
Current name: Boreal Chickadee, *Parus hudsonicus* Forster
Name on plate: two variants
   1. Canadian Titmouse PARUS HUDSONICUS
   2. Hudson's Bay Titmouse PARUS HUDSONICUS
History: Audubon first called this little bird Canada or Canadian Titmouse but later changed it to Hudson's Bay Titmouse. Succeeding ornithologists called it Hudsonian Chickadee and later Brown-capped Chickadee.
Painting and plate depict two adult birds and a young one at bottom. All are in a branch of what is probably a black chokeberry.

Plate CXCV, O.P. 416, One Species, 19 1/2 x 12 1/2
Current name: Ruby-crowned Kinglet, *Regulus calendula* (Linnaeus)
Name on plate: Ruby-crowned Wren REGULUS CALENDULA. Stephens
Painting and plate depict two males in a sheep-laurel.

CXCIV

CXCV

Plate CXCVI, O.P. 230, One Species, 38 1/4 x 25 5/8
Current name: Gyrfalcon, *Falco rusticolus* Linnaeus
Name on plate: two variants
1. Labrador Falcon FALCO LABRADORA
2. Labrador Falcon FALCO ISLANDICUS

History: Gyrfalcons have three color phases: black, white, and gray. In Audubon's day they were considered separate subspecies or even species. Audubon treated them as separate species and called the black-phase birds in Plate CXCVI Labrador Falcons and the white-phase birds in Plate CCCLXVI Iceland or Jer Falcons.
Also in CCCLXVI
Painting and plate depict a male, above, and a female, below (both black phase), on a dead branch with no other background.

CXCVI

Plate CXCVII, O.P. 341, One Species, 25 7/8 x 20 3/4
Current name: Red Crossbill, *Loxia curvirostra* Linnaeus
Name on plate: two variants
1. American Crossbill LOXIA CURVIROSTRA, Linn.
2. Common Crossbill LOXIA CURVIROSTRA. Linn
Painting and plate depict eight birds all in an eastern hemlock: two immatures, top; male, young bird, and two females, center; adult male, lower right; and young bird, lower left.

Plate CXCVIII, O.P. 153, One Species, 19 5/8 x 12 1/4
Current name: Swainson's Warbler, *Limnothlypis swainsonii* (Audubon)
Name on plate: two variants
1. Brown headed Worm eating Warbler SYLVIA SWAINSONII
2. Swainson's Warbler SYLVIA SWAINSONI
   (* Brown-headed Worm-eating Warbler SYLVIA SWAINSONII)

History: One of the plate legends of Plate L was mismarked Swainson's Warbler and the painting also had Swainson's Warbler written on it. The bird in Plate L is an immature Magnolia Warbler and Audubon himself wrote of the confusion caused by this misidentification on plate and painting. Note also that there is a Worm-eating Warbler that looks a little like the Swainson's Warbler, which may account for the variant above. Audubon did paint the Worm-eating Warbler for Plate XXXIV. This bird was painted by Audubon's son John.
Painting depicts one bird in a flame azalea. On the left are fine drawings of bill and toe of a Worm-eating Warbler above another drawing of bill and toe of a Swainson's Warbler for contrast. There are two butterflys in the azalea. The plate is the same except for the elimination of the little drawings.

CXCVII

CXCVIII

Plate CXCIX, O.P. 150, One Species, 19 5/8 x 12 1/4
Current name: Northern Saw-whet Owl, *Aegolius acadicus* (Gmelin)
Other names: often called Saw-whet Owl
Name on plate: Little Owl STRIX ACADICA. Gm
History: Do not confuse this bird with the European Little Owl, *Athene noctua* in Plate CCCCXXXII
Painting and plate depict two birds, the upper on a branch and the lower on a mound clutching a dead rabbit.

CXCIX

Plate CC, O.P. 141, One Species, 12 1/4 x 19 1/2
Current name: Horned Lark, *Eremophila alpestris* (Linnaeus)
Name on plate: Shore Lark ALAUDA ALPESTRIS. Z
History: Note that in Plate CXCII, which depicts Northern Shrikes, there is an impaled Horned Lark in the center.
Painting and plate depict six birds: two chicks in nest, left; third chick over nest; male in summer plumage near nest; female in summer plumage, center; and bird in winter plumage, right. The habitat is a moss- and lichen-covered piece of ground.

CC

Plate CCI, O.P. 94, One Species, 38 x 25 1/2
Current name: Canada Goose, *Branta canadensis* (Linnaeus)
Name on plate: Canada Goose ANSER CANADENSIS. Vieill.
Name on painting: Canada Goose, Anser canadensis Viell.
History: Audubon made another painting of the Canada Goose for Plate CCLXXVII. That goose belongs to one of the populations of Canada Goose that was at one time considered a separate species, and the plate was correctly labeled Hutchin's. The A.O.U. says that for the present it is best to consider the whole complex as one species, Canada Goose.
Also in CCLXXVII
Painting depicts one bird standing on a mound. A background of sea, ice-covered cliffs, and low dark clouds was provided for the plate.

CCI

Plate CCII, O.P. 132, One Species, 20 7/8 x 28 3/8
Current name: Red-throated Loon, *Gavia stellata*
(Pontoppidan)
Name on plate: Red-throated Diver COLYMBUS
SEPTENTRIONALIS
Painting and plate depict four birds against a background
of grasses and pitcher-plants: adult on dry ground in
winter plumage, left; very young bird in water, second
from left; male in breeding plumage in water, second from
right; and female in breeding plumage, right.

Plate CCIII, O.P. 79, One Species, 12 3/4 x 19 1/2
Current name: King Rail, *Rallus elegans* Audubon
Name on plate: two variants
    1. Fresh-water Marsh Hen RALLUS ELEGANS, Aud.
    2. Great Red breasted Rail or Fresh-water Marsh hen
RALLUS ELEGANS. Aud.
Painting and plate depict the left bird standing in the
water and the right bird on a rock with grasses behind.
The left bird was done separately, cut out, and pasted onto
the paper, then the rest was completed in watercolor.

Plate CCIV, O.P. 134, One Species, 19 1/2 x 14 7/8
Current name: Clapper Rail, *Rallus longirostris* Boddaert
Name on plate: Salt Water Marsh Hen RALLUS
CREPITANS. Gm.
    (* Salt-water Marsh Hen, RALLUS CREPITANS,
Gmel.)
Painting is made up of previously painted sections that
depict two birds against a background of grasses. By
looking carefully, one can make out dimly the head of a
bird beneath the breast of the bird on the left. Audubon
must have started to paint a bird but changed his mind
and painted it over with grass. In the plate the habitat is
smoothed out and the foreground is more detailed and
better arranged.

CCII

CCIII

CCIV

CCV

Plate CCV, O.P. 338, One Species, 14 3/4 x 20 3/8
Current name: Virginia Rail, *Rallus limicola* Vieillot
Name on plate: Virginia Rail RALLUS VIRGINIANUS. L
Painting and plate depict two adults, left, and a young bird, right, in shallow water and on a muddy bank. In the painting, done largely in watercolor, the left bird is in pastel.

Plate CCVI, O.P. 388, One Species, 38 1/8 x 25 1/2
Current name: Wood Duck, *Aix sponsa* (Linnaeus)
Name on plate: Summer or Wood Duck ANAS SPONSA. L.
Painting and plate depict four birds in a sycamore tree with a nest covered with resurrection ferns: male, top, with female next to him; male flying, lower left; and female in nest. For the painting Audubon cut out and pasted on the previously painted flying male.

Plate CCVII, O.P. 286, One Species, 25 3/4 x 20 1/2
Current name: Brown Booby, *Sula leucogaster* (Boddaert)
Name on plate: Booby Gannet SULA FUSCA
Painting and plate depict one bird perched high up on a dead tree with sea beyond and a Florida Key in the distance.

CCVI

CCVII

Plate CCVIII, O.P. 291, One Species, 10 1/4 x 19 1/2
Current name: Eskimo Curlew, *Numenius borealis* (Forster)
Name on plate: Esquimaux Curlew NUMENIUS
BOREALIS. Lath.
History: Audubon posed the lower bird lying on the ground
after being shot so as to show the coloration of the inside
of the wing. The only other depiction of a shot bird in
Birds of America is the Black-backed Gull in Plate
CCXLI. All other dead birds were prey, such as the
impaled Horned Lark in Plate CXCII or the ducks in Plate
XVI.
Painting and plate depict a live bird on a rock and a dead
bird below.

CCVIII

Plate CCIX, O.P. 252, One Species, 12 1/8 x 19 3/8
Current name: Wilson's Plover, *Charadrius wilsonia* Ord
Name on plate: Wilson's Plover CHARADRIUS
WILSONIUS
    Also in CCLXXXIV
Painting and plate depict two birds, the one on the right
on a rock with grass behind, and the other standing in the
water. The bird on the right appears again in Plate
CCLXXXIV, which depicts Purple Sandpipers. This is one
of only two instances where the same painting of a bird
appears in two plates; the other is the Bluebird in Plates
CXIII and XXXVI.
SEE COMPOSITE PLATES IN PART I

CCIX

Plate CCX, O.P. 339, One Species, 12 1/4 x 19 1/2
Current name: Least Bittern, *Ixobrychus exilis* (Gmelin)
Name on plate: Least Bittern ARDEA EXILIS. Gm.
Painting depicts two males reaching for a snail on a blade
of grass, and a young bird, left. The foreground shows
muddy mounds and the background a marsh with a boat on
a winding creek and a plantation in the far distance. The
young bird was painted separately and pasted on. The
plate is the same but for the elimination of the plantation
house.

CCX

CCXI

CCXII

CCXIII

Plate CCXI, O.P. 326, One Species, 38 1/8 x 25 1/2
Current name: Great Blue Heron, *Ardea herodias* Linnaeus
Other names: The Great White Heron was formerly
considered a separate species, *Ardea occidentalis*, but is
now treated as a color morph of the Great Blue. The Great
White has also been treated as a subspecies of the Great
Blue.
Name on plate: Great blue Heron ARDEA HERODIAS
  (* Great Blue Heron, ARDEA HERODIAS)
  Also in CCLXXXI (White phase)
Painting and plate alike and depict one bird on a mud bank
by water with grasses.

Plate CCXII, O.P. 11, One Species, 20 7/8 x 26
Current name: Ring-billed Gull, *Larus delawarensis* Ord
Name on plate: two variants
  1. Common Gull LARUS CANUS
  2. Common American Gull LARUS CANUS. L.
Painting and plate depict an adult male, left, and an
immature bird, right, on rocky ground with shells and sea
and sky behind.

Plate CCXIII, O.P. 21, One Species, 12 1/4 x 19 1/2
Current name: Atlantic Puffin, *Fratercula arctica*
(Linnaeus)
Other names: also known as Common Puffin
Name on plate: Puffin MORMON ARCTICUS
Painting and plate are alike except for minor details. The
birds are in spring plumage, male at the right and female
peering out of burrow, and are on a grassy and rocky bank
against a background of water and distant hills. The
painting shows a raft of birds in the water in front of the
hill and a cloud of birds overhead that are not in the
plate.

Plate CCXIV, O.P. 321, One Species, 12 1/4 x 19 1/2
Current name: Razorbill, *Alca torda* Linnaeus
Other names: also known as Razor-billed Auk
Name on plate: two variants
    1. Razor Bill ALCA TORDA
    2. Razor billed Auk ALCA TORDA
Painting and plate alike and depict two adults in spring
plumage floating in the sea with cliffs rising up in the
distance.

CCXIV

Plate CCXV, O.P. 91, One Species, 12 1/4 x 19 1/2
Current name: Red-necked Phalarope, *Phalaropus lobatus*
(Linnaeus)
Other names: also know as Northern Phalarope
Name on plate: Hyperborean phalarope PHALAROPUS
HYPERBOREUS. Lath.
Painting depicts three birds in a calm sea. The female,
left, is standing on a piece of floating seaweed, the male,
right, is swimming, and another female is flying above.
The plate is the same except the birds are closer to each
other.

CCXV

Plate CCXVI, O.P. 247, One Species, 25 1/2 x 38 1/8
Current name: Wood Stork, *Mycteria americana* Linnaeus
Other names: formerly Wood Ibis
Name on plate: Wood Ibiss TANTALUS LOCULATOR
Painting depicts one bird on a muddy bank about to dip his
open bill in the water. The background, in oil, shows a
vista of an open stretch of marsh with a flock of Wood
Storks in the middle distance. The plate is the same
except the trees are more sharply defined and there is
another flock of Wood Storks in the far distance.

CCXVI

CCXVII

CCXVIII

CCXIX

Plate CCXVII, O.P. 115, One Species, 20 3/4 x 25 7/8
Current name: Tricolored Heron, *Egretta tricolor* (Müller)
Other names: until recently Louisiana Heron
Name on plate: Louisiana Heron ARDEA
LUDOVICIANA. Wils.
Painting and plate alike and depict one bird on a Florida
Key overgrown with low dense shrubs and royal palms.

Plate CCXVIII, O.P. 129, One Species, 12 1/4 x 19 1/2
Current name: Common Murre, *Uria aalge* (Pontoppidan)
Other names: formerly Thin-billed Murre
Name on plate: Foolish Guillemot URIA TROILE. Lath.
Painting and plate depict two birds in breeding plumage on
a beach with breaking waves.

Plate CCXIX, O.P. 47, One Species, 17 1/2 x 20 3/8
Current name: Black Guillemot, *Cepphus grylle* (Linnaeus)
Name on plate: Black Guillemot URIA GRYLLE. Lath.
Painting and plate depict a chick, left, squatting on a rock,
an adult in breeding plumage swimming, and an adult in
winter plumage flying above. There is a cliffside in the
left background and mountains in the distance. The chick
was painted by Audubon's son John.

Plate CCXX, O.P. 251, One Species, 12 1/4 x 19 1/2
Current name: Piping Plover, *Charadrius melodus* Ord
Name on plate: Piping Plover CHARADRIUS MELODUS
Painting and plate depict two birds on a rocky shore with
the sea behind.

Plate CCXXI, O.P. 155, One Species, 25 1/2 x 38 1/8
Current name: Mallard, *Anas platyrhynchos* Linnaeus
Name on plate: Mallard Duck ANAS BOSCHAS. L.
Painting depicts two males and two females among grasses
and yellow flowers. The plate is the same except for the
addition of water in the foreground.

Plate CCXXII, O.P. 283, One Species, 20 3/4 x 25 3/4
Current name: White Ibis, *Eudocimus albus* (Linnaeus)
Name on plate: White Ibis IBIS ALBA
Audubon painted the background of the painting in oil and
then cut out and pasted on two previously painted birds,
putting an adult at the left, and an immature at the right.
Both painting and plate depict the birds amid mounds of
mud made by burrowing crayfish. A crayfish is at the left.

CCXX

CCXXI

CCXXII

CCXXIII

CCXXIV

CCXXV

Plate CCXXIII, O.P. 242, One Species, 12 1/4 x 19 3/8
Current name: American Oystercatcher, *Haematopus palliatus* Temminck
Other names: usually called Oystercatcher
Name on plate: two variants
   1. Pied oyster-catcher HAEMATOPUS OSTRALEGUS
   2. American oyster-catcher HAEMATOPUS PALLIATUS
   (* Pied Oyster-catcher, HAEMATOPUS OSTRALEGUS, Linn.)
History: Note that the scientific name *Haematopus ostralegus* belongs to the Eurasian Oystercatcher, an old-world species with old records of straggling to Canada, not portrayed in *Birds of America*.
Painting in watercolor and egg tempera depicts one bird on a flat rock with water all around, mountains in the distance, and a ship in full sail in the middle distance. The plate is the same except that the ship was eliminated and the rock on which the bird is standing is slightly different.

Plate CCXXIV, O.P. 69, One Species, 12 1/4 x 19 3/8
Current name: Black-legged Kittiwake, *Rissa tridactyla* (Linnaeus)
Name on plate: Kittiwake Gull LARUS TRIDACTYLUS. L.
Painting and plate depict an adult in front and a young bird behind standing on rocks.

Plate CCXXV, O.P. 151, One Species, 12 1/4 x 19 3/8
Current name: Killdeer, *Charadrius vociferus* Linnaeus
Name on plate: Killdeer Plover CHARADRIUS VOCIFERUS
Painting depicts a male flying, left, and a female, right, on a clump of rocks. In the plate the male is lower so he seems to be flying straight at the female, and the background is enhanced by more rocks and a view of the sea.

Plate CCXXVI, O.P. 8, One Species, 38 1/8 x 25 1/2
Current name: Whooping Crane, *Grus americana*
(Linnaeus)
Name on plate: two variants
   1. Hooping Crane GRUS AMERICANA
   2. Whooping Crane GRUS AMERICANA
History: Audubon called both this bird and the Sandhill
Crane in Plate CCLXI Hooping Cranes. He thought the
Sandhill was the young of the Whooping, but they are
separate species. This bird, on the very edge of extinction,
is coming back very slowly due to intensive help by man,
but it is a difficult and at times heartbreaking effort.
Painting and plate depict one bird on a bank catching a
baby alligator. Another baby alligator lies dead. There
is water behind and woods beyond.

CCXXVI

Plate CCXXVII, O.P. 187, One Species, 20 3/4 x 25 3/4
Current name: Northern Pintail, *Anas acuta* Linnaeus
Other names: also known as Common Pintail and Pintail
Name on plate: Pin tailed Duck ANAS ACUTA
   (* Pin-tailed Duck ANAS ACUTA)
Painting and plate depict a male in the foreground and a
female behind on a muddy bank with water around and
trees in the distance.

CCXXVII

Plate CCXXVIII, O.P. 322, One Species, 12 1/4 x 19 3/8
Current name: Green-winged Teal, *Anas crecca* Linnaeus
Name on plate: two variants
   1. American Green winged Teal ANAS
CAROLINENSIS
   2. Green winged Teal ANAS CRECCA. Lath.
   (* American Green-winged Teal ANAS
CAROLINENSIS, Lath.)
Name on painting: Green-Winged Teal, Anas Crecca
Painting depicts a female, left, and a male, right, on two
small rocks with a snail shell and a piece of shell on the
bank below with some tufts of grass. The birds are in
watercolor and the habitat is in oil. The plate is the same
except that the shells have been eliminated and a third
rock added right foreground.

CCXXVIII

CCXXIX

CCXXX

CCXXXI

Plate CCXXIX, O.P. 405, One Species, 12 1/4 x 19 1/2
Current name: Greater Scaup, *Aythya marila* (Linnaeus)
Name on plate: Scaup Duck FULIGULA MARILA
Name on painting: Scaup Duck Anas Marila
History: There has been confusion about the identity of
this bird. When Audubon drew these birds he believed
there was only one species of Scaup, known then as
Fuligula marila. He later realized there were two
Scaups: a larger one, *Fuligula marila* (known today as
Aythya marila) and a smaller one, *Fuligula mariloides*
(known today as Lesser Scaup, *Aythya affinis*). After the
prints from Plate CCXXIX were published he wrote that
he had come to believe the birds were Lesser Scaups, but
modern authorities believe he was right in the first place
and that the birds are indeed Greater Scaups, *Aythya
marila*.
Painting depicts a male, left, and a female, right, on a
bank with two shells and a little rock in the foreground
and some grass in the back. In the plate the shells and
little rocks have been eliminated.

Plate CCXXX, O.P. 346, One Species, 12 1/4 x 19 3/8
Current name: Sanderling, *Calidris alba* (Pallas)
Name on plate: two variants
　　1. Ruddy Plover TRINGA ARENARIA
　　2. Sanderling TRINGA ARENARIA
　　Also in CCLXXXV (English name not given, scientific
name in small letters)
Painting and plate depict two birds in winter plumage on a
rocky island with sea and two more rocky isles.
SEE COMPOSITE PLATES IN PART I

Plate CCXXXI, O.P. 182, One Species, 25 1/2 x 38 1/8
Current name: Long-billed Curlew, *Numenius americanus*
Bechstein
Name on plate: Long-billed Curlew NUMENIUS
LONGIROSTRIS
Painting and plate depict two birds on a near shore with a
view of Charleston across the water.

Plate CCXXXII, O.P. 152, One Species, 20 7/8 x 26
Current name: Hooded Merganser, *Lophodytes cucullatus*
(Linnaeus)
Name on plate: Hooded Merganser MERGUS
CUCULLATUS
Painting and plate depict a male, left, and a female,
right, sitting on a small rock surrounded by water and
with grass behind. The painting is in pastel, watercolor,
and stipple.

CCXXXII

Plate CCXXXIII, O.P. 292, One Species, 12 1/4 x 19 1/2
Current name: Sora, *Porzana carolina* (Linnaeus)
Name on plate: two variants
1. Sora or Rail RALLUS CAROLINUS
2. Sora Rail RALLUS CAROLINUS. L.
Painting and plate depict a male, center, a young bird,
left, and another young bird, right, with a little
vegetation.

CCXXXIII

Plate CCXXXIV, O.P. 255, One Species, 13 3/4 x17 3/8
Current name: Ring-necked Duck, *Aythya collaris*
(Donovan)
Name on plate: two variants
1. Tufted Duck FULIGULA RUFITORQUES
2. Ring-necked Duck FULIGULA RUFITORQUES.
Bonap
Painting and plate depict a female, left, and a male,
right, on the ground with no other background.

CCXXXIV

CCXXXV

CCXXXVI

CCXXXVII

Plate CCXXXV, O.P. 61, One Species, 12 1/4 x 19 3/8
Current name: Sooty Tern, *Sterna fuscata* Linnaeus
Name on plate: Sooty Tern STERNA FULIGINOSA
Painting and plate depict one adult in breeding plumage diving through the air.

Plate CCXXXVI, O.P. 418, One Species, 25 1/2 x 38 1/8
Current name: Black-crowned Night-Heron, *Nycticorax nycticorax* (Linnaeus)
Name on plate: Night Heron or Qua bird ARDEA NYCTICORAX. L
Painting and plate depict an adult bird, left, and a young bird, right. The adult is about to catch a frog while the young bird stands by. They are on a muddy bank with marsh grasses and Zephyr Lilys. In the painting the adult bird is done in a combination of pencil, pastel, and watercolor.

Plate CCXXXVII, O.P. 330, One Species, 20 5/8 x 25 3/4
Current name: Whimbrel, *Numenius phaeopus* (Linnaeus)
Other names: formerly Hudsonian Curlew
Name on plate: two variants
   1. Great Esquimaux Curlew NUMENIUS HUDSONICUS, Lath.
   2. Hudsonian Curlew NUMENIUS HUDSONICUS, Lath.
Painting and plate depict one bird in a little clearing amid rocks and grasses.

Plate CCXXXVIII, O.P. 209, One Species, 13 1/4 x 20 7/8
Current name: Marbled Godwit, *Limosa fedoa* (Linnaeus)
Name on plate: Great Marbled Godwit LIMOSA FEDOA,
Vieill.
Two birds were painted separately, cut out, and pasted
onto the paper, and a background of a mound and
vegetation was added. The plate depicts the same scene.

CCXXXVIII

Plate CCXXXIX, O.P. 121, One Species, 12 1/4 x 19 1/4
Current name: American Coot, *Fulica americana* Gmelin
Name on plate: American Coot FULICA AMERICANA.
Gm.
Painting and plate depict one bird on a muddy bank with a
background of marshy grass and water.

Plate CCXL, O.P. 297, One Species, 19 1/2 x 12 1/4
Current name: Roseate Tern, *Sterna dougallii* Montagu
Name on plate: Roseate Tern STERNA DOUGALII. Mont.
(Note that Plate CCLX, Leach's Storm-Petrel, has a
variant misnumbered CCXL)
Painting and plate depict one bird diving earthward
against a blue sky.

CCXXXIX

CCXL

CCXLI

Plate CCXLI, O.P. 226, One Species, 38 1/8 x 25 1/2
Current name: Great Black-backed Gull, *Larus marinus* Linnaeus
Other names: Black-backed Gull
Name on plate: Black Backed Gull LARUS MARINUS
Painting and plate depict one bird crouched on the ground, bleeding from having been shot. In the plate there is a detailed drawing of the gull's foot in the upper right corner. This is one of only two depictions of a shot bird in *Birds of America*; the other is the Eskimo Curlew in Plate CCVIII. All other dead birds were prey, such as the impaled Horned Lark in Plate CXCII and the ducks in Plate XVI.

Plate CCXLII, O.P. 48, One Species, 25 3/4 x 20 1/2
Current name: Snowy Egret, *Egretta thula* (Molina)
Name on plate: Snowy Heron or White Egret ARDEA CANDIDISSIMA. Gm.
Painting and plate depict one bird on a mound with vegetation and water in front. The background is a landscape that stretches across a marsh and water to a Carolina plantation. In the middle distance is the approaching figure of a hunter, which may be Audubon's self-portrait.

CCXLII

Plate CCXLIII, O.P. 65, One Species, 12 1/4 x 19 3/8
Current name: Common Snipe, *Gallinago gallinago* (Linnaeus)
Other names: formerly Wilson's Snipe
Name on plate: American Snipe SCOLOPAX WILSONII
Painting and plate depict three birds on the edge of a river with a view of a South Carolina plantation on the far side.

CCXLIII

Plate CCXLIV, O.P. 385, One Species, 12 1/4 x 19 3/8
Current name: Common Moorhen, *Gallinula chloropus* (Linnaeus)
Other names: formerly Florida Gallinule
Name on plate: Common Gallinule GALLINULA CHLOROPUS
Name on painting: Common Gallinule, Fulica Chloropus
Painting and plate depict one bird on a bank with water and grasses.

CCXLIV

Plate CCXLV, O.P. 254, One Species, 12 1/4 x 21 1/2
Current name: Thick-billed Murre, *Uria lomvia* (Linnaeus)
Other names: formerly Brunnich's Murre
Name on plate: two variants
  1. [No English name] URIA BRUNNICHII
  2. Large-billed Guillemot URIA BRUNNICHII
Painting depicts one bird in flight with no background. In the plate the bird is flying over a moderately rough sea.

CCXLV

Plate CCXLVI, O.P. 185, One Species, 25 1/2 x 38 1/8
Current name: Common Eider, *Somateria mollissima* (Linnaeus)
Name on plate: Eider Duck FULIGULA MOLLISSIMA
Painting and plate depict a male being driven off by a mated pair. The eggs the female has laid are seen on the right. The habitat is a grassy area.

CCXLVI

CCXLVII

CCXLVIII

CCXLIX

Plate CCXLVII, O.P. 367, One Species, 20 5/8 x 29 7/8
Current name: White-winged Scoter, *Melanitta fusca* (Linnaeus)
Other names: The A.O.U. combines the Velvet Scoter, *Melanitta fusca*, of Eurasia and the White-winged Scoter, *Melanitta deglandi*, of North America into one species, *M. fusca*, with the English name White-winged Scoter.
Name on plate: Velvet Duck FULIGULA FUSCA
Painting depicts a female, left, and a male, right, on a rocky beach with sea beyond. In the plate shells are added in the foreground and cliffs in the distance.

Plate CCXLVIII, O.P. 325, One Species, 14 5/8 x 22 1/4
Current name: Pied-billed Grebe, *Podilymbus podiceps* (Linnaeus)
Name on plate: American Pied-bill Dobchick PODICEPS CAROLINENSIS
Painting and plate depict an adult in winter plumage, left, and an adult in breeding plumage, right, swimming, with a bank covered in vegetation behind.

Plate CCXLIX, O.P. 28, One Species, 14 1/4 x 19 1/2
Current name: Tufted Puffin, *Fratercula cirrhata* (Pallas)
Name on plate: two variants
    1. Tufted Auk MORMON CIRRHATUS
    2. Tufted Puffin MORMON CIRRHATUS. Lath.
    (* Tufted Auk MORMON CIRRHATUS, Lath.)
Name on painting: Tufted Auk, Mormon cirrhatus, Temm.
Painting and plate depict two males among small rocks.

Plate CCL, O.P. 146, One Species, 19 3/8 x 12 1/4
Current name: Arctic Tern, *Sterna paradisaea*
Pontoppidan
Name on plate: Arctic Tern STERNA ARCTICA
Painting depicts one bird high in the sky with water and a
tundra coastline. The plate depicts the bird with a dark
cloud behind and nothing but sea below.

Plate CCLI, O.P. 349, One Species, 38 1/8 x 25 1/2
Current name: Brown Pelican, *Pelecanus occidentalis*
Linnaeus
Name on plate: Brown Pelican PELICANUS FUSCUS
Name on painting: Brown Pelican, Pelecanus Fuscus
    Also in CCCCXXI
Painting and plate depict one breeding adult on a branch of
a mangrove.

Plate CCLII, O.P. 175, One Species, 19 3/4 x 26 1/8
Current name: Double-crested Cormorant, *Phalacrocorax*
auritus (Lesson)
Name on plate: two variants
    1. Florida Cormorant CARBO FLORIDANUS
    2. Florida Cormorant PHALACROCORAX
FLORIDANUS
Name on painting: Florida Cormorant, Carbo Floridanus
History: Audubon painted the Double-crested Cormorant
twice for *Birds of America*. He thought he had two
different species, the Florida, this plate, and the Double-
crested, Plate CCLVII.. Today the Florida is considered
to be a subspecies of the Double-crested Cormorant.
    Also in CCLVII
Painting and plate depict one bird standing on a rock above
a beach with a flock of Cormorants just faintly visible in
the distance. In the plate the distant Cormorants are
nearer and more sharply defined.

CCL

CCLI

CCLII

CCLIII

CCLIV

CCLV

Plate CCLIII, O.P. 241, One Species, 15 3/4 x 21 1/4
Current name: Pomarine Jaeger, *Stercorarius pomarinus*
(Temminck)
Name on plate: two variants
   1. Jager LESTRIS POMARINA
   2. Pomarine Jager LESTRIS POMARINUS
Name on painting: Jager, Lestris Pomarina, Temm.
History: It is curious that in the plate titles for the
Pomarine in this plate and the Parasitic in Plate CCLXXII
the spelling is Jager, while for the Long-tailed in Plate
CCLXVII the spelling is Yager.
Painting depicts one bird on a mound with an empty shell.
In the plate the background is enhanced by sea with
curious sharp pointed rocks.

Plate CCLVI (CCLIV), O.P. 171, One Species, 15 3/4 x 21 1/4
Note: This plate was engraved CCLVI by mistake; it
should have been engraved CCLIV. The true Plate CCLVI
is the Reddish Egret. This is one of only three instances
when Havell misengraved the number on a plate, an
incredibly small number considering the of the project.
Current name: Wilson's Phalarope, *Phalaropus tricolor*
(Vieillot)
Name on plate: Wilson's Phalarope, PHALAROPUS
WILSONII, Sabine
Name on painting: Wilson's Phalarope, Phalaropus
wilsonii—Sabine
History: This bird is unusual in that the female is the
more colorful and the male incubates the eggs and raises
the young. Audubon did not know this and so he identified
the female as a male.
Painting and plate depict a male, left, and a female,
right, on a grassy bank near water.

Plate CCLV, O.P. 99, One Species, 15 3/4 x 22 1/2
Current name: Red Phalarope, *Phalaropus fulicaria*
(Linnaeus)
Name on plate: two variants
   1. Red Phalarope PHALAROPUS
PLATYRHYNCHUS
   2. Red Phalarope PHALAROPUS FULICARIUS
Name on painting: Red Phalarope, Phalaropus
platyrhynchus, Temm.
History: Female Phalaropes are more brilliantly colored
and assertive than males. Audubon did not know this and
quite naturally thought the dull bird in the center a
female when it was actually a male, and thought the bird
on the right a male when it was actually a female.
Painting and plate depict a female, left flying, a male,
center, cowering, and another female, right, on a rock. The
plate is enhanced by the addition of sea and mountains.

Plate CCLVI, O.P. 202, One Species, 25 1/2 x 38 1/4
Note: The plate that depicts the Wilson's Phalarope was
mistakenly engraved CCLVI; it should have been CCLIV.
The correct CCLVI is this plate. This is one of only three
instances of misnumbering.
Current name: Reddish Egret, *Egretta rufescens* (Gmelin)
Name on plate: two variants
1. Purple Heron ARDEA RUFESCENS, Buff.
2. Reddish Egret ARDEA RUFESCENS, Buff.
History: Audubon thought birds in white plumage were
the immatures of the birds in reddish plumage. He did not
know that this bird has two color phases, reddish and
white.
Painting and plate depict an adult in white plumage, left,
and another adult in reddish plumage, right, both in a wet
spot with vegetation about.

CCLVI

Plate CCLVII, O.P. 166, One Species, 30 1/4 x 21 5/8
Current name: Double-crested Cormorant, *Phalacrocorax
auritus* (Lesson)
Name on plate: Double-crested Cormorant
PHALACROCORAX DILOPHUS, Swain. & Richards.
History: Audubon painted the Double-crested Cormorant
twice for *Birds of America*. He thought he had two
different species: the Florida, Plate CCLII, and the
Double-crested, this plate. Today the Florida is
considered to be a subspecies of the Double-crested
Cormorant.
    Also in CCLII
Painting and plate depict one bird on a rock above a beach
with a flock of Cormorants just visible in the distance. In
the plate the distant Cormorants are nearer and more
sharply defined.

CCLVII

Plate CCLVIII, O.P. 31, One Species, 14 3/4 x 20 3/8
Current name: Hudsonian Godwit, *Limosa haemastica*
(Linnaeus)
Name on plate: Hudsonian Godwit LIMOSA
HUDSONICA, Swain. & Richards.
Name on painting: Hudsonian Godwit, Limosa Hudsonica,
Swain. and Richard.
Painting and plate depict a male in breeding plumage,
left, and a female, right, on a piece of ground with no
further background. The unusual position of the male
enabled Audubon to illustrate the black color of the inner
wing coverts, a distinguishing mark of the species.

CCLVIII

CCLIX

Plate CCLIX, O.P. 32, One Species, 14 3/4 x 20 3/8
Current name: Horned Grebe, *Podiceps auritus* (Linnaeus)
Name on plate: Horned Grebe PODICEPS CORNUTUS,
Lath.
Name on painting: Horned Grebe, Podiceps cornutus, Lath.
Painting and plate depict a bird in spring plumage, left,
and a bird in winter plumage, right, both on a mound with
water behind and marsh grasses.

Plate CCLX, O.P. 191, One Species, 12 1/4 x 19 3/8
Current name: Leach's Storm-Petrel, *Oceanodroma
leucorhoa* (Vieillot)
Name on plate: two variants
   1.Fork tail Petrel THALASSIDROMA LEACHII
   2.Fork tail Petrel THALASSIDROMA LEACHII—
misnumbered CCXL
(Note that the true CCXL is the Roseate Tern)
   (* Fork-tail Petrel, THALASSIDROMA LEACHII)
Name on painting: Fork Tail Sea Swallows,
Thalassidroma Leachii, - Temm.
Painting and plate depict two birds flying in the trough of
a wave. In the plate the sea is rougher and there is a
cloud-swept sky.

CCLX

Plate CCLXI, O.P. 41, One Species, 38 1/8 x 25 1/2
Current name: Sandhill Crane, *Grus canadensis* (Linnaeus)
Name on plate: Hooping Crane GRUS AMERICANA
History: Audubon called both this bird and the Whooping
Crane in Plate CCXXVI Hooping Crane. He thought this
Sandhill was the young of the Whooping Crane, though
of course they are separate species.
Painting depicts one bird with a background of marsh and
water with hills in the distance. This is probably a
Florida sand hill habitat. In the plate a flock of ten more
cranes has been added in the middle distance.

CCLXI

Plate CCLXII, O.P. 224, One Species, 20 5/8 x 29 7/8
Current name: White-tailed Tropicbird, *Phaethon
lepturus* Daudin
Other names: Yellow-billed Tropicbird
Name on plate: Tropic Bird PHAETON AETHEREUS,
Linn
Painting and plate depict two birds: the left one in flight
and the right one on a rock on a beach with sea behind.

CCLXII

Plate CCLXIII, O.P. 216, One Species, 12 1/8 x 19 1/4
Current name: Curlew Sandpiper, *Calidris ferruginea*
(Pontoppidan)
Name on plate: two variants
    1. Pigmy Curlew TRINGA SUBARQUATA, Temm.
    2. Curlew Sandpiper TRINGA SUBARQUATA, Temm.
Name on painting: Pigmy Curlew, Tringa subarquata,
Temm.
History: Audubon said that he had seen only three of
these birds in all his wanderings, all in New Jersey. His
unfamiliarity with these birds led him to misidentify the
adult in winter plumage as a young bird.
Painting and plate depict a bird in winter plumage, left,
and a bird in summer plumage, right, on a beach with
grass and water around. In the plate the background is
more developed.

CCLXIII

Plate CCLXIV, O.P. 62, One Species, 12 1/4 x 19 3/8
Current name: Northern Fulmar, *Fulmarus glacialis*
(Linnaeus)
Name on plate: Fulmar Petrel PROCELLARIA
GLACIALIS
Name on painting: Fulmar Petrel, Procellaria glacialis. L.
Painting and plate depict one bird on a rock with sea in
the background.

CCLXIV

CCLXV

CCLXVI

CCLXVII

Plate CCLXV, O.P. 172, One Species, 12 1/4 x 19 3/8
Current name: Buff-breasted Sandpiper, *Tryngites subruficollis* (Vieillot)
Name on plate: Buff breasted Sandpiper TRINGA RUFESCENS
   (* Buff-breasted Sandpiper TRINGA RUFESCENS, Vieill.)
Name on painting: Buff breasted Sand-piper. Tringa rufescens. Viele ?
Buff breasted Sandpiper Tringa rufescens, Viellot ?
Painting depicts a male, right, on a rock and a female, left, on a beach. There is a little painted sea and a little pencil sketching to indicate how the background should be. In the plate the background is completed to show calm water, some small evergreen-covered islands, and fields in the distance.

Plate CCLXVI, O.P. 145, One Species, 25 x 38 1/8
Current name: Great Cormorant, *Phalacrocorax carbo* (Linnaeus)
Other names: Black Cormorant, Common Cormorant
Name on plate: Common Cormorant PHALACROCORAX CARBO, Dumont
Painting and plate depict a pair of adults and two chicks high up on a cliffside. In the plate a rough sea at the base of the cliff has been added.

Plate CCLXVII, O.P. 176, One Species, 30 x 21 5/8
Current name: Long-tailed Jaeger, *Stercorarius longicaudus* Vieillot
Name on plate: Arctic Yager LESTRIS PARASITICA
Name on painting: Lestris parasiticus
History: Note that the spelling of Jaeger differs in the three plates that depict Jaegers. For the Pomarine in Plate CCLIII and the Parasitic in Plate CCLXXII the spelling is Jager, while for the Long-tailed in this plate the spelling is Yager. Audubon was confused about the scientific names of the Jaegers; he gives the species name *parasitica*, which properly belongs to the Parasitic, to this Long-tailed.
Painting and plate depict two birds in breeding plumage, the left one in flight and the right one on a rock pile with sea beyond. The plate is enhanced by two small sailboats and tall cliffs in the distance.

Plate CCLXVIII, O.P. 343, One Species, 14 5/8 x 20 3/8
Current name: American Woodcock, *Scolopax minor*
Gmelin
Other names: usually called Woodcock
Name on plate: American Woodcock SCOLOPAX
MINOR, Gmel.
Painting and plate depict three adult birds on muddy
ground with grasses behind.

CCLXVIII

Plate CCLXIX, O.P. 18, One Species, 14 3/4 x 20 5/8
Current name: Common Greenshank, *Tringa nebularia*
(Gunnerus)
Other names: usually called Greenshank
Name on plate: Greenshank TOTANUS GLOTTIS, Temm.
History: Audubon's sighting of this species near Cape
Sable, Florida, has been regarded as questionable. This
bird is a Eurasian species. It has been suggested that what
Audubon saw was a Greater Yellowlegs, but this species is
depicted in Plate CCCVIII, which shows that Audubon
was perfectly clear about the Greater Yellowleg's
appearance. Audubon made the painting in London,
presumably from a preserved specimen in one of the
London collections.
Painting depicts one bird with no background. The plate
has a background of a Spanish fort on the water's edge at
St. Augustine, Florida.

CCLXIX

Plate CCLXX, O.P. 39, One Species, 12 3/8 x 19 1/2
Current name: Wilson's Storm-Petrel, *Oceanites oceanicus*
(Kuhl)
Name on plate: two variants
1. Stormy Petrel THALASSIDROMA WILSONIUS
2. Wilson's Petrel THALASSIDROMA WILSONIUS
(* Stormy Petrel, THALASSIDROMA WILSONII)
Painting depicts two birds in the air over the sea. In the
plate the sea is darker and more defined and a floating
barrel has been added.

CCLXX

CCLXXI

Plate CCLXXI, O.P. 16, One Species, 38 1/8 x 25 1/2
Current name: Magnificent Frigatebird, *Fregata magnificens* Mathews
Other names: often called Frigatebird and also called Man 'O' War Bird
Name on plate: Frigate Pelican TACHYPETES AQUILUS, Viel.
Painting depicts one old male in spring plumage diving with no background. In the lower right are two colorful drawings of the bird's foot. The plate is the same except that the two drawings of the foot are moved to the top.

Plate CCLXXII, O.P. 301, One Species, 20 5/8 x 25 3/4
Current name: Parasitic Jaeger, *Stercorarius parasiticus* (Linnaeus)
Name on plate: Richardson's Jager LESTRIS RICHARDSONII
History: Note that for the Pomarine Jaeger in Plate CCLIII and for the Parastic Jaeger in this plate the spelling is Jager, while for the Long-tailed Jaeger in Plate CCLXVII the spelling is Yager.
Painting depicts an adult atop a cliff and a young bird perched up on a little rock. There is sea in the distance and very faintly indicated mountains beyond. In the plate the background is enhanced with more rocks rising from the sea.

CCLXXII

Plate CCLXXIII, O.P. 429, One Species, 14 7/8 x 20 1/2
Current name: Royal Tern, *Sterna maxima* Boddaert
Name on plate: Cayenne Tern STERNA CAYANA, Lath.
Painting depicts one bird on a rock-strewn beach with water in right background and a crab in the foreground. The plate is similar except that the cliffs, left background, and the sea, right background, are more clearly defined.

CCLXXIII

Plate CCLXXIV, O.P. 195, One Species, 14 3/4 x 20 1/2
Current name: Willet, *Catoptrophorus semipalmatus*
(Gmelin)
Name on plate: Semipalmated Snipe, or Willet
TOTANUS SEMIPALMATUS, Temm.
Painting and plate depict a bird, left, in winter plumage
and a bird, right, in breeding plumage on ground with
small rocks while a third bird in winter plumage is in the
grass behind.

CCLXXIV

Plate CCLXXV, O.P. 232, One Species, 12 1/8 x 19 1/4
Current name: Brown Noddy, *Anous stolidus* (Linnaeus)
Other names: formerly Noddy Tern and formerly Common
Noddy
Name on plate: Noddy Tern STERNA STOLIDA. L.
Painting depicts one bird on a branch of a dead tree with
no other background. In the plate there is a background of
sea and a rocky coastline in which is nestled a little
village. The background is curious as it seems to depict a
rocky northern coast rather than the beach scene Audubon
described in his notes.

CCLXXV

Plate CCLXXVI, O.P. 75, One Species, 25 1/2 x 38 1/8
Current name: King Eider, *Somateria spectabilis*
(Linnaeus)
Name on plate: King Duck FULIGULA SPECTABILIS,
Lath.
Name on painting: King Duck, Fuligula spectabilis, Lath.
Painting and plate depict a male, left, on a rock and a
female, right. The scene is a beach with two razor clams
in the foreground, sea behind, and cliffs rising up on the
right. The light is brighter in the plate.

CCLXXVI

CCLXXVII

CCLXXVIII

CCLXXIX

Plate CCLXXVII, O.P. 116, One Species, 26 x 21 7/8
Current name: Canada Goose, *Branta canadensis*
(Linnaeus)
Name on plate: Hutchins's Barnacle Goose ANSER
HUTCHINSII, Richd. & Swain
Name on painting: Hutchins's barnacle Goose, Anser
Hutchinsii. Richard
History: There is a whole complex of Canada Geese which
at various times have been considered separate species.
Hutchins' Goose (A.O.U. spelling) is one of these. The
A.O.U. at present considers them members of one species,
Canada Goose, *Branta canadensis*. Do not confuse this
goose with the Barnacle Goose in Plate CCXCVI.
   Also in CCI
Painting depicts one bird on a mound with no background.
The plate has a background of sea, ice-covered cliffs, and
dark clouds.

Plate CCLXXVIII, O.P. 72, One Species, 12 1/8 x 19 1/4
Current name: White-rumped Sandpiper, *Calidris
fuscicollis* (Vieillot)
Name on plate: Schinz's Sandpiper TRINGA SCHINZII.
Brehm.
History: Even though the white rump is not evident, the
concensus is that these birds are White-rumped
Sandpipers.
Painting and plate depict a bird in flight, left, and a bird,
right, standing on a shell-strewn beach looking over the
sea with a view of the coastline extending into the
distance. In the plate the vista extends farther into the
background.

Plate CCLXXIX, O.P. 122, One Species, 12 1/8 x 19 1/4
Current name: Sandwich Tern, *Sterna sandvicensis*
Latham
Other names: sometimes known as Cabot's Tern
Name on plate: two variants
   1. Sandwich Tern STERNA CANTIACA, Lath.
   2. Sandwich Tern STERNA BOYSSII
   (* Sandwich Tern, STERNA BOYSSII, Lath.)
History: This bird nests in dense colonies in the British
Isles but it is much rarer here. Audubon was the discoverer
of the Sandwich Tern in this country.
Painting and plate depict one bird on a beach with sea
behind. There is a spiny lobster lying nearby.

Plate CCLXXX, O.P. 189, One Species, 19 5/8 x 12 3/8
Current name: Black Tern, *Chlidonias niger* (Linnaeus)
Name on plate: Black Tern STERNA NIGRA. Lin.
(* Black Tern, STERNA NIGRI. Linn.)
Painting and plate depict a bird in breeding plumage
standing on a rock by the sea while a bird in winter
plumage dives down from on high. The clouds in the plate
are more clearly defined.

Plate CCLXXXI, O.P. 219, One Species, 25 1/2 x 38 1/8
Current name: Great Blue Heron, *Ardea herodias* Linnaeus
Other names: The Great White Heron was formerly
considered a separate species, *Ardea occidentalis*, but it is
now treated as a color morph of the Great Blue. The Great
White has also been treated as a subspecies of the Great
Blue.
Name on plate: Great White Heron ARDEA
OCCIDENTALIS
Name on painting: Ardea occidentalis
History: Audubon was correct in calling this bird Great
White since that is how it was known in his day and until
fairly recently. He painted the Great Blue in its regular
plumage for Plate CCXI.
Also in CCXI
Painting and plate depict one bird with a fish in his beak.
There is a view of Key West across the water. In the
painting there are two dark birds in flight that resemble
Frigatebirds but in the plate these birds are white and
lack the trailing tails.

Plate CCLXXXII, O.P. 12, One Species, 20 5/8 x 25 7/8
Current name: Iceland Gull, *Larus glaucoides* Meyer
Name on plate: White-winged silvery Gull LARUS
LEUCOPTERUS. Bonap.
(* White-winged Silvery Gull, LARUS
LEUCOPTERUS, Bonap.)
Name on painting: White-winged Silvery Gull, Larus
leucopterus Faber
L. arcticus MacGillivray, L. clancoides Temm.
Painting and plate depict an adult in breeding plumage on
a beach with a young bird on a rock just above. In the
plate a mountain is added beyond the sea.

CCLXXX

CCLXXXI

CCLXXXII

CCLXXXIII

CCLXXXIV

CCLXXXV

Plate CCLXXXIII, O.P. 68, One Species, 12 3/8 x 19 5/8
Current name: Greater Shearwater, *Puffinus gravis* O'Reilly
Name on plate: Wandering Shearwater PUFFINUS CINEREUS, Bonap.
Name on painting: Cinerous Petrel Lath. Puffinus cinereus, Cuv.
Painting depicts one bird standing on a rock with just a little blue sky washed in. In the plate the background is developed so that the rock the bird is on seems high up with the sea below and mountains in the background.

Plate CCLXXXIV, O.P. 423, One Species, 12 3/8 x 19 5/8
Current name: Purple Sandpiper, *Calidris maritima* (Brünnich)
Name on plate: Purple Sandpiper TRINGA MARITIMA, Bonap.
Name on painting: Purple Sandpiper, Tringa maritima, Brunn.
The painting depicts a male, left, and a female, right, each on a rock. In the plate the rocks are more developed and the two Purple Sandpipers are moved to the right to make room for the additon of a Wilson's Plover on the left. This Wilson's Plover also appears in Plate CCIX on the right. This is one of only two instances where the same painting of a bird appears in two different plates; the other is the Bluebird in Plates CXIII and XXXVI. Note that the name of the Wilson's Plover does not appear in the legend of Plate CCLXXXIV, although Audubon signaled his intention by writing on the left side of the painting, "Wilson's Plover, Charadrius Wilsonius."

Plate CCLXXXV, O.P. 19, Two Species, 12 1/4 x 19 1/4
Species 1
Current name: Sabine's Gull, *Xema sabini* (Sabine)
Name on plate: Fork-tailed Gull LARUS SABINI, Swain. & Richards.
Name on painting: Fork tailed Gull, Larus Sabinii, Sab.
Species 2
Note: not in original painting, only in plate
Current name: Sanderling, *Calidris alba* (Pallas)
Name on plate: [No English name] TRINGA ARENARIA
Painting depicts one Sabine's Gull on a rock with no other background. In the plate a male Sanderling in spring plumage, which Audubon had painted on a seperate piece of paper, was added on the left; also added was an extensive background of beach, sea, and land in the distance with a grove of trees and a fence.

Plate CCLXXXVI, O.P. 85, One Species, 25 1/2 x 38 1/8
Current name: Greater White-fronted Goose, *Anser albifrons* (Scopoli)
Other names: usually known as White-fronted Goose
Name on plate: White-fronted Goose ANSER ALBIFRONS, Bechst.
 (* White-fronted Goose, Lath., ANSER ALBIFRONS, Bechstein)
Name on painting: White-fronted Goose, Lath., Anser albifrons, Bechst.
Painting and plate depict a male, left, and female, right, with grasses behind. The background is more sharply defined in the plate.

CCLXXXVI

Plate CCLXXXVII, O.P. 206, One Species, 20 5/8 x 30 1/8
Current name: Ivory Gull, *Pagophila eburnea* (Phipps)
Name on plate: Ivory Gull LARUS EBURNEUS, Gm.
 (* Ivory Gull, Lath., LARUS EBURNEUS, Gmel.)
Name on painting: Ivory Gull.Lath., Larus eburneus, Gm.
Painting and plate depict an adult bird, left, on a small rock and a young bird, right, on a beach. There are shells in the foreground and sea and sky in the background.

CCLXXXVII

Plate CCLXXXVIII, O.P. 82, One Species, 14 5/8 x 20 1/4
Current name: Lesser Yellowlegs, *Tringa flavipes* (Gmelin)
Name on plate: Yellow Shank TOTANUS FLAVIPES, Vieill.
Painting and plate depict one bird on the grassy bank of a stream that flows into a small lake, all surrounded by trees.

CCLXXXVIII

CCLXXXIX

CCXC

CCXCI

Plate CCLXXXIX, O.P. 245, One Species, 12 1/4 x 19 1/4
Current name: Solitary Sandpiper, *Tringa solitaria*
Wilson
Name on plate: Solitary Sandpiper TOTANUS
CHLOROPYGIUS, Viell
Painting and plate depict a bird in winter plumage, left,
and a bird in breeding plumage, right, in a watery marsh.
Audubon painted these birds earlier and cut them out and
pasted them onto the paper. In the painting the bird in
winter plumage is standing in unusually deep water, but
Havell corrected this in the plate.

Plate CCXC, O.P. 215, One Species, 12 1/8 x 19 3/8
Current name: Dunlin, *Calidris alpina* (Linnaeus)
Name on plate: Red backed Sandpiper TRINGA ALPINA L
   (* Red-backed Sandpiper TRINGA ALPINA, Linn.)
Name on painting: Red-backed Sandpiper, Tringa alpina,
Lin.
Painting depicts a bird in winter plumage, left, and a bird
in breeding plumage, right, standing on a shell-littered
mound with no other background. In the plate the mound
is at the top of a mountain or cliff with a view of land and
sea below and extending off to the far distance.

Plate CCXCI, O.P. 164, One Species, 38 1/8 x 25 1/2
Current name: Herring Gull, *Larus argentatus* Pontoppidan
Name on plate: Herring Gull LARUS ARGENTATUS,
Brunn.
Painting and plate depict a young bird standing on a clump
of racoon oysters and an adult bird flying above. The
background shows water and beaches. In the painting a
foot protrudes from the flying bird but this was
eliminated in the plate on Audubon's orders.

Plate CCXCII, O.P. 137, One Species, 20 5/8 x 30 1/8
Current name: Great Crested Grebe, *Podiceps cristatus*
(Linnaeus)
Name on plate: Crested Grebe PODICEPS CRISTATUS,
Lath.
Name on painting: Crested Grebe, Podiceps cristatus Lath.
History: This is an old-world species never observed in the
Americas. Audubon drew these birds from preserved
specimens in England, loaned to him by Johr. Gould, in the
mistaken belief he had seen the species in Ohio. He had
it confused with another species.
Painting and plate depict a bird in winter plumage, left,
and a bird in spring plumage, right, both swimming in a
calm sea. Two sketches of the Grebe's foot are upper left
in the painting and upper right in the plate.

CCXCII

Plate CCXCIII, O.P. 87, One Species, 14 3/4 x 20 1/2
Current name: Horned Puffin, *Fratercula corniculata*
(Naumann)
Name on plate: Large billed Puffin MORMON
GLACIALIS.Leach.
 (* Large-billed Puffin, MORMON GLACIAUS,Leach.)
Name on painting: Large-billed Puffin, Mormon
glacialis,Leach
Painting and plate depict two birds in spring plumage, the
left one on a barnacle-encrusted rock and the right one in
the water. Distant mountains were added in the plate.

CCXCIII

Plate CCXCIV, O.P. 422, One Species, 12 1/8 x 19 1/4
Current name: Pectoral Sandpiper, *Calidris melanotos*
(Vieillot)
Name on plate: Pectoral Sandpiper TRINGA
PECTORALIS
Painting and plate depict two adult birds on a shell-
littered beach with the sea beyond. The background in
the plate is enhanced by cliffs in the distance.

CCXCIV

CCXCV

Plate CCXCV, O.P. 162, One Species, 12 1/4 x 19 1/4
Current name: Manx Shearwater, *Puffinus puffinus*
(Brünnich)
Name on plate: Manks Shearwater PUFFINUS
ANGLORUM, Ray
 (* Manx Shearwater PUFFINUS ANGLORUM, Ray)
Name on painting: Manks Puffinus, Puffinus anglorum
Ray.
Painting depicts one bird swimming in the sea. In the
plate the background has cliffs rising from the sea.

CCXCVI

Plate CCXCVI, O.P. 105, One Species, 25 1/2 x 38 1/8
Current name: Barnacle Goose, *Branta leucopsis*
(Bechstein)
Name on plate: Barnacle Goose ANSER LEUCOPSIS
History: Do not confuse this goose with the Canada Goose
in Plate CCLXXVII that Audubon called Hutchin's
Barnacle Goose.
Painting and plate depict two birds on a rocky beach with
a background of water and hills. Audubon used oil for the
background in the painting.

CCXCVII

Plate CCXCVII, O.P. 128, One Species, 20 5/8 x 30 1/4
Current name: Harlequin Duck, *Histrionicus histrionicus*
(Linnaeus)
Name on plate: Harlequin Duck FULIGULA
HISTRIONICA, Bonap.
Painting and plate depict a male, left, standing on a
beach, another male on a rock, and a female crouched on
the beach with a clam shell and lobster claw and sea in
the background. For the painting Audubon cut out two
previously painted birds and pasted them on the right,
then painted the left bird and the background. An
addition of cliffs rising from the sea was made to the
plate.

Plate CCXCVIII, O.P. 125, One Species, 14 3/4 x 20 3/8
Current name: Red-necked Grebe, *Podiceps grisegena* (Boddaert)
Name on plate: Red-necked Grebe PODICEPS RUBRICOLLIS, Lath.
Painting and plate depict an adult in breeding plumage, left, and an adult in winter plumage, right, on a high bank looking over an identation from the sea.

CCXCVIII

Plate CCXCIX, O.P. 38, One Species, 12 1/4 x 19 3/8
Current name: Audubon's Shearwater, *Puffinus lherminieri* Lesson
Name on plate: two variants
  1. Dusky Petrel PUFFINUS OBSCURUS
  2. Dusky Petrel, Lath PUFFINUS OBSCURUS, Cuvier
History: Now that Audubon's Warbler is no longer considered a separate species but instead one of two groups of the Yellow-rumped Warbler, this is the only species bearing Audubon's name.
Painting and plate depict one bird swimming. In the plate a background of mountains in the distance was provided.

CCXCIX

Plate CCC, O.P. 52, One Species, 14 3/4 x 20 1/2
Current name: Lesser Golden-Plover, *Pluvialis dominica* (Müller)
Other names: American Golden-plover
Name on plate: Golden Plover CHARADRIUS PLUVIALIS. L.
History: There is some puzzlement about the identity of these birds. It has been suggested that the two birds on the right may be Greater Golden-Plovers that Audubon drew from specimens in London, but there seems to be no firm ground for this claim.
Painting depicts a moulting bird, left, and two birds in breeding plumage, right. The left bird and the upper right bird were painted separately, cut out, and pasted on. In the plate the left bird is reversed and a background of beach, sea, and distant hills has been added.

CCC

CCCI

CCCII

CCCIII

Plate CCCI, O.P. 238, One Species, 25 1/2 x 38 1/8
Current name: Canvasback, *Aythya valisineria* (Wilson)
Name on plate: Canvas backed Duck FULIGULA
VALLISNERIA, Steph
    (* Canvas-backed Duck, FULIGULA VALLISNERIA,
Steph.)
Painting depicts a male, left, on a bank dipping his bill in
the water, another male, center, in the water, and a
female, right, on a higher bank. In the distance there is
more water, a spit of land, and beyond more water with a
ship. In the plate the vista in the distance was changed
to a view of Baltimore.

Plate CCCII, O.P. 165, One Species, 21 1/8 x 30 3/8
Current name: American Black Duck, *Anas rubripes*
Brewster
Other names: usually called Black Duck
Name on plate: Dusky Duck ANAS OBSCURA. Gm.
History: Old bird books list the name Dusky Duck as an
alternative to Black Duck
Painting and plate depict a male, left, and a female,
right, on ground with marshy grass behind and a view left
of water with mountains beyond. Note how cleverly
Audubon positioned the female so as to illustrate clearly
the white underwing of this species.

Plate CCCIII, O.P. 329, One Species, 14 7/8 x 21
Current name: Upland Sandpiper, *Bartramia longicauda*
(Bechstein)
Other names: until recently Upland Plover
Name on plate: Bartram Sandpiper TOTANUS
BARTRAMIUS, Temm.
History: John Bartram, 1699–1777, was a famous pioneer
botanist who established the still existent Bartram
Gardens in Philadelphia. His son William, 1739–1823,
was a distinguished botanist and ornithologist, most
famous for his journals *Travels*. As Bechstein described
this bird in 1812, it may be assumed the bird was named
for William.
Painting and plate depict two birds, the upper reaching
for an insect and the lower reaching for a snail. The birds
are on rocks with a toadshade nearby and sea and rocky
islets beyond. In the plate the sea, the opposite shore,
and the distant mountains are more clearly defined.

Plate CCCIV, O.P. 51, One Species, 14 3/4 x 21 5/8
Current name: Ruddy Turnstone, *Arenaria interpres*
(Linnaeus)
Name on plate: Turn-stone STREPSILAS INTERPRES. Ill
Name on painting: Turn-stone [more that is faded]
Painting depicts a bird in breeding plumage, left, flying
over water with another bird in winter plumage, right, on
a beach. In the plate the coastline is changed and the sea
is more defined and stretches in the distance to an inlet
and low hills.

CCCIV

Plate CCCV, O.P. 205, One Species, 12 3/8 x 19 1/2
Current name: Purple Gallinule, *Porphyrula martinica*
(Linnaeus)
Name on plate: Purple Gallinule GALLINULA
MARTINICA, Gmel
Painting depicts one bird on a mound on the edge of a
marsh with grass, water, and trees way off. The
background is painted in oil. There are three birds flying
in the distance. In the plate the background is enhanced,
there is more water, the trees on the other side of the
water are more defined, and the three flying birds are
eliminated.

CCCV

Plate CCCVI, O.P. 409, One Species, 25 5/8 x 38 1/4
Current name: Common Loon, *Gavia immer* (Brünnich)
Name on plate: Great Northern Diver or Loon
COLYMBUS GLACIALIS, L.
Painting and plate depict a bird in winter plumage, left,
and a bird in breeding plumage, right, in a grassy clump
with sea and mountains in the distance. In the plate the
mountains have a different configuration.

CCCVI

CCCVII

Plate CCCVII, O.P. 362, One Species, 21 1/4 x 30 1/2
Current name: Little Blue Heron, *Egretta caerulea*
(Linnaeus)
Name on plate: two variants
   1. Blue Heron ARDEA CAERULEA
   2. Blue Crane, or Heron ARDEA COERULEA
Name on painting: Blue Heron, Ardea Caerulea
Painting depicts one bird looking over a swampy area
with patches of water and trees beyond. Just over the back
of the bird one can faintly discern a pencilled outline of a
bird Audubon wished included. The plate is the same
except for the addition of a white-plumaged immature
standing in the middle distance. Havell did not include
the bird that Audubon indicated in pencil. The habitat
depicted is near Charleston, South Carolina.

CCCVIII

Plate CCCVIII, O.P. 380, One Species, 14 7/8 x 21
Current name: Greater Yellowlegs, *Tringa melanoleuca*
(Gmelin)
Name on plate: Tell-tale Godwit or Snipe TOTANUS
MELANOLEUCUS, Vieill.
Painting and plate depict two birds in winter plumage on
the near bank of a river. On the far bank is a Florida farm
with three buildings. There are seven Vultures in one of
the trees.

Plate CCCIX, O.P. 56, One Species, 19 3/8 x 15 1/4
Current name: Common Tern, *Sterna hirundo* Linnaeus
Name on plate: Great Tern STERNA HIRUNDO. L.
Name on painting: Common Tern, Sterna Hyrundo
Painting and plate depict one bird diving against a
background of sky.

CCCIX

Plate CCCX, O.P. 347, One Species, 14 5/8 x 21 1/8
Current name: Spotted Sandpiper, *Actitis macularia*
(Linnaeus)
Name on Plate: Spotted Sandpiper TOTANUS
MACULARIUS
Painting and plate depict two birds on either side of a
stream. In the painting the background is lightly
indicated in pencil. In the plate the background is
developed to show a continuation of the stream across a
marsh with fallen trees and woods beyond. The scene is
near Bayou Sarah, Louisiana.

CCCX

Plate CCCXI, O.P. 410, One Species, 38 1/4 x 25 3/4
Current name: American White Pelican, *Pelecanus
erythrorhynchos* Gmelin
Other names: usually called White Pelican
Name on plate: American White Pelican PELICANUS
AMERICANUS, Aud.
Painting depicts one adult bird standing on a rock with
some water on the left and a dark cloudy sky. In the plate
there is green by the rock and beyond a lovely night
landscape of water and shore with trees. This is one of
only three night scenes in *Birds of America*; the others are
found in Plate CXXI, Snowy Owl, and in Plate CLXXI,
Common Barn-Owl.

Plate CCCXII, O.P. 229, One Species, 21 1/4 x 30 1/4
Current name: Oldsquaw, *Clangula hyemalis* (Linnaeus)
Name on plate: Long-tailed Duck FULIGULA
GLACIALIS
Painting and plate depict an adult male in summer
plumage, left, and another adult male in winter plumage,
right, on rocks while a female with her chicks swims in
the water in front of them. In the plate a mountain was
added in the far distance.

CCCXI

CCCXII

CCCXIII

CCCXIV

CCCXV

Plate CCCXIII, O.P. 353, One Species, 14 3/4 x 20 1/2
Current name: Blue-winged Teal, *Anas discors* Linnaeus
Name on plate: Blue-Winged Teal ANAS DISCORS
   (* Blue-winged Teal, ANAS DISCORS, Linn.)
Name on painting: Blue Winged Teal, Anas Discors
Painting depicts a male, left, and a female, above and
behind, flying low over a pond. In the plate the birds are
shown high in the air with a view of land and water
below.

Plate CCCXIV, O.P. 366, One Species, 14 3/4 x 20 1/2
Current name: Laughing Gull, *Larus atricilla* Linnaeus
Name on plate: Black-headed Gull LARUS ATRICILLA.
L.
Name on painting: Laughing Gull, Larus atricilla Linn.
Painting and plate depict an adult in spring plumage,
front, and a young bird, behind, with no background.

Plate CCCXV, O.P. 192, One Species, 12 1/4 x 19 1/2
Current name: Red Knot, *Calidris canutus* (Linnaeus)
Name on plate: Red-breasted Sandpiper TRINGA
ISLANDICA. L.
Name on painting: Red breasted Sandpiper, Tringa
islandica, L.
Painting depicts a bird in breeding plumage, above, and
another in winter plumage, below, on a spit of beach
jutting out into a rough sea with a full-rigged sailing ship
in the background. In the plate the sea is calm and the
ship has been eliminated.

Plate CCCXVI, O.P. 64, One Species, 38 1/4 x 25 5/8
Current name: Anhinga, *Anhinga anhinga* (Linnaeus)
Other names: formerly American Anhinga, sometimes
called Water Turkey
Name on plate: Black-bellied Darter PLOTUS
ANHINGA
Name on painting: Black Bellied Darter or Snake Bird
Plotus Melanogaster
            Common name "Bec à Lancette"
History: Bec à Lancette was the name used for this species
by the French speaking Creoles around New Orleans
Painting depicts a male and a female, below, on a tree
stump with no further background. In the plate a
background of water stretching to trees in the distance was
provided, with five more Anhingas in the middle
distance in the water and on a tree stump sticking out of

CCCXVI

Plate CCCXVII, O.P. 29, One Species, 21 1/4 x 30 1/4
Current name: Surf Scoter, *Melanitta perspicillata*
(Linnaeus)
Name on plate: Black, or Surf Duck FULIGULA
PERSPICILLATA
Painting and plate depict a male, left, perched on a rock
with a female, right, below him on a beach with shells
and sea beyond. In the plate cliffs rising from the sea
were added on the right.

CCCXVII

Plate CCCXVIII, O.P. 270, One Species, 14 5/8 x 20 3/8
Current name: American Avocet, *Recurvirostra americana*
Gmelin
Name on plate: American Avocet RECURVIROSTRA
AMERICANA
Painting depicts one adult bird in winter plumage
reaching for a snail with other birds in the far distance,
all against a background of water, bank, rocks, and
grasses. In the plate the bird is in spring plumage with
pinkish-tan head and neck. An insect replaces the snail,
and a young bird appears in the middle distance.

CCCXVIII

Plate CCCXIX, O.P. 170, One Species, 19 1/2 x 12 1/4
Current name: Least Tern, *Sterna antillarum* (Lesson)
Name on plate: Lesser Tern STERNA MINUTA. L.
Name on painting: Lesser Tern, Sterna minuta, L.
Painting and plate depict a young bird, above, and an
adult bird, below, both in flight against a background of
sky. For the painting, Audubon did the two birds
separately, cut them out, and pasted them onto the paper.

Plate CCCXX, O.P. 118, One Species, 14 3/4 x 20 1/2
Current name: Least Sandpiper, *Calidris minutilla*
(Vieillot)
Name on plate: Little Sandpiper TRINGA PUSILLA,
Wils.
Name on painting: Least sand piper
Painting and plate depict two birds at a little pool at the
bottom of a small rapids with rocks about. In the plate
the background was greatly enhanced so that the stream
extends well back, banked on the sides with tall trees
about.

CCCXIX

Plate CCCXXI, O.P. 35, One Species, 25 5/8 x 35 1/4
Current name: Roseate Spoonbill, *Ajaia ajaja* (Linnaeus)
Name on plate: Roseate Spoonbill PLATALEA AJAJA, L.
Painting depicts one bird on the right against a background
of reeds. On the left is a very light indication of a
pencilled-in background. In the plate this background was
developed into a vista of land and water with bushy trees
extending to hills in the far distance.

CCCXX

CCCXXI

Plate CCCXXII, O.P. 221, One Species, 20 5/8 x 26
Current name: Redhead, *Aythya americana* (Eyton)
Name on plate: Red-headed Duck FULIGULA FERINA,
Steph.
History: Painted from specimens given to Audubon by his
friend Daniel Webster.
Painting and plate depict a female, left, and a male,
right, on a sloping bank. In the plate a background of
smooth sea and mountains beyond was provided.

CCCXXII

Plate CCCXXIII, O.P. 355, One Species, 21 x 21 1/8
Current name: Black Skimmer, *Rynchops niger* Linnaeus
Name on plate: Black Skimmer or Shearwater
RHINCOPS NIGRA, L.
Painting depicts one bird flying low over the sea in a
skimming position. There is a protruding rock at the left
and a ship in full sail behind it. In the plate the rock and
the ship were eliminated and the bird is shown flying
over a dark sea.

CCCXXIII

Plate CCCXXIV, O.P. 43, One Species, 21 1/8 x 16 7/8
Current name: Bonaparte's Gull, *Larus philadelphia*
(Ord)
Distribution: western Canada, coastal western U.S.,
central and eastern U.S.
Name on plate: Bonapartian Gull LARUS BONAPARTII.
Swain.and Rich.
History: Charles Lucien Bonaparte, Prince of Canino and
Musignano and a nephew of Napoleon, was the youngest
and most colorful personality of the Philadelphia
scientific community. He was an eminent ornithologist
and wrote a supplement to Alexander Wilson's classic on
birds. He had a stormy relationship with Audubon, one
minute good friends, the next at odds.
Painting depicts an adult bird and an immature bird
standing while another adult flies overhead. All three
birds were painted separately, cut out, and pasted onto
the paper. In the process, part of the lower bill of the
flying bird was torn off. In the plate a background of sea
and rocks looming up on the left was provided.

CCCXXIV

CCCXXV

CCCXXVI

CCCXXVII

Plate CCCXXV, O.P. 406, One Species, 14 7/8 x 20 1/2
Current name: Bufflehead, *Bucephala albeola* (Linnaeus)
Name on plate: Buffel-headed Duck FULIGULA
ALBEOLA
Painting and plate depict a male, right, and a female,
left, standing in front of a clump of grass.

Plate CCCXXVI, O.P. 268, One Species, 25 5/8 x 38 1/4
Current name: Northern Gannet, *Sula bassanus* (Linnaeus)
Other names: also known as Gannet
Name on plate: Gannet SULA BASSANA, Lacep.
Name on painting: Gannet
Painting depicts a young bird, front, and an adult, behind,
on a rocky foreground. The sea is beyond with a large rock
rising up at the left, around which is a cloud of birds. In
the plate the sea is much rougher and there are many
Gannets flying about in the distance. The scene is Gannet
Rock in the Gulf of St. Lawrence.

Plate CCCXXVII, O.P. 287, One Species, 21 x 30 1/4
Current name: Northern Shoveler, *Anas clypeata* Linnaeus
Name on plate: Shoveller Duck ANAS CLYPEATA, L.
Painting and plate depict a male, left, and a female,
right, both reaching for an insect in the grass. The
painting was first done in watercolor, then painted over in
oil.

Plate CCCXXVIII, O.P. 101, One Species, 14 7/8 x 20 1/2
Current name: Black-necked Stilt, *Himantopus mexicanus*
(Müller)
Name on plate: Long-legged Avocet HIMANTOPUS
NIGRICOLLIS, Vieill.
Name on painting: Long legged Plover, Charadrius
Himantopus
Painting depicts one male bird standing on a rocky beach
with a wind-swept sea and hills beyond. There are two
boats under sail. All of this background was eliminated in
the plate and the bird is shown standing on a rocky beach
with smooth sea and sky behind.

CCCXXVIII

Plate CCCXXIX, O.P. 98, One Species, 12 1/4 x 19 1/2
Current name: Yellow Rail, *Coturnicops noveboracensis*
(Gmelin)
Name on plate: Yellow-breasted Rail RALLUS
NOVEBORACENSIS, Bonap.
Name on painting: New York Rail, Rallus (Crex)
noveboracensis
Painting depicts one bird perched on low rocks on a bank by
water with trees and woods beyond. Audubon first
surrounded the birds with reeds that he later painted out,
but they are still faintly visible. The plate is roughly the
same but the dead sapling on the left was eliminated and
the background was more finely drawn to show the river
winding away between its banks.

CCCXXIX

Plate CCCXXX, O.P. 71, One Species, 12 1/4 x 19 1/2
Current name: Semipalmated Plover, *Charadrius
semipalmatus* Bonaparte
Name on plate: Ring Plover CHARADRIUS
SEMIPALMATUS
Name on painting: Ring Plover Tringa Hiaticula
Painting depicts male leaning down off a rock in pursuit of
a snail, while female stands off to the right. In the plate
the background is developed to show sea beyond and low
mountains in the distance.

CCCXXX

CCCXXXI

CCCXXXII

CCCXXXIII

Plate CCCXXXI, O.P. 275, One Species, 25 5/8 x 38 1/4
Current name: Common Merganser, *Mergus merganser*
Linnaeus
Name on plate: Goosander MERGUS MERGANSER, L.
Name on painting: Goosander
Painting depicts a female, left, swimming in the water
while the male, right, is on a bank. There is no further
background. In the plate the background was developed to
show a view of the falls at Cohoes in upper New York
state.

Plate CCCXXXII, O.P. 305, One Species, 21 1/4 x 30 1/8
Current name: Labrador Duck, *Camptorhynchus
labradorius* (Gmelin)
Name on plate: Pied Duck FULIGULA LABRADORA
History: The skins of these birds were given to Audubon by
his friend Daniel Webster. The last known individual of
this species was taken on December 12, 1878, in Elmira,
New York.
Painting depicts a female, left, and a male, right, on a
rocky foreground with the sea beyond, a boat in the
distance and a rim of land in the far distance. The
painting is primarily in watercolor with rocks in the
foreground in oil. In the plate the sea is calmer, the boat
and distant land have been eliminated, and cliffs have
been added on the right.

Plate CCCXXXIII, O.P. 78, One Species, 20 1/4 x 22 3/8
Current name: Green-backed Heron, *Butorides striatus*
(Linnaeus)
Other names: formerly Green Heron
Name on plate: Green Heron ARDEA VIRESCENS, L.
History: The A.O.U. includes *virescens* in the species
Butorides striatus.
Painting and plate depict an adult bird in the foreground
with a young bird behind reaching for what seems to be a
luna moth. They are in the midst of some vegetation by a
little pool. The painting was done in watercolor, pencil,
and pastel.

Plate CCCXXXIV, O.P. 244, One Species, 15 1/8 x 21
Current name: Black-bellied Plover, *Pluvialis squatarola*
(Linnaeus)
Name on plate: Black-bellied Plover CHARADRIUS
HELVETICUS
Painting depicts a bird in breeding plumage, left, and a
bird in winter plumage, right, standing on a rocky beach
with the sea in the background. The left bird was painted
separately, cut out, and pasted on. In the plate the bird in
breeding plumage was moved to the foreground and the
bird in winter plumage was moved behind. A chick was
added from a separate painting by Audubon, which is now
owned by the New-York Historical Society.

CCCXXXIV

Plate CCCXXXV, O.P. 161, One Species, 12 1/4 x 19 3/8
Current name: Short-billed Dowitcher, *Limnodromus
griseus* (Gmelin)
Name on plate: Red-breasted Snipe SCOLOPAX GRISEA,
Gm.
Painting depicts a bird in winter plumage, left, and a bird
in summer plumage, right, with no background. In the
plate the birds are on a muddy bank with water in the
foreground and water and coastline beyond with rocks
surfacing from the water.

CCCXXXV

Plate CCCXXXVI, O.P. 361, One Species, 38 1/4 x 25 5/8
Current name: Yellow-crowned Night-Heron, *Nycticorax
violaceus* (Linnaeus)
Name on plate: Yellow-Crowned Heron ARDEA
VIOLACEA, L.
(* Yellow-crowned Heron, ARDEA VIOLACEA, Linn.)
Painting depicts a male, below, and an immature, above,
perched in a dead tree entwined with smilax with no
other background. In the plate there is a background of a
broad expanse of water with a coastline of cliffs in the
distance.

CCCXXXVI

CCCXXXVII

CCCXXXVIII

CCCXXXIX

Plate CCCXXXVII, O.P. 371, One Species, 22 7/8 x 28 1/8
Current name: American Bittern, *Botaurus lentiginosus*
(Rackett)
Name on plate: American Bittern ARDEA MINOR
Name on painting: American Bittern
History: According to Audubon this painting was done
entirely by his son, John Woodhouse Audubon.
Painting and plate depict two birds standing on a muddy
bank against a background of marshy grasses.

Plate CCCXXXVIII, O.P. 296, One Species, 18 1/2 x 23 7/8
Current name: Hybrid bird Mallard x Gadwall, *Anas
platyrhynchos x strepera*
Name on plate: Bemaculated Duck ANAS GLOCITANS
Name on painting: Bemaculated Duck ?
History: Audubon agonized over the identity of this duck.
At first he called it Bemaculated, meaning spotted, then
Brewer's in honor of his friend Thomas Mayo Brewer, a
youthful ornithologist from Roxbury, Massachusetts.
Later on he wrote that he thought it might be a hybrid of
a Mallard and a Gadwall, and this time he was correct.
Painting and plate depict one male amid grass reaching
for a snail. The painting is in pencil, watercolor, pastel,
and oil.

Plate CCCXXXIX, O.P. 300, One Species, 12 3/8 x 19 7/8
Current name: Dovekie, *Alle alle* (Linnaeus)
Other names: sometimes called Little Auk
Name on plate: Little Auk URIA ALLE, Temm.
Name on painting: Little Auk
Painting and plate depict a bird in breeding plumage,
right, on a rock and a bird in winter plumage, left,
swimming with a large shrimp in its mouth. Distant
mountains were added in the plate.

Plate CCCXL, O.P. 158, One Species, 12 1/2 x 19 3/8
Current name: British Storm-Petrel, *Hydrobates pelagicus*
(Linnaeus)
Name on plate: Least Stormy-Petrel THALASSIDROMA
PELAGICA
History: Although this species is considered to be
accidental in North America, Audubon collected several
while becalmed on the Newfoundland banks.
Painting depicts two birds flying over blue sea that is only
casually daubed on. In the plate the sea stretches all the
way across the paper and is more clearly defined. In both
painting and plate there is something just under the bill of
the bird on the right. In the painting it looks like a small
island in the sea. In the plate it looks as though it may be
a piece of seaweed the bird is about to pick up.

CCCXL

Plate CCCXLI, O.P. 169, One Species, 25 5/8 x 38 1/4
Current name: Great Auk, *Pinguinus impennis* (Linnaeus)
Name on plate: Great Auk ALCA IMPENNIS, L.
Name on painting: Great Auk, Alca Impennis, Linn.
History: This species became extinct by 1844 due to
relentless persecution by sealers. The generic name of the
bird relates to the fact that the bird was once widely
known as Penguin. Audubon never saw this bird and had
only one authentic account of its occurence off North
American coast, this from Henry Havell, brother of his
engraver.
Painting depicts one bird on a low rock and another
swimming in the sea with no further background. In the
plate the sea is far rougher and there are massive cliffs.
In the painting only one foot shows on the swimming bird,
but in the plate the bird's other foot stretches out behind.

CCCXLI

Plate CCCXLII, O.P. 248, One Species, 21 1/4 x 30 3/8
Current name: Common Goldeneye, *Bucephala clangula*
(Linnaeus)
Name on plate: Golden-Eye Duck FULIGULA
CLANGULA
(* Golden-eye Duck FULIGULA CLANGULA)
Name on painting: Golden eyed Duck
History: Some maintain that when Audubon painted
Barrow's Goldeneye he did not realize it was a different
species from the Common Goldeneye, but note that the
scientific names on the plate are different. Also note that
Audubon has the cheek patches placed correctly in each
species.
For purposes of comparison:
Plate CCCXLII
Current name: Common Goldeneye, *B. clangula*
Plate name: Golden Eye Duck FULIGULA CLANGULA
Plate CCCCIII
Current name: Barrow's Goldeneye, *B. islandica*
Plate name: Golden-eye Duck CLANGULA VULGARIS
Painting, in watercolor, pastel, and pencil, and plate
depict a male, left, and a female, right, flying against a
blue sky.

CCCXLII

CCCXLIII

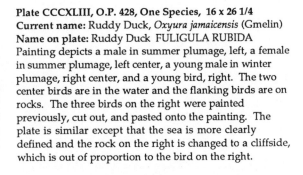

Plate CCCXLIII, O.P. 428, One Species, 16 x 26 1/4
Current name: Ruddy Duck, *Oxyura jamaicensis* (Gmelin)
Name on plate: Ruddy Duck FULIGULA RUBIDA
Painting depicts a male in summer plumage, left, a female
in summer plumage, left center, a young male in winter
plumage, right center, and a young bird, right. The two
center birds are in the water and the flanking birds are on
rocks. The three birds on the right were painted
previously, cut out, and pasted onto the painting. The
plate is similar except that the sea is more clearly
defined and the rock on the right is changed to a cliffside,
which is out of proportion to the bird on the right.

CCCXLIV

Plate CCCXLIV, O.P. 159, One Species, 12 1/2 x 19 7/8
Current name: Stilt Sandpiper, *Calidris himantopus*
(Bonaparte)
Name on plate: Long-legged Sandpiper TRINGA
HIMANTOPUS
Name on painting: Long legged Sandpiper, Tringa
himantopus, Bonap.
Painting depicts two birds with no background. In the
plate the birds are on a rocky rise by a beach and sea.

CCCXLV

Plate CCCXLV, O.P. 282, One Species, 15 x 20
Current name: American Wigeon, *Anas americana* Gmelin
Other names: usually called Wigeon
Name on plate: American Widgeon ANAS AMERICANA.
Gm,
Name on painting: American Widgeon, Anas Americana
History: Note the old spelling, Widgeon, compared to
modern day Wigeon.
Painting depicts a male, left, and a female, right,
standing on rocks with a background of water and trees in
the distance. In the plate the male was moved to the
right and the female to the left.

Plate CCCXLVI, O.P. 278, One Species, 25 5/8 x 38 1/4
Current name: Arctic Loon, *Gavia arctica* (Linnaeus)
Name on plate: Black-throated Diver COLYMBUS
ARCTICUS. L.
Name on painting: Black-throated Diver, Colymbus
arcticus
Painting and plate depict two birds in breeding plumage,
left and right, and a bird in winter plumage, center, all on
a bank and in water with marsh grasses. In the plate
mountains were added in the distance.

CCCXLVI

Plate CCCXLVII, O.P. 314, One Species, 26 3/8 x 22 1/8
Current name: Smew, *Mergellus albellus* (Linnaeus)
Name on plate: Smew or White Nun MERGUS
ALBELLUS
History: This bird is a rare visitor to our northern shores.
Audubon's claim that he shot a female on Lake Barataria
near New Orleans in 1819 is generally discounted. He
probably drew the birds from specimens in England.
Painting and plate depict a male in the air and a female
in the water with cliffs behind. In the plate the water
and cliffs are more sharply defined.

CCCXLVII

Plate CCCXLVIII, O.P. 234, One Species, 16 7/8 x 24 7/8
Current name: Gadwall, *Anas strepera* Linnaeus
Name on plate: Gadwall Duck ANAS STREPERA, L.
Painting depicts a female, left, and a male, right, with no
background. In the plate the two birds are perched atop a
rocky cliff with water far below.

CCCXLVIII

CCCXLIX

CCCL

Plate CCCXLIX, O.P. 414, One Species, 12 1/4 x 19 1/2
Current name: Black Rail, *Laterallus jamaicensis* (Gmelin)
Name on plate: two variants
   1. Least Water-hen RALLUS JAMAICENSIS. Gmel.
   2. Least Water-hen,Edwards,RALLUS JAMAICENSIS, Gmel.
Name on painting: Least Waterhen-Edwards, Rallus Jamaicensis, Gmel.
History: Titian Peale, son of Charles Wilson Peale, supplied the birds that served as models for this painting. Painting depicts an adult, left, and a young bird, right, with no background. In the plate the birds are on a bank by water with tall grass and low clouds.

Plate CCCL, O.P. 199, One Species, 12 1/4 x 19 3/8
Current name: Mountain Plover, *Charadrius montanus* Townsend
Name on plate: Rocky Mountain Plover CHARADRIUS MONTANUS, Townsend
Name on painting: Rocky Mountain Plover, Charadrius montana, Townsend
Painting depicts one adult female with no background. In the plate the bird is on a grassy spot high up in mountains with more mountains in the distance.

Plate CCCLI, O.P. 34, One Species, 38 1/4 x 25 5/8
Current name: Great Gray Owl, *Strix nebulosa* Forster
Name on plate: Great Cinereous Owl STRIX CINEREA, Gmelin.
Name on painting: Great Cinerous Owl
Painting depicts one bird on a dead branch with no other background. In the plate the branch shoots up on the right and there is a background of white clouds.

CCCLI

Plate CCCLII, O.P. 239, One Species, 30 3/8 x 21 1/4
Current name: Black-shouldered Kite, *Elanus caeruleus* (Desfontaines)
Other names: The birds in this plate were once called White-tailed Kites, *Elanus leucurus*, but they are now considered members of the *leucurus* group of the Black-shouldered Kite.
Name on plate: Black-Winged Hawk FALCO DISPAR, Temm.
　(* Black-winged Hawk, FALCO DISPAR, Temm.)
Name on painting: Black winged Hawk
Painting depicts one bird perched on a branch and another flying in pursuit of an insect. The plate is the same except that the insect was eliminated.

CCCLII

Plate CCCLIII, O.P. 73, Three Species, 19 7/8 x 14 1/2
<u>Species 1</u>
Current name: Bushtit, *Psaltriparus minimus* (Townsend)
Name on plate: Chestnut-crowned Titmouse PARUS MINIMUS, Townsend
Name on painting: Chestnut crowned Titmouse, Parus minimus, Townsend
<u>Species 2</u>
Current name: Black-capped Chickadee, *Parus atricapillus* Linnaeus
Name on plate: Black-capt Titmouse PARUS ATRICAPILLUS, Wils.
Name on painting: Black-capt Titmouse, Parus atricapillus, Wils.
<u>Species 3</u>
Current name: Chestnut-backed Chickadee, *Parus rufescens* Townsend
Name on plate: Chestnut-backed Titmouse PARUS RUFESCENS, Townsend
Name on painting: Chestnut-backed Titmouse, Parus rufescens Townsend
Painting and plate depict six birds representing three species. There are a pair of Chestnut-backed Chickadees, left, a pair of Bushtits, right, and a pair of Black-capped Chickadees, bottom. There is a Bushtit's nest, upper center, to which feathers cling. All are in branches of a willow oak.

CCCLIII

Plate CCCLIV, O.P. 370, Two Species, 12 3/8 x 19 7/8
<u>Species 1</u>
Current name: Scarlet Tanager, *Piranga olivacea* (Gmelin)
Name on plate: Scarlet Tanager TANAGRA RUBRA, L.
Name on painting: Scarlet Tanager, Tanagra rubra, L.
<u>Species 2</u>
Current name: Western Tanager, *Piranga ludoviciana* (Wilson)
Name on plate: Louisiana Tanager TANAGRA LUDOVICIANA, Wils.
Name on painting: Louisiana Tanager, Tanagra ludoviciana, Wils.
Painting and plate depict two male Western Tanagers, top, and a pair of Scarlet Tanagers, below. All the birds are in a branch of red-bay, also called sweet bay.
SEE COMPOSITE PLATES IN PART I

CCCLIV

CCCLV

Plate CCCLV, O.P. 345, One Species, 19 1/2 x 12 3/8
Current name: Seaside Sparrow, *Ammodramus maritimus* (Wilson)
Name on plate: MacGillivray's Finch FRINGILLA MACGILLIVRAII
History: Audubon named this bird MacGillivray's Finch after William MacGillivray. It is still considered a valid subspecies of the Seaside Sparrow. The painting was done by Audubon's son John, and one can see that the birds do not have the usual animation Audubon gave them.
Also in XCIII
Painting and plate depict two birds in a marsh with two butterflies above.

Plate CCCLVI, O.P. 124, One Species, 38 1/4 x 25 5/8
Current name: Northern Harrier, *Circus cyaneus* (Linnaeus)
Other names: sometimes referred to as Harrier, formerly and often still called Marsh Hawk
Name on plate: Marsh Hawk FALCO CYANEUS
Painting and plate depict a young bird, top, on a branch, an adult bird on a branch, center, and another young bird, bottom, devouring its prey. Distant mountains and more detail in the water were added to the plate.

Plate CCCLVII, O.P. 154, One Species, 25 1/2 x 21 1/4
Current name: Black-billed Magpie, *Pica pica* (Linnaeus)
Other names: formerly American Magpie, usually called Magpie
Name on plate: American Magpie CORVUS PICA
Painting and plate depict a bird, top, in flight and another, below, on a dead branch.

CCCLVI

CCCLVII

Plate CCCLVIII, O.P. 107, One Species, 20 1/2 x 14 3/4
Current name: Pine Grosbeak, *Pinicola enucleator*
(Linnaeus)
Name on plate: Pine Grosbeak PYRRHULA
ENUCLEATOR
Name on painting: Pine Grosbeak, Phrrhula enucleator
Painting and plate depict an immature bird, top, a female,
center, and a male, bottom, all in a pine tree. Note the
sores on the feet of the adult male, which Audubon
thought were caused by the resinous material exuded by
the pines.

CCCLVIII

Plate CCCLIX, O.P. 288, Three Species, 21 3/4 x 14
Species 1
Current name: Say's Phoebe, *Sayornis saya* (Bonaparte)
Name on plate: Say's Flycatcher MUSCICAPA SAYA,
Bonap.
Name on painting: Say's Flycatcher, Muscicapa Saya,
Bonap.
History: Thomas Say, author of *American Entomology*,
was a contemporary of Audubon's. Audubon shipped
insects to Say while on his travels.
Species 2
Current name: Scissor-tailed Flycatcher, *Tyrannus*
forficatus (Gmelin)
Name on plate: Swallow Tailed Flycatcher MUSCICAPA
FORFICATA, Gme.
    (* Swallow-tailed Flycatcher, MUSCICAPA
FORFICATA, Gmel.)
Name on painting: Swallow-tailed Flycatcher, Muscicapa
forficata, Gme.
Species 3
Current name: Western Kingbird, *Tyrannus verticalis* Say
Distribution: western U.S., tip of Florida
Name on plate: Arkansaw Flycatcher MUSCICAPA
VERTICALIS, Bonap.
Name on painting: Arkansaw Flycatcher, Muscicapa
verticalis, Bonap.
SEE CHART OF ORIGINAL PAINTING 288

CCCLIX

Plate CCCLX, O.P. 328, Two Species, 19 3/4 x 12 3/8
Species 1
Current name: Rock Wren, *Salpinctes obsoletus* (Say)
Name on plate: Rock Wren TROGLODYTES OBSELATA,
Say.
Species 2
Current name: Winter Wren, *Troglodytes troglodytes*
(Linnaeus)
Name on plate: Winter Wren SYLVIA TROGLODYTES,
Name on painting: Winter Wren
Painting depicts three Winter Wrens, the top bird on a
branch of a dead sapling and the two bottom birds on a
clump of moss-covered rocks. Audubon cut out a previously
painted Rock Wren and pasted it on at left center. The
bird is in a perching position but there is nothing for it to
perch on. In the plate another branch extends out from the
dead sapling affording a perch for the bird.

CCCLX

CCCLXI

CCCLXII

CCCLXIII

Plate CCCLXI, O.P. 392, One Species, 25 5/8 x 38 1/4
Current name: Blue Grouse, *Dendragapus obscurus* (Say)
Name on plate: Long-tailed or Dusky Grous TETRAO OBSCURUS
Painting and plate depict a male, left, and a female, right, with high cliffs, waterfall, distant lake, and high hills. In the plate there is more detail in the background.

Plate CCCLXII, O.P. 417, Four Species, 26 1/8 x 21 7/8
Species 1
Current name: Clark's Nutcracker, *Nucifraga columbiana* (Wilson)
Name on plate: Clark's Crow CORVUS COLUMBIANUS, Wils.
Name on painting: Clark's Crow, Corvus columbianus, Wils—
History: This species was named for William Clark, co-leader of the Lewis and Clark expedition to the West.
Species 2
Current name: Scrub Jay, *Aphelocoma coerulescens* (Bosc)
Name on plate: Ultramarine Jay CORVUS ULTRAMARINUS
Name on painting: Ultramarine Jay, Corvus ultramarinus
History: Audubon painted the Scrub Jay twice, once from an eastern specimen, Plate LXXXVII, and once from a western specimen, which he thought to be a new species and named Ultramarine Jay, in this plate. It had, however, been named previously. Both populations are now considered subspecies of *A. coerulescens*.
    Also in LXXXVII
Species 3
Current name: Steller's Jay, *Cyanocitta stelleri* (Gmelin)
Name on plate: Stellers Jay CORVUS STELLERII
    (* Steller's Jay CORVUS STELLERI)
Name on painting: Stellers Jay, Corvus Stellerii
Species 4
Current name: Yellow-billed Magpie, *Pica nuttalli* (Audubon)
Name on plate: Yellow billed Magpie CORVUS NUTALLII, Aud.
    (* Yellow-billed Magpie CORVUS NUTALLII)
Name on painting: Yellow-billed Magpie, Corvus Nutallii, Aud.
History: Audubon named the species in honor of his friend Thomas Nuttall, the Boston ornithologist. Nuttall discovered the bird and Audubon described it.
Painting and plate depict five birds representing four species, all feeding in a sweetgum tree. The Scrub Jay is at the top, the Steller's Jay is second from the top, the Yellow-billed Magpie is at the center, and a pair of Clark's Nutcrackers are at the bottom.

Plate CCCLXIII, O.P. 323, One Species, 19 3/4 x 12 1/2
Current name: Bohemian Waxwing, *Bombycilla garrulus* (Linnaeus)
Name on plate: Bohemian Chatterer BOMBYCILLA GARRULA
Painting and plate depict two birds in a mountain ash.

Plate CCCLXIV, O.P. 304, One Species, 19 5/8 x 12 3/8
Current name: White-winged Crossbill, *Loxia leucoptera* Gmelin
Name on plate: White-winged Crossbill LOXIA LEUCOPTERA Gm.
Painting and plate depict two males, bottom and right, an immature, center, and a female, top, all in what may be a green alder.

Plate CCCLXV, O.P. 119, One Species, 12 3/8 x 19 5/8
Current name: Lapland Longspur, *Calcarius lapponicus* (Linnaeus)
Name on plate: Lapland Long-spur FRINGILLA LAPONICA
　(* Lapland Longspur, FRINGILLA LAPONICA)
Name on painting: Emberiza laponica, Lapland Long Spur
Painting and plate depict a male in winter plumage, left, a young bird, center, and a male in breeding plumage. Audubon pasted onto the painting a previously done pastel of the male in winter plumage on a rocky mound. The other two birds are in watercolor with no background. In the plate there is an extensive vista of rocks in the foreground, and a lake and distant mountains.

Plate CCCLXVI, O.P. 431, One Species, 38 1/4 x 25 5/8
Current name: Gyrfalcon, *Falco rusticolus* Linnaeus
Name on plate: Iceland or Jer Falcon FALCO ISLANDICUS, Lath
History: In Audubon's day the black, white, and gray phases of this species were considered separate species. Today it is known that these are color morphs of one species, Gyrfalcon *Falco rusticolus*.
　Also in CXCVI (black phase)
Painting depicts two birds in the white phase. The upper bird is flying down and the lower bird is perched on a high lichen-covered cliff. There is water below and more rocks and cliffsides in the background. In the plate the rock in the foreground is not lichen-covered and the background is not as defined as in the painting.

CCCLXIV

CCCLXV

CCCLXVI

CCCLXVII

CCCLXVIII

CCCLXIX

Plate CCCLXVII, O.P. 144, One Species, 29 1/4 x 21 3/4
Current name: Band-tailed Pigeon, *Columba fasciata* Say.
Name on plate: Band-tailed Pigeon COLUMBA
FASCIATA, Say.
Name on painting: Band-tailed Pigeon, Columba fasciata,
Say.
Painting and plate depict a female, above, and a male,
below, on a flowering branch of western or mountain
dogwood.

Plate CCCLXVIII, O.P. 350, One Species, 16 1/4 x 21 3/8
Current name: Rock Ptarmigan, *Lagopus mutus* (Montin)
Name on plate: Rock Grous TETRAO RUPESTRIS, Leach.
    Also in CCCCXVIII
Painting and plate depict two birds in summer plumage,
left, and a bird in winter plumage, right, on a rise in a
meadow with a river and mountains beyond. The
landscape in the painting is mostly in oil.

Plate CCCLXIX, O.P. 318, Two Species, 19 3/4 x 14 1/2
Species 1
Current name: Varied Thrush, *Ixoreus naevius* (Gmelin)
Name on plate: Varied Thrush TURDUS NAEVIUS, Gm.
Name on painting: Varied Thrush, Turdus naevius, Gm.
    Also in CCCCXXXIII
Species 2
Current name: Sage Thrasher, *Oreoscoptes montanus*
(Townsend)
Name on plate: Mountain Mocking bird ORPHEUS
MONTANUS, Townsend
(* Mountain Mocking Bird ORPHEUS MONTANUS,
Towns.)
Name on painting: Mountain Mock-bird, Orpheus
montanus, Townsend
History: The Sage Thrasher was known in Audubon's day
as Mountain Mockingbird .
Painting and plate depict a Sage Thrasher at top and a
pair of Varied Thrushes, below, in a branch of mistletoe.
SEE COMPOSITE PLATES IN PART I

Plate CCCLXX, O.P. 92, One Species, 12 3/8 x 19 3/4
Current name: American Dipper, *Cinclus mexicanus*
Swainson
Other names: sometimes called Dipper and North
American Dipper
Name on plate: American Water Ouzel CINCLUS
AMERICANUS
   Also in CCCCXXXV
Painting and plate depict two birds on rocks by a stream
with a vista of hilly country. In the painting the
landscape is in oil and the birds are in pencil, watercolor,
pastel, and oil

CCCLXX

Plate CCCLXXI, O.P. 399, One Species, 25 5/8 x 38 1/4
Current name: Sage Grouse, *Centrocercus urophasianus*
(Bonaparte)
Name on plate: Cock of the Plains TETRAO
UROPHASIANUS
Painting and plate depict a female, left, and a male,
right, on grassy ground. The background in the plate is
more clearly defined.

CCCLXXI

Plate CCCLXXII, O.P. 354, One Species, 27 3/8 x 23 3/4
Current name: Swainson's Hawk, *Buteo swainsoni*
Bonaparte
Name on plate: Common Buzzard BUTEO VULGARIS
Name on painting: Common Buzzard, Buteo vulgaris
History: Audubon was not familiar with this bird and
painted it from a skin he bought from his friend Dr.
Townsend, who shot it near the Columbia River.
Painting depicts one bird diving on a hare that is
crouching on the ground. The ground is painted under the
hare but is only pencilled in on the left. There is a finely
detailed portrayal of a horned lizard on the left. In the
plate there is a background of a river with a farm on the
far bank. The lizard is not in this plate but does appear in
Plate CCCLXXXVI, which depicts a Great Egret.

CCCLXXII

CCCLXXIII

CCCLXXIV

CCCLXXV

Plate CCCLXXIII, O.P. 220, Two Species, 19 1/2 x 12 3/8
Species 1
Current name: Black-headed Grosbeak, *Pheucticus melanocephalus* (Swainson)
Name on plate: Spotted Grosbeak FRINGILLA MACULATA
Name on painting: Spotted Grosbeak, Fringilla maculata
Species 2
Current name: Evening Grosbeak, *Coccothraustes vespertinus* (Cooper)
Name on plate: Evening Grosbeak FRINGILLA VESPERTINA, Cooper
Name on painting: Evening Grosbeak, Fringilla vespertina, Cooper
  Also in CCCCXXIV
Painting depicts an Evening Grosbeak, top, and three Black-headed Grosbeaks, below: two males at the center and a female at the left. All are perched on bare, thin branches. In the plate the birds are arranged slightly differently. The Evening Grosbeak is still at the top. One of the male Black-headed Grosbeaks is at the center and the other male and the female are at the bottom peering up at a butterfly. Note that in addition to writing "Evening Grosbeak" and "Spotted Grosbeak" on the painting, Audubon also wrote "Pine Grosbeak." He may have originally intended to include the Pine Grosbeak but he evidently changed his mind for in darker ink was added the note "Plate 358," referring to Plate CCCLVIII, which does depict the Pine Grosbeak.
SEE COMPOSITE PLATES IN PART I

Plate CCCLXXIV, O.P. 277, One Species, 19 1/2 x 14 3/4
Current name: Sharp-shinned Hawk, *Accipter striatus* Vieillot
Name on plate: Sharp-shinned Hawk FALCO VELOX, Wilson
Name on painting: Slate-coloured Hawk, Falco velox
History: If Audubon wished to use a painting of a bird that he had already finished in *Birds of America*, his usual custom was to cut it out, paste it onto the paper, and then complete the painting. In this case he painted copies of two earlier drawings. At first he thought the male at top was a different species than the female Sharp-shinned Hawk below and he named it Slate-coloured Hawk, but later he realized both were Sharp-shinned Hawks. Painting and plate depict a male, top, about to feed on a mouse and a female, below, both perched on a dead tree.

Plate CCCLXXV, O.P. 360, One Species, 19 1/2 x 12 3/8
Current name: Common Redpoll, *Carduelis flammea* (Linnaeus)
Other names: usually referred to as Redpoll
Name on plate: Lesser Red-Poll FRINGILLA LINARIA, L.
  (* Lesser Red-poll, FRINGILLA LINARIA, Linn.)
Painting and plate depict a male, above, and a female, below, on a branch of snowberry.

Plate CCCLXXVI, O.P. 334, One Species, 25 5/8 x 38 1/4
Current name: Trumpeter Swan, *Cygnus buccinator*
Richardson
Name on plate: Trumpeter Swan CYGNUS
BUCCINATOR
   Also in CCCCVI
Painting and plate depict one bird amid grass and
washed-up seaweed.

CCCLXXVI

Plate CCCLXXVII, O.P. 149, One Species, 21 x 33 1/4
Current name: Limpkin, *Aramus guarauna* (Linnaeus)
Name on plate: Scolopaceus Courlan ARAMUS
SCOLOPACEUS, Viell
Painting depicts one bird with a very lightly pencilled
indication of a background. In the plate the background
was developed to show the bird on the grassy top of a cliff
overlooking a river, with trees and shoreline in the
distance.

Plate CCCLXXVIII, O.P. 253, One Species, 26 1/8 x 21 5/8
Current name: Northern Hawk-Owl, *Surnia ulula*
(Linnaeus)
Other names: known as Hawk Owl
Name on plate: Hawk Owl STRIX FUNEREA
Painting depicts two birds with no background. In the
plate the birds are perched on a dead tree trunk.

CCCLXXVII

CCCLXXVIII

Plate CCCLXXIX, O.P. 37, One Species, 19 5/8 x 12 3/8
Current name: Rufous Hummingbird, *Selasphorus rufus* (Gmelin)
Name on plate: Ruff-necked Humming-bird TROCHILUS RUFUS, Latham
Name on painting: Ruff-necked Hummingbird, Trochilus rufus
Painting and plate depict two males, above, and a female, below, perched on her nest, all in a Spider-flower. Note that Havell obeyed Audubon's instructions to put the nest in the plate nearer to the lower leaves than it is in the painting.

Plate CCCLXXX, O.P. 126, One Species, 20 3/4 x 15 3/4
Current name: Boreal Owl, *Aegolius funereus* (Linnaeus)
Name on plate: Tengmalm's Owl STRIX TENGMALMI
Painting and plate alike and depict two birds, each perched on its own small branch with no further background.

Plate CCCLXXXI, O.P. 265, One Species, 25 5/8 x 38 1/4
Current name: Snow Goose, *Chen caerulescens* (Linnaeus)
Other names: At one time it was considered that there were two species: Blue Goose, *Chen caerulescens*, and Snow Goose, *Chen hyperborea*. Now these two are considered color morphs of one species, Snow Goose, *Chen caerulescens*.
Name on plate: Snow Goose ANSER HYPERBOREUS, Pallas
History: Audubon thought that the Blue Goose was the immature of the Snow Goose.
Painting and plate depict one bird in the white phase, left, and one bird in the blue phase, right, both on a beach with sea and sky behind.

CCCLXXIX

CCCLXXX

CCCLXXXI

Plate CCCLXXXII, O.P. 393, One Species, 21 5/8 x 29 1/4
Current name: Sharp-tailed Grouse, *Tympanuchus phasianellus* (Linnaeus)
Name on plate: Sharp-tailed Grous TETRAO PHASIANELLUS
Painting depicts two birds on a grassy ground, with a berried plant at left and a vague background. In the plate the background is developed to show a winding stream emptying into a stretch of water, with mountains in the distance.

CCCLXXXII

Plate CCCLXXXIII, O.P. 390, One Species, 19 3/4 x 12 1/2
Current name: Long-eared Owl, *Asio otus* (Linnaeus)
Name on plate: Long-eared Owl STRIX OTUS
Painting and plate depict one bird on a dead branch.

Plate CCCLXXXIV, O.P. 411, One Species, 19 5/8 x 12 3/8
Current name: Dickcissel, *Spiza americana* (Gmelin)
Name on plate: Black-throated Bunting FRINGILLA AMERICANA
Name on painting: Black [word faded—"throat" or "throated"] Bunting Emberiza americana
Painting depicts a male, right, perched on a spray of butter-and-eggs and a female on a reed. In the plate there are more reeds below.

CCCLXXXIII

CCCLXXXIV

CCCLXXXV

CCCLXXXVI

CCCLXXXVII

Plate CCCLXXXV, O.P. 204, Two Species, 19 1/8 x 15 7/8
<u>Species 1</u>
Current name: Bank Swallow, *Riparia riparia* (Linnaeus)
Name on plate: two variants
  1. Bank Swallow HIRUNDO RIPARIA
  2. Bank Swallow HIRUNDO VIPARIA
<u>Species 2</u>
Current name: Violet-green Swallow, *Tachycineta thalassina* (Swainson)
Name on plate: Violet-Green Swallow HIRUNDO THALASSINUS, Swain.
  (* Violet-green Swallow, HIRUNDO MALASSINUS, Swain.)
Painting depicts two Violet-green Swallows, top, and four Bank Swallows, below, with no background. In the plate the two Violet-greens are flying high while of the four Banks one is flying, one is clinging to a nest hole, and two young are peering from a nest hole. The background is a high cliff with sky behind.

Plate CCCLXXXVI, O.P. 389, One Species, 25 5/8 x 38 1/4
Current name: Great Egret, *Casmerodius albus* (Linnaeus)
Other names: formerly American Egret, formerly Common Egret
Name on plate: White Heron ARDEA ALBA, Linn.
Name on painting: Great White Heron, Ardea alba
History: Audubon made a preliminary painting for this plate that is in the New-York Historical Society. The final painting that was used is quite different and it is hard to understand why the first one was not used as it surely is one of Audubon's most beautiful works. Perhaps its black background caused a problem. Audubon wrote "Great White Heron" on the painting but caught his error in time to have "White Heron" in the legend. The Great White Heron is in Plate CCLXXXI.
Painting depicts one male bird on a beach with grasses. In the plate there is a horned lizard ahead of the bird's beak. This is the lizard from O.P. 354, which depicts a Swainson's Hawk, that was left out of Plate CCCLXXII; as a desert animal, it is out of place in this wet habitat.

Plate CCCLXXXVII, O.P. 108, One Species, 21 7/8 x 26 1/8
Current name: Glossy Ibis, *Plegadis falcinellus* (Linnaeus)
Name on plate: Glossy Ibis IBIS FALCINELLUS
Name on painting: Glossy Ibis, Ibis falcinellus
Painting depicts one male bird with no background. In the plate the bird is on a bank by a river with a farmhouse, outbuilding, and fence on the opposite shore.

Plate CCCLXXXVIII, O.P. 266, Three Species, 19 3/4 x 12 3/8
Species 1
Current name: Northern Oriole, *Icterus galbula* (Linnaeus)
Other names: At one time the Baltimore Oriole, *I. Galbula*, and the Bullock's Oriole, *I. bullockii*, were considered separate species. These are now merged.
Name on plate: Bullock's Oriole ICTERUS BULLOCKII
Name on painting: Icterus bullockii, Swainson
   Also in XII (Baltimore group) and CCCCXXXIII (Baltimore & Bullock's groups)
Species 2
Current name: Tricolored Blackbird, *Agelaius tricolor* (Audubon)
Name on plate: Nuttall's Starling ICTERUS TRICOLOR, Aud.
History: Audubon named this bird for his friend Thomas Nuttall, a Boston ornithologist. Nuttall and John Kirk Townsend went on a collecting expedition to the Rockies and the Columbia River and Audubon purchased skins from them from which he painted most of the birds from that region that appear in *Birds of America.*
Species 3
Current name: Yellow-headed Blackbird, *Xanthocephalus xanthocephalus* (Bonaparte)
Name on plate: Yellow-headed Troopial ICTERUS XANTHOCEPHALUS, Bonap.
Name on painting: Yellow-headed Troupial, Icterus icterocephalus, Bonap.
SEE CHART OF ORIGINAL PAINTING 266 IN PART III
SEE COMPOSITE PLATES IN PART I

CCCLXXXVIII

Plate CCCLXXXIX, O.P. 402, One Species, 19 3/4 x 12 1/4
Current name: Red-cockaded Woodpecker, *Picoides borealis* (Vieillot)
Name on plate: Red-Cockaded Woodpecker PICUS QUERULUS, Wils.
   (* Red-cockaded Woodpecker, PICUS QUERULUS, Wils.)
Name on painting: Red Cockaded Woodpecker, Picus Querellus
Painting and plate depict a female bird, top, and two male birds, center and bottom, all on a tree trunk. For the painting Audubon first painted the center male on the tree trunk. He then cut out two separately painted birds, a female and another male, and pasted them on.

CCCLXXXIX

Plate CCCXC, O.P. 293 and 359, Three Species, 19 5/8 x 12 1/4
Species 1 (in O.P. 293)
Current name: Lark Bunting, *Calamospiza melanocorys* Stejneger
Name on plate: Prairie Finch FRINGILLA BICOLOR, Townsend
Name on painting: Prairie Finch . Fringilla bicolor, Townsend
Species 2 (in O.P. 359)
Current name: Lark Sparrow, *Chondestes grammacus* (Say)
Name on plate: Lark Finch FRINGILLA GRAMMACA, Say.

CCCXC

Name on painting: Lark Finch, Fringilla grammaca, Say.
<u>Species 3</u> **(in O.P. 293)**
Current name: Song Sparrow, *Melospiza melodia* (Wilson)
Name on plate: Brown Song Sparrow FRINGILLA
CINEREA, Gmel.
Name on painting: Brown Song Sparrow, Fringilla cinerea,
Gmel.
History: The bird depicted here is an individual of a west
coast subspecies.
   Also in XXV
SEE CHARTS OF ORIGINAL PAINTINGS 293 AND 359

CCCXCI

Plate CCCXCI, O.P. 312, One Species, 25 5/8 x 38 1/4
Current name: Brant, *Branta bernicla* (Linnaeus)
Name on plate: Brant Goose ANSER BERNICLA
Painting and plate depict two birds standing on low rocks
with water front and back and low hills in the distance.
The habitat, done in oil in the painting, is clearer and
crisper in the plate.

Plate CCCXCII, O.P. 102, One Species, 21 7/8 x 26
Current name: Harris' Hawk, *Parabuteo unicinctus*
(Temminck)
Name on plate: Louisiana Hawk BUTEO HARRISI, Aud.
History: Audubon named this bird *Buteo harrisi* in honor of
his devoted friend Edward Harris, a gentleman farmer
and naturalist whom Audubon met in New York. Harris
bought paintings from Audubon when Audubon was
penniless and discouraged, and also accompanied him on

CCCXCII

two expeditions. This bird had been previously named by
Temminck, but Audubon's appellation survives in the
English name.
Painting and plate depict one bird perched on a branch
with no other background.

Plate CCCXCIII, O.P. 186, Three Species, 19 1/2 x 12 3/8
<u>Species 1</u>
Current name: Mountain Bluebird, *Sialia currucoides*
(Bechstein)
Name on plate: Arctic Blue-bird SIALIA ARCTICA,
Swain.
   (* Arctic Blue Bird, SIALIA ARCTICA, Swain.)
Name on painting: Arctic blue bird, Sylvia arctica
<u>Species 2</u>
Current name: Townsend's Warbler, *Dendroica townsendi*
(Townsend)
Name on plate: Townsend's Warbler SYLVIA
TOWNSENDI, Nuttall
Name on painting: Townsend's W^{r} Sylvia Townsendii,
Aud.

CCCXCIII

<u>Species 3</u>
Current name: Western Bluebird, *Sialia mexicana*
Swainson
Name on plate: Western Blue-bird SIALIA
OCCIDENTALIS, Townsend
   (* Western Blue Bird, SIALIA OCCIDENTALIS,
Towns.)
Name on painting: Western blue Bird, Sialia occidentalis,
Townsend

Painting depicts eleven birds representing six species. Havell put five birds in this plate and six birds in Plate CCCXCV.

SEE CHART OF ORIGINAL PAINTING 186 IN PART III

CCCXCIV

Plate CCCXCIV, O.P. 280 and 359, Four Species, 19 5/8 x 12 1/4

Species 1 **(in O.P. 359)**
Current name: Chestnut-collared Longspur, *Calcarius ornatus* (Townsend)
Name on plate: Chestnut-coloured Finch PLECTROPHANES ORNATA, Towns.
Name on painting: Chestnut collared Finch, Fringilla ornata Townsend.
Species 2 **(in O.P. 359)**
Current name: Golden-crowned Sparrow, *Zonotrichia atricapilla* (Gmelin)
Name on plate: Black crown Bunting, Lath EMBERIZA ATRICAPILLA, Gmel.
   (* Black Crown Bunting, Lath., EMBERIZA ATRICAPILLA, Gmel.)
Name on painting: Black and Yellow crowned Finch, [smudge] atricapilla, Gmel.
Species 3 **(in O.P. 280)**
Current name: Hooded Siskin, *Carduelis magellanica* (Vieillot)
Name on plate: Black-headed Siskin FRINGILLA MAGELLANICA Vieill.
   (* Black Crown Bunting,Lath., EMBERIZA ATRICAPILLA, Gmel.)
Name on painting: Black-headed Siskin, Fringilla magellanica
History: Audubon collected this bird in Henderson, Kentucky. It is usually regarded as an escape from captivity. This species is native to South America.
Species 4 **(in O.P. 359)**
Current name: Rufous-sided Towhee, *Pipilo erythrophthalmus* (Linnaeus)
Name on plate: Arctic Ground Finch PIPILO ARCTICA, Swains.
Name on painting: Arctic ground Finch, Fringilla arctica
History: The birds depicted here are of the western *maculatus* group, once known as the Spotted Towhee and considered a separate species.
   Also in XXIX
SEE CHARTS OF ORIGINAL PAINTINGS 280 AND 359

CCCXCV

CCCXCVI

CCCXCVII

Plate CCCXCV, O.P. 186, Three Species, 19 5/8 x 12 1/4
<u>Species 1</u>
Current name: Black-throated Gray Warbler, *Dendroica nigrescens* (Townsend)
Name on plate: Black-throated gray Warbler SYLVIA NIGRESCENS, Townsend.
   (* Black-throated Gray Warbler, SYLVIA NIGRESCENS, Towns.)
Name on painting: Black throated Gray W^r, S. nigrescens, Townsend
<u>Species 2</u>
Current name: Hermit Warbler, *Dendroica occidentalis* (Townsend)
Name on plate: Hermit Warbler SYLVIA OCCIDENTALIS, Townsend
Name on painting: Hermit W^r, Sylvia occidentalis, Townsend
<u>Species 3</u>
Current name: Yellow-rumped Warbler, *Dendroica coronata* (Linnaeus)
Other names: The Myrtle Warbler and Audubon's Warbler, until recently considered two species, are now combined as Yellow-rumped Warbler.
Name on plate: Audubon's Warbler SYLVIA AUDUBONI, Townsend
Name on painting: Audubon's W^r, Sylvia audubonii, Nuttall
   Also in CLIII (Myrtle group)
Painting depicts eleven birds representing six species. Six of the birds appear in this plate and five in Plate CCCXCIII.
SEE CHART OF ORIGINAL PAINTING 186 IN PART III

Plate CCCXCVI, O.P. 222, One Species, 25 5/8 x 38 1/4
Current name: Glaucous Gull, *Larus hyperboreus* Gunnerus
Name on plate: Burgomaster Gull LARUS GLAUCUS, Brunnich
Painting and plate depict an adult bird, left, and a young bird, right, standing on a rocky outcrop with sky behind. In the plate there is water far below the rocks on the left with a rocky coast beyond.

Plate CCCXCVII, O.P. 179, One Species, 21 5/8 x 29 3/8
Current name: Scarlet Ibis, *Eudocimus ruber* (Linnaeus)
Name on plate: Scarlet Ibis IBIS RUBRA, Viell.
History: The Scarlet Ibis is a rare vagrant to the United States and is considered accidental in Texas, Florida, and Alabama. Audubon said he had only seen three in the whole country. It has been suggested that what he saw were Roseate Spoonbills, but this seems ridiculous since Audubon knew well what a Roseate Spoonbill looked like. See Roseate Spoonbill, Plate CCCXXI, O.P. 35.
Painting depicts an adult, left, and a young bird, right, with no background. In the plate they are on a bank with water and islands beyond.

Plate CCCXCVIII, O.P. 359 and 424, Three Species, 19 1/2 x 12 1/4
Species 1 (in O.P. 424)
Current name: Clay-colored Sparrow, *Spizella pallida* (Swainson)
Name on plate: Clay-coloured Finch EMBERIZA PALLIDA, Swains
Name on painting: Clay-coloured Bunting, Emberiza pallida, Swainson & Richardson
History: William Swainson was a British zoologist who at first heaped praise on Audubon, but they later disagreed.
Species 2 (in O.P. 424)
Current name: Dark-eyed Junco, *Junco hyemalis* (Linnaeus)
Other names: The Oregon Junco, *J. oreganus*, and the Slate-colored Junco, *J. hyemalis*, are now one species.
Name on plate: Oregon Snow Finch FRINGILLA OREGONA, Towns.
Name on painting: Oregon Snow Bird, Fringilla oregona, Townsend
    Also in XIII (Slate-colored group)
Species 3 (in O.P. 359)
Current name: Lazuli Bunting, *Passerina amoena* (Say)
Name on plate: Lazuli Finch FRINGILLA AMOENA
Name on painting: Lazuli Finch, Fringilla amoena, Say.—
    Also in CCCCXXIV
SEE CHARTS OF ORIGINAL PAINTINGS 359 AND 424 IN PART III TO SORT OUT THIS EXTREMELY COMPLICATED SHIFTING AROUND OF BIRDS SEE COMPOSITE PLATES IN PART I

CCCXCVIII

Plate CCCXCIX, O.P. 327, Three Species, 19 1/2 x 12 1/4
Species 1
Current name: Blackburnian Warbler, *Dendroica fusca* (Müller)
Name on plate: Blackburnian w. SYLVIA BLACKBURNIAE
Name on painting: Blackburnian W^{r}, Sylvia blackburnia
    Also in CXXXIV and CXXXV
Species 2
Current name: Black-throated Green Warbler, *Dendroica virens* (Gmelin)
Name on plate: Black-throated green Warbler SYLVIA VIRENS
    (* Black-throated Green Warbler, SYLVIA VIRENS)
Name on painting: Black-throated Green Warbler, Sylvia virens, Lath.
Species 3
Current name: MacGillivray's Warbler, *Oporornis tolmiei* (Townsend)
Name on plate: Mourning Warbler SYLVIA PHILADELPHIA
Name on painting: Mourning Warbler, Sylvia philadelphia, Wils.
History: It was not until after this plate was published bearing the name Mourning Warbler that Audubon decided this bird was a different species. He named it *Trichas macgillivrayi*, after William MacGillivray, but it had in the meantime already been named by Townsend. MacGillivray assisted Audubon in the writing of the *Ornithological Biography*. Today MacGillivray's name

CCCXCIX

CCCC

CCCCI

is perpetuated in the English name of this species. The Mourning Warbler is not depicted in *Birds of America*. Painting depicts nine birds representing five species. Havell put five of the birds in this plate and four in Plate CCCCXIV.
SEE CHART OF ORIGINAL PAINTNG 327

Plate CCCC, O.P. 280, Five Species, 20 x 12 1/2
Species 1
Current name: Lesser Goldfinch, *Carduelis psaltria* (Say)
Name on plate: Arkansaw Siskin FRINGILLA SPALTRIA
Name on painting: Arkansaw Siskin, Fringilla Psaltria, Say
  Also in CCCCXXXIII
Species 2
Current name: Hoary Redpoll, *Carduelis hornemanni* Holböll
Name on plate: Mealy Red-poll LINOTA BOREALIS
Name on painting: Linola flavirostris ?
Species 3
Current name: Smith's Longspur, *Calcarius pictus* (Swainson)
Name on plate: Buff-breasted Finch, EMBERIZA PICTA
Species 4
Current name: Townsend's Bunting, *Emberiza townsendi* Audubon
Name on plate: Townsend's Finch EMBERIZA TOWNSENDI
Name on painting: Townsend's Finch, Fringilla Townsendi, Aud
History: John Kirk Townsend, Audubon's friend and member of the Wyeth expedition, shot this bird in Pennsylvania. Audubon painted it, described it, and named it for Townsend. The skin is in the Smithsonian Institution with Audubon's name on its ticket. It is the only known specimen of its kind and ornithologists suspect it may be a mutation of a Dickcissel or a hybrid Dickcissel x Blue Grosbeak.
Species 5
Current name: Western Tanager, *Piranga ludoviciana* (Wilson)
Name on plate: Louisiana Tanager TANAGRA LUDOVICIANA
  Also in CCCLIV
Painting depicts six birds representing six species. Five appear in this plate and the sixth in Plate CCCXCIV.
SEE CHART OF ORIGINAL PAINTINGS 280 AND 359

Plate CCCCI, O.P. 274, One Species, 25 5/8 x 38 1/4
Current name: Red-breasted Merganser, *Mergus serrator* Linnaeus
Name on plate: Red-breasted Merganser MERGUS SERRATOR, L.
Painting depicts a female flying, left, and a male in the water, right, with a little blue water brushed in under the female. In the plate a background of water, marsh grasses, and flowering pitcher plants was developed.

Plate CCCCII, O.P. 112, Four Species, 18 5/8 x 28
Species 1
Current name: Ancient Murrelet, *Synthliboramphus antiquus* (Gmelin)
Name on plate: Black-throated Guillemot MERGULUS ANTIQUUS, Bonap.
Name on painting: Mergulus antiquus, Bonap. Black-throated Guillemot
Species 2
Current name: Crested Auklet, *Aethia cristatella* (Pallas)
Name on plate: Curled-Crested Auk PHALERIS SUPERCILIATA, Bonap.
    (* Curled-crested Auk PHALERIS SUPERCILIATA)
Name on painting: Phaleris superciliata, Bonap., Curled-crested Auk
Species 3
Current name: Least Auklet, *Aethia pusilla* (Pallas)
Name on plate: Nobbed-billed Auk PHALERIS NODIROSTRIS, Bonap.
Name on painting: Phaleris nodirostris, Bonap., Knobbed-billed Auk
Species 4
Current name: Rhinoceros Auklet, *Cerorhinca monocerata* (Pallas)
Name on plate: Horned-billed Guillemot CERATORRHINA OCCIDENTALIS, Bonap.
Name on painting: Ceratorrhina Occidentalis, Bonap., Horned-billed Guillemot
Painting depicts five birds representing four species with no background. From left to right they are Crested Auklet, Ancient Murrelet with young, Least Auklet a little below, and Rhinoceros Auklet. In the plate there is a background of water, ice floes, and mountains. The birds are rearranged and from left to right are Ancient Murrelet and young on floe, Least Auklet swimming, Crested Auklet reversed and swimming, and Rhinoceros Auklet.

CCCCII

CCCCIII

Plate CCCCIII, O.P. 109, One Species, 12 1/4 x 19 1/2
Current name: Barrow's Goldeneye, *Bucephala islandica* (Gmelin)
Name on plate: Golden-eye Duck CLANGULA VULGARIS
Name on painting: Golden-eye Duck, Clangula (smudge)
History: Some maintain that when Audubon painted Barrow's Goldeneye he did not realize it was a different species from the Common Goldeneye, but note that the scientific names on the plate legends are different. Also note that Audubon has correctly placed the cheek patches on each species.
For purposes of comparison:
    Plate CCCXLII:
Current name: Common Goldeneye, *B. clangula*
Plate name: Golden-Eye Duck FULIGULA CLANGULA
    Plate CCCCIII:
Current name: Barrow's Goldeneye, *B. islandica*
Plate name: Golden-eye Duck CLANGULA VULGARIS
Painting depicts one male in a swimming position but with no background. In the plate the bird is swimming on a moderately rough sea.

CCCCIV

Plate CCCCIV, O.P. 235, One Species, 12 3/8 x 19 5/8
Current name: Eared Grebe, *Podiceps nigricollis* Brehm
Name on plate: Eared Grebe PODICEPS AURITUS
History: Audubon made this painting from skins loaned to him by Lord Stanley, later Lord Derby.
Painting depicts a bird in summer plumage, left, and a bird in winter plumage, right, standing on a mound by a quiet backwater. In the plate grassy mounds and mountains in the distance were added.

CCCCV

Plate CCCCV, O.P. 413, One Species, 12 3/8 x 19 1/2
Current name: Semipalmated Sandpiper, *Calidris pusilla* (Linnaeus)
Name on plate: Semipalmated Sandpiper TRINGA SEMIPALMATA, Wils.
Painting depicts two birds with no background. In the plate the birds are on a bank with shells strewn about and sea beyond with two rocky islets.

CCCCVI

Plate CCCCVI, O.P. 7, One Species, 25 5/8 x 38 1/4
Current name: Trumpeter Swan, *Cygnus buccinator* Richardson
Name on plate: Trumpeter Swan CYGNUS BUCCINATOR. Richardson
Also in CCCLXXVI
Painting depicts one bird floating on calm water. In the plate the bird is reaching for a floating insect and there are ripples in the water caused by the movements of the Swan.

Plate CCCCVII, O.P. 168, One Species, 21 5/8 x 28 3/8
Current name: Light-mantled Albatross, *Phoebetria palpebrata* (Forster)
Other names: Sooty Albatross
Name on plate: Dusky Albatros DIOMEDEA FUSCA
Name on painting: Brown Albatros, Diomedea fusca
History: Audubon was erroneously told that the skin from which he painted this bird had been collected in Oregon. The bird lives on subantarctic islands.
Painting depicts one bird with no background. In the plate the bird is standing on a rocky shore looking over the sea. The perspective of the sea in relation to the shore is out of balance.

CCCCVII

Plate CCCCVIII, O.P. 261, One Species, 16 5/8 x 21 7/8
Current name: Black Scoter, *Melanitta nigra* (Linnaeus)
Other names: Common Scoter
Name on plate: American Scoter Duck FULIGULA AMERICANA
Painting depicts two birds in a swimming position but with no background. In the plate the birds are swimming in the sea.

CCCCVIII

Plate CCCCIX, O.P. 309, Two Species, 15 1/4 x 24 3/4
<u>Species 1</u>
Current name: Forster's Tern, *Sterna forsteri* Nuttall
Name on plate: Havell's Tern STERNA HAVELLI, Aud.
Name on painting: Black billed Tern, Sterna Ludovicianus
History: Audubon did not recognize this bird as a Forster's Tern in winter plumage and thought he had a new species. He named it in honor of his engraver Robert Havell. It is sad that Audubon did not name a truly new species for Havell and thus perpetuate the name of the man whose genius contributed so much to *Birds of America*.
<u>Species 2</u>
Current name: Trudeau's Tern, *Sterna trudeaui* Audubon
Name on plate: Trudeau's Tern STERNA TRUDEAUI, Aud.
Name on painting: Sterna Trudeaui
History: Audubon said he received this bird from his friend Dr. James Trudeau. Dr. Trudeau told Audubon that he shot the bird in New Jersey, that others were with it, and that he had heard more had been sighted on Long Island, New York. The A.O.U. says the Trudeau's Tern (also called Snow-crowned Tern) breeds in Chile and Argentina. The specimen from which Audubon described this species still exists; the question is whether the locality is correct.
Painting depicts a Trudeau's Tern, left, and a Forster's Tern in winter plumage, right. Audubon painted the Trudeau's Tern with only the sketchiest indication of background. He then pasted on at right a previously painted picture of a Forster's Tern on a rocky ground. In the plate the Trudeau's Tern is below and the Forster's Tern above reversed, both standing on a shell-strewn cliff looking over an inland sea with ships in the distance. Note that the plate legends are not under the birds they identify but are reversed.

CCCCIX

Plate CCCCX, O.P. 210, One Species, 19 3/8 x 15 7/8
Current name: Gull-billed Tern, *Sterna nilotica* Gmelin
Name on plate: Marsh Tern STERNA ANGLICA, Montagu
Name on painting: Marsh Tern Sterna anglica
Painting depicts one bird in spring plumage diving in
pursuit of an insect that is not painted but just faintly
indicated in pencil. In the plate the insect is fully
developed.

Plate CCCCXI, O.P. 258, One Species, 25 5/8 x 38 1/4
Current name: Tundra Swan, *Cygnus columbianus* (Ord)
Other names: Until recently the North American bird was
known as the Whistling Swan and the Old World bird as
Bewick's Swan. The A.O.U. now considers them to be
conspecific and uses the English name of Tundra Swan.
Name on plate: Common American Swan CYGNUS
AMERICANUS, Sharpless
Painting depicts one bird swimming with a background of
woods. In the plate there is a brighter light, the bird is
more submerged in the water, and there are yellow water
lilies in the foreground.

CCCCX

CCCCXI

Plate CCCCXII, O.P. 262, Two Species, 23 3/4 x 27 1/2
Species 1
Current name: Brandt's Cormorant, *Phalacrocorax
penicillatus* (Brandt)
Name on plate: Townsend's Cormorant
PHALACROCORAX TOWNSENDI, Aud.
History: Audubon painted this bird from a specimen
collected by his friend John Kirk Townsend on the
Columbia River. Audubon, not realizing the bird had
already been described by Brandt, named it for Townsend.
Species 2
Current name: Pelagic Cormorant, *Phalacrocorax pelagicus*
Pallas
Name on plate: Violet-green Cormorant
PHALACROCORAX RESPLENDENS, Aud.
History: Audubon painted this bird from a specimen
collected by his friend John Kirk Townsend on the
Columbia River. Audubon, not realizing the bird had
already been described by Pallas, named it Violet-green
Cormorant.
Painting depicts an adult Pelagic Cormorant, left, and a
young Brandt's Cormorant, right, with no background. In
the plate the birds are on a rocky bluff looking over the
sea far below.

CCCCXII

Plate CCCCXIII, O.P. 142, One Species, 12 1/4 x 19 1/2
Current name: California Quail, *Callipepla californica* (Shaw)
Name on plate: Californian Partridge PERDIX CALIFORNICA, Lath.
History: Although quail and partridge are quite different, quail were, and still are, sometimes referred to as partridge.
Painting depicts a male, right, and a female, left, with no background. In the plate they are standing high up in a clearing on a hill with a vista of rolling countryside, a river, and distant low mountains.

CCCCXIII

Plate CCCCXIV, O.P. 327, Two Species, 19 1/2 x 12 1/4
<u>Species 1</u>
Current name: Cape May Warbler, *Dendroica tigrina* (Gmelin)
Name on plate: Cape May Warbler SYLVIA MARITIMA, Wils.
Name on painting: Cape May Warbler, Sylvia maritima, Wils.
<u>Species 2</u>
Current name: Golden-winged Warbler, *Vermivora chrysoptera* (Linnaeus)
Name on plate: Golden-winged Warbler SYLVIA CHRYSOPTERA, Lath.
Name on painting: Golden-winged Warbler, Sylvia chrysoptera, Lath.
Painting depicts nine birds representing five species. Havell put four of these birds into this plate and the other five into Plate CCCXCIX.
SEE CHART OF ORIGINAL PAINTING 327 IN PART III

CCCCXIV

Plate CCCCXV, O.P. 123, Two Species, 19 1/2 x 12 1/2
<u>Species 1</u>
Current name: Brown Creeper, *Certhia americana* Bonaparte
Other names: This bird had usually been considered conspecific with the European form *C. familiaris*. The A.O.U. now considers them separate species.
Name on plate: Brown Creeper CERTHIA FAMILIARIS, Lin.
Name on painting: Brown Creeper, Certhia familiaris
<u>Species 2</u>
Current name: Pygmy Nuthatch, *Sitta pygmaea* Vigors
Name on plate: Californian Nuthatch SITTA PYGMEA, Vig.
Name on painting: Sitta pygmea, Vigors
For the painting Audubon painted two Pygmy Nuthatches on a tree trunk. Then he cut out two previously painted Brown Creepers and pasted them on. The top of the tree trunk was not completed, just pencilled in. In the plate the tree trunk is completed and the Brown Creeper at top is reversed.

CCCCXV

CCCCXVI

CCCCXVII

Plate CCCCXVI, O.P. 333, Five Species, 38 1/4 x 25 5/8
<u>Species 1</u>
Current name: Hairy Woodpecker, *Picoides villosus* (Linnaeus)
Name on plate: Hairy Woodpecker PICUS VILLOSUS. Linn.
Name on painting: Hairy Woodpecker, Picus villosus L.
    Also in CCCCXVII
<u>Species 2</u>
Current name: Lewis' Woodpecker, *Melanerpes lewis* (Gray)
Name on plate: Lewis' Woodpecker PICUS TORQUATUS, Wils.
Name on painting: Lewis Woodpecker Picus Torquatus, Wils.
<u>Species 3</u>
Current name: Northern Flicker, *Colaptes auratus* (Linnaeus)
Other names: also known as Common Flicker. The three northern groups of this species, Yellow-shafted, Red-shafted, and Gilded, were once thought separate species but are now considered one, Northern Flicker.
Name on plate: Red-shafted Woodpecker PICUS MEXICANUS, Aud.
Name on painting: Red Shafted Woodpecker, Picus mexicanus Swain.
    Also in XXXVII (Yellow-shafted group)
<u>Species 4</u>
Current name: Red-bellied Woodpecker, *Melanerpes carolinus* (Linnaeus)
Name on plate: Red-bellied Woodpecker PICUS CAROLINUS, Linn.
Name on painting: Red bellied Woodpecker, Picus carolinus L.
<u>Species 5</u>
Current name: Red-breasted Sapsucker, *Sphyrapicus ruber* (Gmelin)
Other names: sometimes considered a subspecies of the Yellow-bellied Sapsucker, *S. varius*.
Name on plate: Red-breasted Woodpecker PICUS RUBER, Lath.
Name on painting: Red breasted Woodpecker, Picus flaviventris, Viell.
Audubon also wrote "Red-cockaded Woodpecker, Picus guerulus" on his painting but did not paint this species here. It is in Plate CCCLXXXIX.
SEE CHART OF ORIGINAL PAINTING 333 IN PART III

Plate CCCCXVII, O.P. 97, Two Species, 30 1/2 x 22 1/2
<u>Species 1</u>
Current name: Three-toed Woodpecker, *Picoides tridactylus* (Linnaeus)
Other names: Northern Three-toed Woodpecker
Name on plate: Three-toed Woodpecker PICUS HIRSUTIS, Vieil.
History: Do not confuse this species with the bird in Plate CXXXII, which is called Black-backed Woodpecker, *Picoides arcticus* (sometimes called Black-backed Three-toed Woodpecker).

Species 2

Current name: Hairy Woodpecker, *Picoides villosus* (Linnaeus)

Name on plate: Of the ten birds in this plate, two are Three-toed Woodpeckers. Audubon thought the remaining eight represented five species:
Maria's Woodpecker PICUS MARTINI, Aud.
Phillips' Woodpecker PICUS PHILLIPSI, Aud.
Canadian Woodpecker PICUS CANADENSIS, Buff.
Harris's Woodpecker PICUS HARRISI, Aud.
Audubon's Woodpecker PICUS AUDUBONI, Trudeau
Today these are all considered part of *P. villosus*.
   Also in CCCCXVI

Painting depicts ten birds representing two species; third bird from top is a male Three-toed Woodpecker, female is just below left. The rest of the birds are Hairy Woodpeckers. There is a partially painted tree, which is completed in the plate, and the Three-toed Woodpeckers are moved to upper right, male below and female above.

CCCCXVIII

Plate CCCCXVIII, O.P. 308, Two Species, 16 3/4 x 22 7/8
Species 1

Current name: Rock Ptarmigan, *Lagopus mutus* (Montin)
Name on plate: American Ptarmigan TETRAO MUTUS, Leach

Name on painting: American Ptarmigan
   Also in CCCLXVIII
Species 2

Current name: White-tailed Ptarmigan, *Lagopus leucurus* (Richardson)

Name on plate: White-tailed Grous TETRAO LEUCURUS, Swains.

For the painting Audubon pasted on two previously painted birds: a Rock Ptarmigan changing from summer to winter plumage at left and a White-tailed Ptarmigan in winter plumage at right. In the plate the birds are atop a cliff with mountains in the background.

CCCCXIX

Plate CCCCXIX, O.P. 299, Three Species, 19 1/2 x 12 3/8
Species 1

Current name: Gray Jay, *Perisoreus canadensis* (Linnaeus)
Name on plate: Canada Jay CORVUS CANADENSIS, Linn.

History: The bird here is a darker form of this species than the one in Plate CVII.
   Also in CVII
Species 2

Current name: Hermit Thrush, *Catharus guttatus* (Pallas)
Name on plate: Little Tawny Thrush TURDUS MINOR, Gm.
   Also in LVIII
Species 3

Current name: Townsend's Solitaire, *Myadestes townsendi* (Audubon)

Name on plate: PTILIOGONY'S TOWNSENDI, Aud
History: Audubon described this species and named it for his friend Townsend, who sent him the skin from Oregon. Painting depicts a Hermit Thrush, top, a Townsend's Solitaire, middle, and Gray Jay, bottom, with no background. In the plate all three are in a tree.

Plate CCCCXX, O.P. 272, One Species, 19 3/8 x 12 1/4
Current name: Red-winged Blackbird, *Agelaius phoeniceus* (Linnaeus)
Name on plate: Prairie Starling ICTERUS GUBERNATOR, Aud.
  Also in LXVII
Painting and plate depict a female, above, and a male, below, in a budding branch.

Plate CCCCXXI, O.P. 396, One Species, 25 5/8 x 38 1/4
Current name: Brown Pelican, *Pelecanus occidentalis* Linnaeus
Name on plate: Brown Pelican PELICANUS FUSCUS
  Also in CCLI
Painting and plate depict one young bird on a muddy bank with beach and sea beyond and a boat and a lighthouse in the distance. In the painting the bird is in pencil, watercolor, and pastel, and the landscape in oil.

CCCCXX

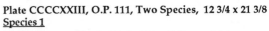

Plate CCCCXXII, O.P. 88, One Species, 38 1/4 x 25 5/8
Current name: Rough-legged Hawk, *Buteo lagopus* (Pontoppidan)
Name on plate: Rough-legged Falcon BUTEO LAGOPUS
Name on painting: Rough-legged Falcon, Buteo lagopus
  Also in CLXVI
Painting and plate depict an adult male, left, and a young bird, right, on a bare branch.

Plate CCCCXXIII, O.P. 111, Two Species, 12 3/4 x 21 3/8
<u>Species 1</u>
Current name: Crested Bobwhite, *Colinus cristatus* (Linnaeus)
Name on plate: Thick-legged Partridge PERDIX NEOXENUS, Aud.
  (* Thick-legged Partridge PERDIX NEOXENUS. Aud.)
History: Audubon drew this bird from a specimen in the Museum of the Zoological Society of London. It should not have been included in *Birds of America*. It is a Central American species.
<u>Species 2</u>
Current name: Mountain Quail, *Oreortyx pictus* (Douglas)
Name on plate: Plumed Partridge PERDIX PLUMIFERA, Gould.
Name on painting: Plumed Partridge, Ortyx plumifera, Gould.
History: Although quail and partridge are quite different, quail were, and still are, sometimes referred to as partridge.
Painting depicts a male Mountain Quail, left, a female Mountain Quail, center, and a Crested Bobwhite, right, with no background. In the plate the Crested Bobwhite is reversed and the birds are on grassy ground with mountains in the distance.

CCCCXXI

CCCCXXII

Plate CCCCXXIV, O.P. 284, Six Species, 20 x 13 1/4
Species 1
Current name: Brown-headed Cowbird, *Molothrus ater*
(Boddaert)
Other names: usually called Cowbird
Name on plate: Cow pen Bird ICTERUS PECORIS, Bonap.
   (* Cow-pen bird, ICTERUS PECORIS, Bonap.)
Name on painting: Cowpen
   Also in XCIX
Species 2
Current name: Fox Sparrow, *Passerella iliaca* (Merrem)
Name on plate: Brown Longspur PLECTROPHANES
TOWNSENDI, Aud.
   Also in CVIII
Species 3
Current name: House Finch, *Carpodacus mexicanus*
(Müller)
Name on plate: Crimson-necked Bull Finch PYRRHULA
FRONTALIS, Bonap.
   (* Crimson-necked Bull-finch, PYRRHULA
FRONTALIS, Bonap.)
History: Audubon painted this bird from a specimen
loaned to him by the famous British painter and
ornithologist John Gould.
Species 4
Current name: Lazuli Bunting, *Passerina amoena* (Say)
Name on plate: Lazuli Finch FRINGILLA AMOENA,
Say.
   Also in CCCXCVIII
Species 5
Current name: Evening Grosbeak, *Coccothraustes*
vespertinus (Cooper)
Name on plate: Evening Grosbeak FRINGILLA
VESPERTINA, Cooper
Name on painting: Evening Grosbeak
   Also in CCCLXXIII
Species 6
Current name: Rosy Finch, *Leucosticte arctoa* (Pallas)
Name on plate: Grey-crowned Linnet LINARIA
TEPHROCOTIS, Swains.
SEE CHART OF ORIGINAL PAINTING 284 IN PART III

Plate CCCCXXV, O.P. 420, One Species, 19 1/2 x 12 1/4
Current name: Anna's Hummingbird, *Calypte anna*
(Lesson)
Name on plate: Columbian Humming Bird TROCHILUS
ANNA, Lesson.
Name on painting: Trochilus anna, Lesson
Painting depicts three males flying, one male perched,
and a female on a nest, all with no background. Just below
the upper right bird there is a pencilled reproduction of
the bird indicating that Audubon wished the bird moved
down, but Havell did not do this. In the plate the birds
are in the branch of a flowering bush.

CCCCXXIII

CCCCXXIV

CCCCXXV

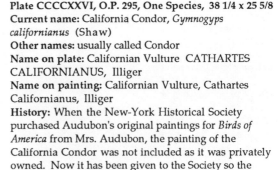

Plate CCCCXXVI, O.P. 295, One Species, 38 1/4 x 25 5/8
Current name: California Condor, *Gymnogyps californianus* (Shaw)
Other names: usually called Condor
Name on plate: Californian Vulture CATHARTES CALIFORNIANUS, Illiger
Name on painting: Californian Vulture, Cathartes Californianus, Illiger
History: When the New-York Historical Society purchased Audubon's original paintings for *Birds of America* from Mrs. Audubon, the painting of the California Condor was not included as it was privately owned. Now it has been given to the Society so the collection is complete except for the two that are lost. This species is close to extinction.
Painting and plate depict one bird standing on a large curving branch.

CCCCXXVI

Plate CCCCXXVII, O.P. 178, One Species, 21 3/4 x 27 1/4
Current name: American Black Oystercatcher, *Haematopus bachmani* Audubon
Other names: formerly Black Oystercatcher
Name on plate: White-legged Oyster-catcher HAEMATOPUS BACHMANI, Aud.
and Slender-billed Oyster-catcher HAEMATOPUS TOWNSENDI, Aud.
History: Although Audubon thought he had two species here, the concensus is that both birds are American Black Oystercatchers. Audubon named one for his friend John Kirk Townsend, the ornithologist, and the other for John Bachman.
Painting depicts two birds with no background. In the plate the habitat is rocky with water in the distance.

CCCCXXVII

Plate CCCCXXVIII, O.P. 139, One Species, 18 5/8 x 16 1/8
Current name: Surfbird, *Aphriza virgata* (Gmelin)
Name on plate: Townsend's Sandpiper TRINGA TOWNSENDI, Aud.
Painting depicts two birds in flight, one over the other. Audubon cut out two previously done paintings and pasted them onto the paper but did not add a background. In the plate the birds are closer together and there is a background of sea and sky.

CCCCXXVIII

Plate CCCCXXIX, O.P. 148, One Species, 12 3/4 x 21 3/8
Current name: Steller's Eider, *Polysticta stelleri* (Pallas)
Name on plate: Western Duck FULIGULA STELLERI.
Bonap.
Name on painting: Western Duck
Painting depicts one male bird with no background. In the
plate the bird is on a bank overlooking the sea. Behind
the grass on the right Havell added the head and
shoulders of another male but this bird does not fit
comfortably into the scene and seems oddly out of
proportion.

CCCCXXIX

Plate CCCCXXX, O.P. 198, One Species, 12 1/4 x 19 1/8
Current name: Marbled Murrelet, *Brachyramphus
marmoratus* (Gmelin)
Name on plate: Slender-billed Guillemot URIA
TOWNSENDI, Aud
History: Audubon did not know this species had already
been described by Gmelin; thinking he had a new species
he named it for his friend John Kirk Townsend. Audubon
mistook the plumages of these birds and thought the bird
in spring plumage was a female and the bird in winter
plumage a male.
Painting depicts bird in spring plumage, left, and bird in
winter plumage, right, with no background. In the plate
the birds are on top of high cliffs with the sea far below.

CCCCXXX

Plate CCCCXXXI, O.P. 74, One Species, 38 1/4 x 25 5/8
Current name: Greater Flamingo, *Phoenicopterus ruber*
Linnaeus
Other names: If the Old World populations are considered
a separate species, *P. roseus*, then the New World
populations of *P. ruber* would be called the American
Flamingo.
Name on plate: American Flamingo PHOENICOPTERUS
RUBER, Linn.
Painting depicts one bird with no background. In the plate
the bird is on one of many mudflats, with water between
them. There are eight other Flamingos in the middle and
far distance. At the top there are detailed drawings of
the bird's foot and various views of the beak.

CCCCXXXI

CCCCXXXII

CCCCXXXIII

Plate CCCCXXXII, O.P. 401, Four Species, 21 3/4 x 26
<u>Species 1</u>
Current name: Burrowing Owl, *Athene cunicularia*
(Molina)
Name on plate: Burrowing Owl STRIX CUNICULARIA
and Large-headed Burrowing Owl STRIX CALIFORNICA
History: Audubon thought the bird farthest left top and
the bird farthest left bottom were two different species
but they are in fact both Burrowing Owls.
<u>Species 2</u>
Current name: Little Owl, *Athene noctua* (Scopoli)
Name on plate: Little night Owl STRIX NOCTUA, Lath
      (* Little Night Owl, STRIX NOCTUA, Lath.)
History: Audubon was told the skin from which he
painted this bird came from Nova Scotia but it did not. It
is strictly a European bird and a favorite of the Greeks,
who portray it on coins and friezes. Do not confuse this
bird with the Northern Saw-whet Owl in Plate CXCIX,
which Audubon called Little Owl.
<u>Species 3</u>
Current name: Northern Pygmy-Owl, *Glaucidium gnoma*
Wagler
Name on plate: Columbian Owl STRIX
PASSERINOIDES, Temm.
<u>Species 4</u>
Current name: Short-eared Owl, *Asio flammeus*
(Pontoppidan)
Name on plate: Short eared Owl STRIX BRACHYOTUS,
Wils.
      (* Short-eared Owl, STRIX BRACHYOTUS, Wils.)
SEE CHART OF ORIGINAL PAINTING 401 IN PART III

Plate CCCCXXXIII, O.P. 183, Four Species, 20 3/8 x 14 1/8
<u>Species 1</u>
Current name: Lesser Goldfinch, *Carduelis psaltria* (Say)
Name on plate: Mexican Goldfinch CARDUELIS
MEXICANUS, Swains.
    Also in CCCC
<u>Species 2</u>
Current name: Northern Oriole, *Icterus galbula* (Linnaeus)
Other names: The Baltimore Oriole, *I. galbula*, and the
Bullock's Oriole, *I. bullockii*, are sometimes considered two
species but the A.O.U. combines them into one.
Name on plate: Bullock's Oriole ICTERUS BULLOCKII,
Swains.
and Baltimore Oriole ICTERUS BALTIMORE, Bonap.
Name on painting: Icterus bullocki, Swainson
    Also in XII (Baltimore) and CCCLXXXVIII (Bullock's)
<u>Species 3</u>
Current name: Northern Waterthrush, *Seiurus
noveboracensis* (Gmelin)
Name on plate: Common Water Thrush TURDUS
AQUATICUS, Wilson.
<u>Species 4</u>
Current name: Varied Thrush, *Ixoreus naevius* (Gmelin)
Name on plate: Varied Thrush TURDUS NOEVIUS,
Lath.
Name on painting: Varied Robbin
    Also in CCCLXIX
SEE CHART OF ORIGINAL PAINTING 183 IN PART III

Plate CCCCXXXIV, O.P. 302, Six Species, 19 1/2 x 12 1/4
Species 1
Current name: Western Wood-Pewee, *Contopus sordidulus* Sclater
Name on plate: Short-legged Pewee MUSCICAPA PHOEBE, Lath.
Name on painting: Muscicapa Phoebe, [Short-legged Pewit Flycatcher]
Species 2
Current name: Black Phoebe, *Sayornis nigricans* (Swainson)
Name on plate: Rocky Mountain Flycatcher TYRANNULA NIGRICANS, Swains.
Name on painting: Rocky Mountain Flycatcher, Muscicapa Nigricans
Species 3
Current name: Blue Mountain Warbler, *Sylvia montana* Wilson
Name on plate: Blue Mountain Warbler SYLVIA MONTANA, Wilson.
History: This species was first identified by Wilson. Audubon painted it from a specimen in the Zoological Society of London. It has yet to be satisfactorily identified with any known species.
Species 4
Current name: Least Flycatcher, *Empidonax minimus* (Baird and Baird)
Name on plate: Little Tyrant Flycatcher TYRANNULA PUSILLA, Swains.
Species 5
Current name: Red-eyed Vireo, *Vireo olivaceus* (Linnaeus)
Name on plate: Bartram's Viroe VIREO BARTRAMI, Swains.
Species 6
Current name: Small-headed Flycatcher, *Sylvania microcephala* Ridgway
Name on plate: Small headed Flycatcher MUSCICAPA MINUTA, Wils.
   (* Small-headed Flycatcher, MUSCICAPA MINUTA, Wils.)
History: Wilson first named and published a drawing of this bird, saying he found it in New Jersey. Audubon said he found it in Louisville in 1808, claiming Wilson copied the drawing from one he showed him in 1810. In 1885 Ridgway renamed the bird *S. microcephal* as *M. minuta* was preoccupied. No other like it has been found.
SEE CHART OF ORIGINAL PAINTING 302 IN PART III

CCCCXXXIV

CCCCXXXV

Plate CCCCXXXV, O.P. 276, One Species, 19 1/2 x 12 1/4
Current name: American Dipper, *Cinclus mexicanus* Swainson
Name on plate: Columbian Water Ouzel CINCLUS TOWNSENDI, Aud.
and Arctic Water Ouzel, CINCLUS MORTONI, Townsend
History: Audubon correctly identified this bird in Plate CCCLXX, but was misled here by immature plumage.
   Also in CCCLXX
Painting depicts immature male, right, on a rock and immature female, left, with no background. In the plate the birds are on tall rocks with a stream between, cascading over rocks in the distance.

PART THREE

CHARTS OF CONFUSING ORIGINAL PAINTINGS

For the majority of paintings and plates it is a simple matter to describe the position of the birds, but for those that have a multiplicity of species the situation is more complicated. When Audubon sent Havell a painting in which there were several birds, Havell often would rearrange the birds for a more pleasing effect. If Havell thought there were too many birds, he would put some in different plates. In one instance, the birds in one painting are distributed among three plates. These thirteen charts of original paintings are for these complicated situations.

ORIGINAL PAINTING 183　　　PLATE CCCCXXXIII

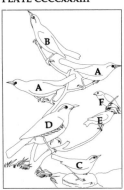

O.P. 183, Plate
CCCCXXXIII
The painting depicts seven
birds representing four
species with no back-
ground. The same birds
appear in the plate, ar-
ranged differently, with
the six top birds perched
in leafless branches and
the bottom one on a rock.

A *Northern Oriole* F Bullock's Oriole　**B** *Northern Oriole M*
Bullock's Oriole　**C** *Northern Waterthrush* Common Water
Thrush　**D** *Varied Thrush* Varied Thrush　**E** *Lesser Goldfinch M*
Mexican Goldfinch　**F** *Lesser Goldfinch F* Mexican Goldfinch

---

ORIGINAL PAINTING 186

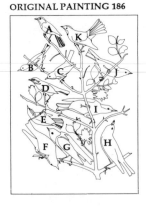

PLATE CCCXCIII　　　　　　　PLATE CCCXCV

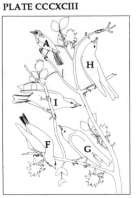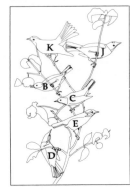

O.P. 186, Plates CCCXCIII
and CCCXCV
The painting depicts
eleven birds representing
six species. Five of these
birds appear in Plate
CCCXCIII perched in a
branch of strawberry-
shrub and six appear in
Plate CCCXCV perched in
leafy fruited branches.
This is one of two times
Havell made two plates
from one painting, thus
accounting for the fact that
there are two more plates
than paintings.

A *Townsend's Warbler M* Townsend's Warbler　**B** *Hermit
Warbler F* Hermit Warbler　**C** *Hermit Warbler M* Hermit
Warbler　**D** *Black-throated Gray Warbler* Black-throated Gray
Warbler　**E** *Black-Throated Gray Warbler* Black-Throated Gray
Warbler　**F** *Western Bluebird F* Western Blue-bird　**G** *Western
Bluebird M* Western Blue-bird　**H** *Mountain Bluebird M.* Artic
Blue-bird　**I** *Mountain Bluebird F* Artic Blue-bird　**J** *Yellow-
rumped Warbler, Imm* Audubon's Warbler　**K** *Yellow-rumped
Warbler M* Audubon's Warbler

ORIGINAL PAINTING 266

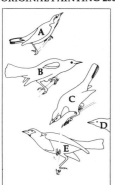

PLATE CCCLXXXVIII

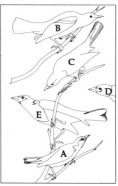

A *Northern Oriole M* Bullock's Oriole   B *Tricolored Blackbird*
Nuttal's Starling   C *Yellow-headed Blackbird F* Yellow-headed
Troopial   D *Yellow-headed Blackbird, Imm Head* Yellow-headed
Troopial   E *Yellow-headed Blackbird M* Yellow-headed
Troopial

O.P. 266, Plate
CCCLXXXVIII
The painting depicts five
birds representing three
species with no back-
ground. All five birds
appear in the plate,
arranged differently, and
perched on leafless
branches.

ORIGINAL PAINTING 280

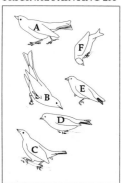

PLATE CCCC

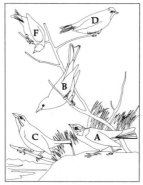

A *Smith's Longspur M* Buff-breasted Finch   B *Western Tanager*
F *Louisana Tanager*   C *Townsend's Bunting* Townsend's Finch
D *Hoary Redpoll* Mealy Red-poll   E *Hooded Siskin* Black-
headed Siskin   F *Lesser Goldfinch M* Arkansaw Siskin

O.P. 280, Plate CCCC
The painting depicts six
birds representing six
species and has no
background. Five of the
birds appear in this plate,
which depicts the birds on
dead branches with one
atop a cliff, all overlooking
a marsh with winding
river and distant hills.
Havell put the sixth bird,
the Hooded Siskin, in Plate
CCCXCIV.

ORIGINAL PAINTING 284

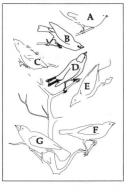

PLATE CCCCXXIV

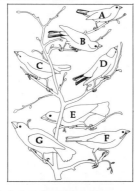

A *Lazuli Bunting* Lazuli Finch   B *House Finch M* Crimson-
necked Bull Finch   C *Brown-headed Cowbird, Imm* Cow pen
Bird   D *Rosy Finch* Grey-crowned Linnet   E Evening
Grosbeak F Evening Grosbeak   F *Fox Sparrow* Brown
Longspur   G *Evening Grosbeak, Young M* Evening Grosbeak

O.P. 284, Plate CCCCXXIV
The painting depicts seven
birds representing six
species. Two of the
birds—the House Finch
and the Rosy Finch—are
painted, the rest are in
pencil. There is no back-
ground but a lightly pen-
cilled branch. In the plate,
all seven birds are
arranged almost the same,
fully colored, and perched
on a leafless branch. It is
interesting to speculate
who was responsible for
turning the lightly
pencilled birds into the
finished paintings that
appear in the plate.

ORIGINAL PAINTING 288   PLATE CCCLIX

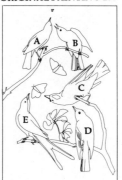
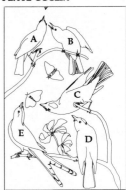

O.P. 288, Plate CCCLIX
The painting depicts five
birds representing three
species perched in
branches with two moths.
The top two birds are
eyeing a bee. The plate is
exactly the same.

A *Say's Phoebe* Say's Flycatcher **B** *Say's Phoebe* Say's
Flycatcher **C** *Western Kingbird* Arkansaw Flycatcher **D**
Western Kingbird Arkansaw Flycatcher **E** *Scissor-tailed
Flycatcher* Swallow Tailed Flycatcher

O.P. 293, Plate CCCXC
The painting depicts three
birds representing two
species with no back-
ground except a few small
branches. All three birds
appear in the plate, plus a
Lark Sparrow from O.P.
359. The plate has a
background of grass, a
small rock, a small dead
tree, and a leafy reed.
In addition to writing the
names of the Lark Bun-
tings and the Song
Sparrow (which he called
Prairie Finch and Brown
Song Sparrow) directly on
the painting, Audubon
also wrote Black-throated
Bunting, which we know
today as Dickcissel. He
may have meant to paint
these birds but sent the
painting off to Havell
before doing so. These
birds do not appear in the
plate but, as noted, Havell
did add the Lark Sparrow.

ORIGINAL PAINTING 293   PLATE CCCXC

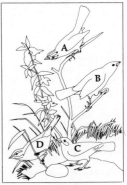

A *Lark Sparrow* Lark Finch **B** *Lark Bunting* M Prairie Finch
C *Lark Bunting* F Prairie Finch **D** *Song Sparrow* Brown Song
Sparrow

ORIGINAL PAINTING 302

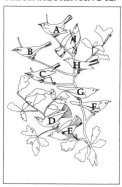

PLATE CCCCXXXIV

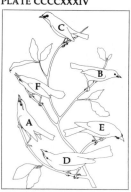

A *Red-eyed Vireo* Bartram's Viroe **B** *Small-headed Flycatcher* Small headed Flycatcher **C** *Least Flycatcher* Little Tyrant Flycatcher **D** *Black Phoebe* Rocky Mountain Flycatcher **E** *Western Wood-Pewee* Short-legged Pewee **F** *Blue Mountain Warbler* Blue Mountain Warbler

O.P. 302, Plate CCCCXXXIV
The painting depicts six species with no background. All six appear in the plate, arranged differently, perched in a branch with a few large leaves.

ORIGINAL PAINTING 327

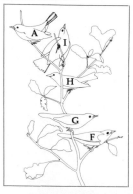

PLATE CCCXCIX

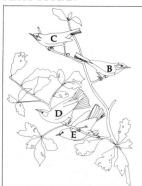

PLATE CCCCXIV

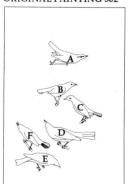

A *Black-throated Green Warbler* M Black-throated Green Warbler **B** *Golden-winged Warbler* M Golden-winged Warbler **C** *Golden-winged Warbler* F Golden-winged Warbler **D** *Cape May Warbler* M Cape May Warbler **E** *Cape May Warbler* F Cape May Warbler **F** *MacGillivray's Warbler* F Mourning Warbler **G** *MacGillivray's Warbler* M Mourning Warbler **H** *Blackburnian Warbler* F Blackburnian Warbler **I** *Black-throated Green Warbler* F Black-throated Green Warbler

O.P. 327, Plates CCCXCIX and CCCCXIV
The painting depicts nine birds representing five species in a branch of water oak. Five of the birds appear in Plate CCCXCIX and four in Plate CCCCXIV, all in branches of water oak. This is one of two times Havell made two plates from one painting, thus accounting for the fact that there are two more plates than paintings.

ORIGINAL PAINTING 333

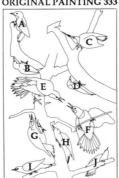

PLATE CCCCXVI

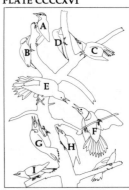

O.P. 333, Plate CCCCXVI
The painting depicts ten
birds representing five
species, all in two thick
branches of a dead tree.
All ten birds are arranged
the same way in the plate
but for one minor differ-
ence and a background in
which the two branches
are merged into one.

A *Hairy Woodpecker* Hairy Woodpecker B *Hairy Woodpecker*
Hairy Woodpecker C *Red-bellied Woodpecker* M Red-bellied
Woodpecker D *Red-bellied Woodpecker* F Red-bellied
Woodpecker E *Northern Flicker, Imm* Red-shafted Woodpecker
F *Northern Flicker* Red-shafted Woodpecker G *Lewis'*
Woodpecker Lewis' Woodpecker H *Lewis' Woodpecker* Lewis'
Woodpecker I *Red-breasted Sapsucker* Red-breasted Woodpecker
J *Red-breasted Sapsucker* Red-breasted Woodpecker

ORIGINAL PAINTING 359

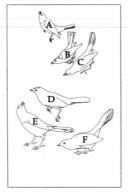

PLATE CCCXC

PLATE CCCXCIV

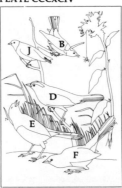

PLATE CCCXCVIII

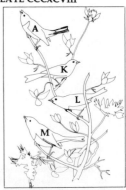

O.P. 359, Plates CCCXC,
CCCXCIV, and
CCCXCVIII
The painting depicts six
birds representing five
species with no back-
ground. One of the birds
appears in Plate CCCXC
with others from another
painting, four appear in
Plate CCCXCIV with one
other from another
painting, and the sixth
appears in Plate CCXCVIII
with others from another
painting.

A *Lazuli Bunting* M Lazuli Finch B *Chestnut-collared Longspur* M
Chestnut-coloured Finch C *Lark Sparrow* M Lark Finch D *Golden-*
crowned Sparrow M Black crown Bunting E *Rufous- sided Towhee* F
Artic Ground Finch F *Rufous-Sided Towhee* M Artic Ground Finch
G *Lark Bunting* Prairie Finch H *Lark Bunting* Prairie Finch I *Song*
Sparrow Brown Song Sparrow J *Hooded Siskin* Black-headed Siskin
K *Clay-colored Sparrow* Clay-coloured Finch L *Dark-eyed Junco*
Oregon Snow Finch M *Dark-Eyed Junco* Oregon Snow Finch

ORIGINAL PAINTING 401

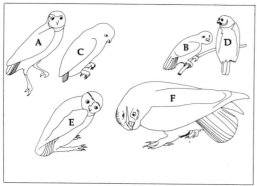

PLATE CCCCXXXII

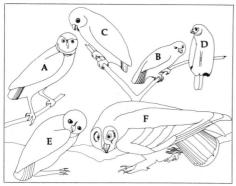

A *Burrowing Owl* Burrowing Owl B *Northern Pygmy Owl*
Columbian Owl C *Little Owl* Little Night Owl D *Northern
Pygmy-Owl* Columbian Owl E *Burrowing Owl* Large-headed
Burrowing Owl F *Short-eared Owl* Short eared Owl

O.P. 401, Plate
CCCCXXXII
The painting depicts six
birds representing four
species with no back-
ground but for one small
branch. All six birds are in
the plate, two on the
ground and four on dead
branches. There are hills
in the distance.

ORIGINAL PAINTING 424   **PLATE CCCXCVIII**

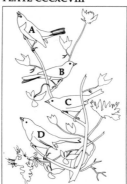

A *Lazuli Bunting* Lazuli Finch B *Clay-colored Sparrow* M
Clay-coloured Finch C *Dark-eyed Junco* F Oregon Snow Finch
D *Dark-eyed Junco* M Oregon Snow Finch

O.P. 424, Plate CCCXCVIII
The painting depicts three
birds representing two
species with no back-
ground. All three birds
appear in the plate in a
branch of a flowering tree,
along with a Lazuli
Bunting from O.P. 359.
Audubon indicated on the
painting that he wished a
pair of Common Redpolls
added, but the Lazuli
Bunting was added
instead.

PART FOUR

INDEX OF CURRENT NAMES

The names of all the birds in *Birds of America* as they are known today, cross-indexed to the names as they appear in the plate legends; listed as is customary in ornithological indexes.

Sparrow, Henslow's, *Ammodramus henslowii*
Henslow's Bunting EMBERIZA HENSLOWII
Plate LXX (some marked 70), O.P. 89

Sparrow, Lark, *Chondestes grammacus*
Lark Finch FRINGILLA GRAMMACA
Plate CCCXC, O.P. 359

Sparrow, Lincoln's, *Melospiza lincolnii*
Lincoln Finch FRINGILLA LINCOLNII
Plate CXCIII, O.P. 167

Sparrow, Savannah, *Passerculus sandwichensis*
Savannah Finch FRINGILLA SAVANNA
Plate CIX, O.P. 246

Sparrow, Seaside, *Ammodramus maritimus*
Sea-side Finch FRINGILLA MARITIMA
Plate XCIII (some marked 93), O.P. 33

MacGillivray's Finch FRINGILLA MACGILLIVRAII
Plate CCCLV, O.P. 345

Sparrow, Sharp-tailed, *Ammodramus caudacutus*
Sharp-tailed Finch FRINGILLA CAUDACUTA
Plate CXLIX, O.P. 163

Sparrow, Song, *Melospiza melodia*
Song Sparrow FRINGILLA MELODIA
Plate XXV (some marked 25), O.P. 256

Brown Song Sparrow FRINGILLA CINEREA
Plate CCCXC, O.P. 293

Sparrow, Swamp, *Melospiza georgiana*
Swamp Sparrow SPIZA PALUSTRIS (marked 64)
Swamp Sparrow FRINGILLA PALUSTRIS
Plate LXIV, O.P. 331

Sparrow, Vesper, *Pooecetes gramineus*
Grass Finch or Bay-winged Bunting FRINGILLA GRAMINEA
Bay-winged Bunting FRINGILLA GRAMINEA (marked 94)
Plate XCIV, O.P. 217

Sparrow, White-crowned, *Zonotrichia leucophrys*
White-crowned Sparrow FRINGILLA LEUCOPHRYS
Plate CXIV, O.P. 340

Sparrow, White-throated, *Zonotrichia albicollis*
White Throated Sparrow FRINGILLA PENNSYLVANICA
Plate VIII, O.P. 337

Spoonbill, Roseate, *Ajaia ajaja*
Roseate Spoonbill PLATALEA AJAJA
Plate CCCXXI, O.P. 35

Stilt, Black-necked, *Himantopus mexicanus*
Long-legged Avocet HIMANTOPUS NIGRICOLLIS
Plate CCCXXVIII, O.P. 101

Stork, Wood, *Mycteria americana*
Wood Ibiss TANTALUS LOCULATOR
Plate CCXVI, O.P. 247

Storm-Petrel, British, *Hydrobates pelagicus*
Least Stormy-Petrel THALASSIDROMA PELAGICA
Plate CCCXL, O.P. 158

Storm-Petrel, Leach's, *Oceanodroma leucorhoa*
Fork-tail Petrel THALASSIDROMA LEACHII
Plate CCLX, O.P. 191

Storm-Petrel, Wilson's, *Oceanites oceanicus*
Stormy Petrel THALASSIDROMA WILSONIUS
Wilson's Petrel THALASSIDROMA WILSONIUS
Plate CCLXX, O.P. 39

Surfbird, *Aphriza virgata*
Townsend's Sandpiper TRINGA TOWNSENDI
Plate CCCCXXVIII, O.P. 139

Swallow, Bank, *Riparia riparia*
Bank Swallow HIRUNDO RIPARIA
Bank Swallow HIRUNDO VIPARIA
Plate CCCLXXXV, O.P. 204

Swallow, Barn, *Hirundo rustica*
Barn Swallow HIRUNDO AMERICANA
Plate CLXXIII, O.P. 117

Swallow, Cliff, *Hirundo pyrrhonota*
Republican or Cliff Swallow HIRUNDO FULVA
Plate LXVIII (some marked 68), O.P. 133

Swallow, Tree, *Tachycineta bicolor*
White-bellied Swallow HIRUNDO BICOLOR
Green-blue or White Bellied Swallow HIRUNDO BICOLOR
(mislabeled 100)

211

Warbler, Myrtle. *See* Warbler, Yellow-
rumped

Warbler, Nashville, *Vermivora ruficapilla*
Nashville Warbler SYLVIA RUBRICAP-
ILLA
Plate LXXXIX (some marked 89), O.P. 63

Warbler, Orange-crowned, *Vermivora
celata*
Orange-crowned Warbler SYLVIA
CELATA
Plate CLXXVIII, O.P. 190

Warbler, Palm, *Dendroica palmarum*
Palm Warbler SYLVIA PALMARUM
Yellow red poll Warbler SYLVIA
PETECHIA
Plate CLXIII, O.P. 332

Yellow Red-poll Warbler SYLVIA
PETECHIA
Plate CXLV, O.P. 368

Warbler, Parula. *See* Parula, Northern

Warbler, Pine, *Dendroica pinus*
Vigor's Warbler SYLVIA VIGORSII
Vigors Vireo VIREO VIGORSII (marked
30)
Plate XXX, O.P.23

Pine Creeping Warbler SYLVIA PINUS
Plate CXL, O.P. 211

Warbler, Prairie, *Dendroica discolor*
Prairie Warbler SYLVIA DISCOLOR
Plate XIV (some marked 14), O.P. 260

Warbler, Prothonotary, *Protonotaria citrea*
Prothonotary Warbler DACNIS
PROTONOTARIUS
Prothonotary Warbler SYLVIA PRO-
TONOTARIUS
Plate III, O.P. 93

Warbler, Swainson's, *Limnothlypis
swainsonii*
Brown headed Worm eating Warbler
SYLVIA SWAINSONII
Swainson's Warbler SYLVIA SWAIN-
SONI
Plate CXCVIII, O.P. 153

Warbler, Tennessee, *Vermivora peregrina*
Tennessee Warbler SYLVIA PERE-
GRINA
Plate CLIV, O.P. 80

Warbler, Townsend's, *Dendroica townsendi*
Townsend's Warbler SYLVIA
TOWNSENDI

Warbler, Prothonotary, *Protonotaria citrea*
Prothonotary Warbler DACNIS
PROTONOTARIUS
Prothonotary Warbler SYLVIA PRO-
TONOTARIUS
Plate III, O.P. 93

Warbler, Swainson's, *Limnothlypis
swainsonii*
Brown headed Worm eating Warbler
SYLVIA SWAINSONII
Swainson's Warbler SYLVIA SWAIN-
SONI
Plate CXCVIII, O.P. 153

Warbler, Tennessee, *Vermivora peregrina*
Tennessee Warbler SYLVIA PERE-
GRINA
Plate CLIV, O.P. 80

Warbler, Townsend's, *Dendroica townsendi*
Townsend's Warbler SYLVIA
TOWNSENDI
Plate CCCXCIII, O.P. 186

Warbler, Wilson's, *Wilsonia pusilla*
Green Black-capt Flycatcher MUSCI-
CAPA PUSILLA
Green Black-capt Flycatcher MUSCI-
CAPA WILSONII
Plate CXXIV, O.P. 378

Warbler, Worm-eating, *Helmitheros
vermivorus*
Worm eating Warbler SYLVIA VERMI-
VORA
Plate XXXIV (some marked 34), O.P. 379

Warbler, Yellow, *Dendroica petechia*
Blue-eyed yellow Warbler SYLVIA
AESTIVA (some marked 95)
Yellow-poll Warbler SYLVIA AESTIVA
Plate XCV, O.P. 147

Rathbone Warbler SYLVIA RATH-
BONIA
Plate LXV (some marked 65), O.P. 383

Children's Warbler SYLVIA CHIL-
DRENI (some marked 35)
Children's Warbler SYLVIA CHIL-
DRENII
Plate XXXV, O.P. 263

Warbler, Yellow-rumped, *Dendroica
coronata*
Yellow-Crown Warbler SYLVIA
CORONATA
Yellow rump Warbler SYLVIA
CORONATA
Plate CLIII, O.P. 127

Wood-Pewee, Eastern, *Contopus virens*
Wood Pewee MUSCICAPA VIRENS
Plate CXV, O.P. 381

Wood-Pewee, Western, *Contopus sordidulus*
Short legged Pewee MUSCICAPA PHOEBE
Plate CCCCXXXIV, O.P. 302

Wren, Bewick's, *Thryomanes bewickii*
Bewick's Wren TROGLODYTES BEWICKII
Bewick's Long-tailed Wren TROGLO-DYTES BEWICKII (marked 18)
Plate XVIII, O.P. 240

Wren, Carolina, *Thryothorus ludovicianus*
Great Carolina Wren TROGLODYTES LUDOVICIANUS
Plate LXXVIII (some marked 78), O.P. 113

Wren, House, *Troglodytes aedon*
House Wren TROGLODYTES AEDON
Plate LXXXIII (some marked 83), O.P. 4

Wood Wren TROGLODYTES AMERI-CANA
Plate CLXXIX, O.P. 427

Wren, Long-billed Marsh. *See* Wren, Marsh

Wren, Marsh, *Cistothorus palustris*
Marsh Wren TROGLODYTES PALUS-TRIS
Plate C (some mislabeled 98), O.P. 336

Wren, Rock, *Salpinctes obsoletus*
Rock Wren TROGLODYTES OBSELATA
Plate CCCLX, O.P. 328

Wren, Sedge, *Cistothorus platensis*
Nuttall's lesser-marsh Wren TROGLO-DYTES BREVIROSTRIS
Plate CLXXV, O.P. 394

Wren, Short-billed Marsh. *See* Wren, Sedge

Wren, Winter, *Troglodytes troglodytes*
Winter Wren SYLVIA TROGLODYTES
Plate CCCLX, O.P. 328

Yellowlegs, Greater, *Tringa melanoleuca*
Tell-tale Godwit or Snipe TOTANUS MELANOLEUCUS
Plate CCCVIII, O.P. 380

Yellowlegs, Lesser, *Tringa flavipes*
Yellow Shank TOTANUS FLAVIPES
Plate CCLXXXVIII, O.P. 82

Yellowthroat, Common, *Geothlypis trichas*
Roscoe's Yellow-throat SYLVIA ROSCO
Plate XXIV (some marked 24), O.P. 294

Yellow-breasted Warbler SYLVIA TRICHAS
Maryland Yellow Throat SYLVIA TRICHAS (marked 23)
Plate XXIII, O.P. 407

PART FIVE

INDEX OF PLATE NAMES

The names of all the birds in *Birds of America* as they appear in the plate legends, cross-indexed to the names as they are known today; listed alphabetically.

Plate CCCXXXI, O.P. 275

Goshawk FALCO PALUMBARIUS
Northern Goshawk, *Accipiter gentilis*
Plate CXLI, O.P. 17

Grass Finch or Bay-winged Bunting
FRINGILLA GRAMINEA
Vesper Sparrow, *Pooecetes gramineus*
Plate XCIV, O.P. 217

Gray Tyrant TYRANNUS GRISENS
Gray Kingbird, *Tyranuus dominicensis*
Plate CLXX, O.P. 358

Great American Cock MALEAGRIS
GALLOPAVO
Wild Turkey, *Meleagris gallopavo*
Plate I, O.P. 1

Great American Hen & Young MELEAG-
RIS GALLOPAVO
Wild Turkey, *Meleagris gallopavo*
Plate VI, O.P. 5

Great American Sea Eagle. *See* Bird of
Washington

Great American Shrike or Butcher Bird
LANIUS SEPTENTRIONALIS
Northern Shrike, *Lanius excubitor*
Plate CXCII, O.P. 173

Great Auk ALCA IMPENNIS
Great Auk, *Pinguinus impennis*
Plate CCCXLI, O.P. 169

Great blue Heron ARDEA HERODIAS
Great Blue Heron, *Ardea herodias*
Plate CCXI, O.P. 326

Great Carolina Wren TROGLODYTES
LUDOVICIANUS
Carolina Wren, *Thryothorus ludovicianus*
Plate LXXVIII (some marked 78), O.P. 113

Great Crested Flycatcher MUSCICAPA
CRINITA
Great Crested Flycatcher, *Myiarchus
crinitus*
Plate CXXIX, O.P. 335

Great Cinereous Owl STRIX CINEREA
Great Gray Owl, *Strix nebulosa*
Plate CCCLI, O.P. 34

Great cinerous Shrike or Butcher Bird
LANIUS EXCUBITOR
Northern Shrike, *Lanius excubitor*
Plate CXCII, O.P. 173

Great Esquimaux Curlew NEWMENIUS

HUDSONICUS
Whimbrel, *Numenius phaeopus*
Plate CCXXXVII, O.P. 330

Great-footed Hawk FALCO PEREGRINUS
Peregrine Falcon, *Falco peregrinus*
Plate XVI (some marked 16), O.P. 315

Great Horned Owl STRIX VIRGINIANA
Great horned Owl STRIX VIRGINIANA
(marked 61)
Great Horned Owl, *Bubo virginianus*
Plate LXI, O.P. 412

Great Marbled Godwit LIMOSA FEDOA
Marbled Godwit, *Limosa fedoa*
Plate CCXXXVIII, O.P. 209

Great Northern Diver or Loon CO-
LYMBUS GLACIALIS
Common Loon, *Gavia immer*
Plate CCCVI, O.P. 409

**Great Red breasted Rail or Fresh-water
Marsh hen**
RALLUS ELEGANS
King Rail, *Rallus elegans*
Plate CCIII, O.P. 79

Great Tern STERNA HIRUNDO
Common Tern, *Sterna hirundo*
Plate CCCIX, O.P. 56

Great White Heron ARDEA OCCIDEN-
TALIS
Great Blue Heron, *Ardea herodias*
Plate CCLXXXI, O.P. 219

Green Black-capt Flycatcher MUSCICAPA
PUSILLA
Green Black-capt Flycatcher MUSCICAPA
WILSONII
Wilson's Warbler, *Wilsonia pusilla*
Plate CXXIV, O.P. 378

Green-blue or White Bellied Swallow
HIRUNDO BICOLOR
Tree Swallow, *Tachycineta bicolor*
Plate C (marked 100), O.P. 397 (misla-
beled—should be XCVIII)

Green Heron ARDEA VIRESCENS
Green-backed Heron, *Butorides striatus*
Plate CCCXXXIII, O.P. 78

Greenshank TOTANUS GLOTTIS
Common Greenshank, *Tringa nebularia*
Plate CCLXIX, O.P. 18

Green winged Teal ANAS CRECCA
Green-winged Teal, *Anas crecca*
Plate CCXXVIII, O.P. 322

PART SIX

INDEX OF PAINTING NAMES

The names of the birds as Audubon wrote them on the paintings, cross-indexed to the plate names and current names; listed alphabetically.

Audubon did not always label his paintings, and of those he did, many have writing too faint to decipher.

If there are variants of the name on the plate as given in this list, the reader is warned by the addition of a small "v" in parentheses. Refer to the plate in Part II.

American Bittern - O.P. 371
Plate Name: American Bittern - Plate CCCXXXVII
Current Name: American Bittern

American Ptarmigan - O.P. 308
Plate Name: American Ptarmigan - Plate CCCCXVIII
Current Name: Rock Ptarmigan

American Redstart - O.P. 365
Plate Name: American Redstart - Plate XL
Current Name: American Redstart

American Widgeon - O.P. 282
Plate Name: American Widgeon - Plate CCCXLV
Current Name: American Wigeon

Arctic blue bird - O.P. 186
Plate Name: Arctic Blue-bird - Plate CCCXCIII
Current Name: Mountain Bluebird

Arctic ground Finch - O.P. 359
Plate Name: Arctic Ground Finch - Plate CCCXCIV
Current Name: Rufous-sided Towhee

Ardea occidentalis - O.P. 219
Plate Name: Great White Heron - Plate CCLXXXI
Current Name: Great Blue Heron

Arkansaw Flycatcher - O.P. 288
Plate Name: Arkansaw Flycatcher - Plate CCCLIX
Current Name: Western Kingbird

Arkansaw Siskin - O.P. 280
Plate Name: Arkansaw Siskin - Plate CCCC
Current Name: Lesser Goldfinch

Audubon's W$_-^r$ - O.P. 186
Plate Name: Audubon's Warbler - Plate CCCXCV
Current Name: Yellow-rumped Warbler

Autumnal Warbler - O.P. 364
Plate Name: Autumnal Warbler - Plate LXXXVIII
Current Name: Bay-breasted Warbler

Band-tailed Pigeon - O.P. 144
Plate Name: Band-tailed Pigeon - Plate CCCLXVII
Current Name: Band-tailed Pigeon

Barred Owl - O.P. 188
Plate Name: Barred Owl - Plate XLVI

Current Name: Barred Owl

Bay breasted Warbler - O.P. 103
Plate Name: Bay-breasted Warbler - Plate LXIX
Current Name: Bay-breasted Warbler

Bay-winged Bunting - O.P. 217
Plate Name: Grass Finch, or Bay-winged Bunting - Plate XCIV
Current Name: Vesper Sparrow

Belted Kingfisher - O.P. 257
Plate Name: Belted Kingfisher - Plate LXXVII
Current Name: Belted Kingfisher

Bemaculated Duck ? - O.P. 296
Plate Name: Bemaculated Duck - Plate CCCXXXVIII
Current Name: Hybrid Duck

Bewick's long-tailed Wren - O.P. 240
Plate Name: Bewick's Wren - Plate XVIII (v)
Current Name: Bewick's Wren

Black & Yellow Warblers - O.P. 136
Plate Name: Black & Yellow Warbler - Plate CXXIII
Current Name: Magnolia Warbler

Black and Yellow crowned Finch - O.P. 359
Plate Name: Black crown Bunting - Plate CCCXCIV
Current Name: Golden-crowned Sparrow

Black Bellied Darter or Snake Bird - O.P. 64
Plate Name: Black-bellied Darter - Plate CCCXVI
Current Name: Anhinga

Black billed Tern - O.P. 309
Plate Name: Havell's Tern - Plate CCCCIX
Current Name: Forster's Tern

Blackburnian W$_-^r$ - O.P. 327
Plate Name: Blackburnian W. - Plate CCCXCIX
Current Name: Blackburnian Warbler

Black burnian Warbler - O.P. 404
Plate Name: Blackburnian Warbler - Plate CXXXV
Current Name: Blackburnian Warbler

Black-capt Titmouse - O.P. 73
Plate Name: Black-capt Titmouse - Plate

CCCLIII
Current Name: Black-capped Chickadee

Black-headed Siskin - O.P. 280
Plate Name: Black-headed Siskin - Plate CCCXCIV
Current Name: Hooded Siskin

Blackpoll Warbler - O.P. 197
Plate Name: Black-poll Warbler - Plate CXXXIII
Current Name: Black-poll Warbler

Black throat Bunting - O.P. 411
Plate Name: Black-throated Bunting - Plate CCCLXXXIV
Current Name: Dickcissel

Black-throated Diver - O.P. 278
Plate Name: Black-throated Diver - Plate CCCXLVI
Current Name: Arctic Loon

Black throated Gray W$_-^r$ - O.P. 186
Plate Name: Black-throated gray Warbler - Plate CCCXCV
Current Name: Black-throated Gray Warbler

Black-throated Green Warbler - O.P. 327
Plate Name: Black throated Green Warbler -.Plate CCCXCIX
Current Name: Black-throated Green Warbler

Black-throated Guillemot - O.P. 112
Plate Name: Black-throated Guillemot - Plate CCCCII
Current Name: Ancient Murrelet

Black Warrior - O.P. 174
Plate Name: Black Warrior - Plate LXXXVI
Current Name: Red-tailed Hawk

Black winged Hawk - O.P. 239
Plate Name: Black winged Hawk - Plate CCCLII
Current Name: Black-shouldered Kite

Blue-eyed yellow-Warbler - O.P. 147
Plate Name: Yellow-poll Warbler - Plate XCV (v)
Current Name: Yellow Warbler

Blue Green Warbler - O.P. 233
Plate Name: Blue-green Warbler - Plate XLIX
Current Name: Cerulean Warbler

Blue Heron - O.P. 362
Plate Name: Blue Crane, or Heron -

Plate CCCVII (v)
Current Name: Little Blue Heron

Blue Jay - O.P. 70
Plate Name: Blue Jay - Plate CII
Current Name: Blue Jay

Blue Winged Teal - O.P. 353
Plate Name: Blue-Winged Teal - Plate CCCXIII
Current Name: Blue-winged Teal

Blue Yellow Back Wabler - O.P. 10
Plate Name: Blue Yellow-backed Warbler - Plate XV
Current Name: Northern Parula

Broad-winged Hawk - O.P. 259
Plate Name: Broad-winged Hawk - Plate XCI
Current Name: Broad-winged Hawk

Brown Albatros - O.P. 168
Plate Name: Dusky Albatros - Plate CCCCVII
Current Name: Light-mantled Albatross

Brown Creeper - O.P. 123
Plate Name: Brown Creeper - Plate CCCCXV
Current Name: Brown Creeper

Brown Pelican - O.P. 349
Plate Name: Brown Pelican - Plate CCLI
Current Name: Brown Pelican

Brown Song Sparrow - O.P. 293
Plate Name: Brown Song Sparrow - Plate CCCXC
Current Name: Song Sparrow

Buff breasted Sandpiper (and)
Buff breasted Sand-Piper - O.P. 172
Plate Name: Buff breasted Sandpiper - Plate CCLXV
Current Name: Buff-breasted Sandpiper

Californian Vulture - O.P. 295
Plate Name: Californian Vulture - Plate CCCCXXVI
Current Name: California Condor

Canada Flycatcher - O.P. 46
Plate Name: Canada Warbler - Plate CIII
Current Name: Canada Warbler

Canada Goose - O.P. 94
Plate Name: Canada Goose - Plate CCI
Current Name: Canada Goose

Cape May Warbler - O.P. 327

Plate Name: Cape May Warbler - Plate
CCCCXIV
Current Name: Cape May Warbler

Carbonated Warbler - O.P. 348
Plate Name: Carbonated Warbler - Plate
LX
Current Name: Carbonated Warbler

Carolina Parrot - O.P. 223
Plate Name: Carolina Parrot - Plate
XXVI
Current Name: Carolina Parakeet

Cedar Bird - O.P. 9
Plate Name: Cedar Bird - Plate XLIII
Current Name: Cedar Waxwing

Cerulean Warbler - O.P. 415
Plate Name: Azure Warbler - Plate
XLVIII (v)
Current Name: Cerulean Warbler

Chestnut-backed Titmouse - O.P. 73
Plate Name: Chestnut-backed Titmouse
- Plate CCCLIII
Current Name: Chestnut-backed
Chickadee

Chestnut collared Finch - O.P. 359
Plate Name: Chestnut-coloured Finch -
Plate CCCXCIV
Current Name: Chestnut-collared
Longspur

Chestnut crowned Titmouse - O.P. 73
Plate Name: Chestnut-crowned
Titmouse - Plate CCCLIII
Current Name: Bushtit

Chestnut-sided Warbler - O.P. 369
Plate Name: Chestnut-sided Warbler -
Plate LIX (v)
Current Name: Chestnut-sided Warbler

Chipping Sparrow - O.P. 430
Plate Name: Chipping Sparrow - Plate
CIV
Current Name: Chipping Sparrow

Chuck Wills widow - O.P. 196
Plate Name: Chuck-will's-Widow -
Plate LII (v)
Current Name: Chuck-will's-widow

Cinerous Petrel - O.P. 68
Plate Name: Wandering Shearwater -
Plate CCLXXXIII
Current Name: Greater Shearwater

Clark's Crow - O.P. 417
Plate Name: Clark's Crow - Plate

CCCLXII
Current Name: Clark's Nutcracker

Clay-coloured Bunting - O.P. 424
Plate Name: Clay-coloured Finch - Plate
CCCXCVIII
Current Name: Clay-colored Sparrow

Common Buzzard - O.P. 354
Plate Name: Common Buzzard - Plate
CCCLXXII
Current Name: Swainson's Hawk

Common Gallinule - O.P. 385
Plate Name: Common Gallinule - Plate
CCXLIV
Current Name: Common Moorhen

Common Tern - O.P. 56
Plate Name: Great Tern - Plate CCCIX
Current Name: Common Tern

Connecticut Warbler - O.P. 386
Plate Name: Connecticut Warbler -
Plate CXXXVIII
Current Name: Connecticut Warbler

Cow Bunting - O.P. 59
Plate Name: Cow-pen Bird - Plate XCIX
(v)
Current Name: Brown-headed Cowbird

Cowpen - O.P. 284
Plate Name: Cow pen bird - Plate
CCCCXXIV
Current Name: Brown-headed Cowbird

Crested Grebe - O.P. 137
Plate Name: Crested Grebe - Plate
CCXCII
Current Name: Great Crested Grebe

Crested Titmouse - O.P. 298
Plate Name: Crested Titmouse - Plate
XXXIX
Current Name: Tufted Titmouse

Curled-crested Auk - O.P. 112
Plate Name: Curled-Crested Auk - Plate
CCCCII
Current Name: Crested Auklet

Cuvier's Wren - O.P. 207
Plate Name: Cuvier's Regulus - Plate
LV
Current Name: Cuvier's Kinglet

Cypress Swamp Fly Catcher - O.P. 6
Plate Name: Bonaparte Fly Catcher -
Plate V (v)
Current Name: Canada Warbler

Current Name: Northern Flicker

Red-shouldered Hawk - O.P. 249
Plate Name: Red-shouldered Hawk - Plate LVI
Current Name: Red-shouldered Hawk

Red-winged Starling - O.P 324
Plate Name: Red winged Starling or Marsh Blackbird - Plate LXVII (v)
Current Name: Red-winged Blackbird

Republican Cliff Swallow - O.P. 133
Plate Name: Republican or Cliff Swallow - Plate LXVIII
Current Name: Cliff Swallow

Rice Bird - O.P. 373
Plate Name: Rice Bird - Rice Bunting - Plate LIV (v)
Current Name: Bobolink

Ring Plover - O.P. 71
Plate Name: Ring Plover - Plate CCCXXX
Current Name: Semipalmated Plover

Rocky Mountain Flycatcher - O.P. 302
Plate Name: Rocky Mountain Fly-catcher - Plate CCCCXXXIV
Current Name: Black Phoebe

Rocky Mountain Plover - O.P. 199
Plate Name: Rocky Mountain Plover - Plate CCCL
Current Name: Mountain Plover

Rough-legged Falcon - O.P. 88
Plate Name: Rough-legged Falcon - Plate CCCCXXII
Current Name: Rough-legged Hawk

Ruby throated Humming-bird - O.P. 237
Plate Name: Ruby-throated Humming Bird - Plate XLVII (v)
Current Name: Ruby-throated Hummingbird

Ruffed Grous - O.P. 227
Plate Name: Ruffed Grouse - Plate XLI
Current Name: Ruffed Grouse

Ruff-necked Hummingbird - O.P. 37
Plate Name: Ruff-necked Humming-bird - Plate CCCLXXIX
Current Name: Rufous Hummingbird

Savannah Finch - O.P. 246
Plate Name: Savannah Finch - Plate CIX
Current Name: Savannah Sparrow

Say's Flycatcher - O.P. 288

Plate Name: Say's Flycatcher - Plate CCCLIX
Current Name: Say's Phoebe

Scarlet Tanager - O.P. 370
Plate Name: Scarlet Tanager - Plate CCCLIV
Current Name: Scarlet Tanager

Scaup - O.P. 405
Plate Name: Scaup Duck - Plate CCXXIX
Current Name: Greater Scaup

Sea Eagle - O.P. 228
Plate Name: Bird of Washington - Plate XI (v)
Current Name: Bald Eagle

Sea Side Finch - O.P. 33
Plate Name: Sea-side Finch - Plate XCIII
Current Name: Seaside Sparrow

Sharp tailed Finch - O.P. 163
Plate Name: Sharp-tailed Finch - Plate CXLIX
Current Name: Sharp-tailed Sparrow

Short-legged Pewit Flycatcher - O.P. 302
Plate Name: Short legged Pewee - Plate CCCCXXXIV
Current Name: Western Wood-Pewee

Sitta pygmea - O.P. 123
Plate Name: Californian Nuthatch - Plate CCCCXV
Current Name: Pygmy Nuthatch

Slate-coloured Hawk - O.P. 277
Plate Name: Sharp-shinned Hawk - Plate CCCLXXIV
Current Name: Sharp-shinned Hawk

Small green crested Flycatcher - O.P. 408
Plate Name: Small Green Crested Flycatcher - Plate CXLIV
Current Name: Acadian Flycatcher

Solitary Flycatcher - O.P. 313
Plate Name: Solitary Flycatcher or Vireo - Plate XXVIII (v)
Current Name: Solitary Vireo

Song Sparrow - O.P. 256
Plate Name: Song Sparrow - Plate XXV
Current Name: Song Sparrow

Spotted Grosbeak - O.P. 220
Plate Name: Spotted Grosbeak - Plate CCCLXXIII
Current Name: Black-headed Grosbeak

Current Name: Whip-poor-will

White Crowned Bunting - O.P. 340
Plate Name: White-crowned Sparrow - Plate CXIV
Current Name: White-crowned Sparrow

White Eyed Flycatcher - O.P. 77
Plate Name: White eyed Flycatcher, or Vireo - Plate LXIII (v)
Current Name: White-eyed Vireo

White fronted Goose - O.P. 85
Plate Name: White-fronted Goose - Plate CCLXXXVI
Current Name: Greater White-fronted Goose

White-headed Eagle - O.P. 2
Plate Name: White headed Eagle - Plate XXXI (v)
Current Name: Bald Eagle

White-winged Silvery Gull - O.P. 12
Plate Name: White-winged silvery Gull - Plate CCLXXXII
Current Name: Iceland Gull

Wilson's Phalarope - O.P. 171
Plate Name: Wilson's Phalarope - Plate CCLVI
(mislabeled—should be CCLIV)
Current Name: Wilson's Phalarope

Winter Hawk - O.P. 42
Plate Name: Winter Hawk - Plate LXXI (v)
Current Name: Red-shouldered Hawk

Winter Wren - O.P. 328
Plate Name: Winter Wren - Plate CCCLX
Current Name: Winter Wren

Wood Pewee Flycatcher - O.P. 381
Plate Name: Wood Pewee - Plate CXV
Current Name: Eastern Wood-Pewee

Wood Thrush - O.P. 279
Plate Name: Wood Thrush - Plate LXXIII
Current Name: Wood Thrush

Yellow-billed Magpie - O.P. 417
Plate Name: Yellow billed Magpie - Plate CCCLXI
Current Name: Yellow-billed Magpie

Yellow-breasted Chat - O.P. 243
Plate Name: Yellow-breasted Chat - Plate CXXXVII
Current Name: Yellow-breasted Chat

Yellow-headed Troupial - O.P. 266
Plate Name: Yellow-headed Troopial - Plate CCCLXXXVIII
Current Name: Yellow-headed Blackbird

Yellow Red Poll Warbler - O.P. 368 and 332
Plate Name: Yellow Red-poll Warbler - Plate CXLV (368)
Yellow red poll Warbler - Plate CLXIII (332) (v)
Current Name: Palm Warbler

Yellow rump Warbler - O.P. 127
Plate Name: Yellow-Crown Warbler - Plate CLIII (v)
Current Name: Yellow-rumped Warbler

Yellow Throated Vireo - O.P. 83
Plate Name: Yellow-throated Vireo - Plate CXIX
Current Name: Yellow-throated Vireo

Yellow Throat Warbler - O.P. 14
Plate Name: Yellow Throated Warbler - Plate LXXXV
Current Name: Yellow-throated Warbler

Yellow Winged Sparrow - O.P. 273
Plate Name: Yellow-winged Sparrow - Plate CXXX
Current Name: Grasshopper Sparrow

BIBLIOGRAPHY

American Ornithologists Union. *Check-list of North American Birds.* 6th ed. Lawrence, Kans.: Allen Press, 1983.

Audubon, John James. *The Birds of America.* Engraved, Printed, and Coloured by R. Havell. 4 vols. London, 1827–1838.

———. *The Birds of America.* Introduction by William Vogt. New York: Macmillan Co., 1937. 500 illustrations in color.

———. *Ornithological Biography.* 5 vols. Edinburgh, 1838.

Baker, Cathleen Ann. *Audubon's Birds of America: A technical examination and condition survey of the four volume set belonging to Syracuse University.* Unpublished thesis, 1985.

Bannon, Lois Elmer, and Clark, Taylor. *Handbook of Audubon Prints.* Gretna, La.: Pelican Publishing, 1980.

Chamberlin, Walter. *Etching and Engraving.* New York: Viking Press, 1972.

Christie, Manson and Woods International. *John James Audubon, "The Birds of America."* Catalogue of the sale of plates from the Delaware Art Museum copy of *The Birds of America.* Christies, Houston; sale number 5172, October 15–16, 1982.

Ford, Alice. *John James Audubon.* Norman, Okla.: University of Oklahoma Press, 1964.

Fries, Waldemar H. *The Double Elephant Folio—The Story of Audubon's "Birds of America."* Chicago: American Library Association, 1973. Anyone researching *Birds of America* owes a deep debt of gratitude to Mr. Fries, who spent sixteen years travelling with Mrs. Fries in search of all manner of detailed information about the Double Elephant Folio.

Gruson, Edward S. *Words for Birds.* New York: Times Books, Quadrangle Books, 1972.

The Original Water-color Paintings by John James Audubon for "The Birds of America." Introduction by Marshall B. Davidson. New York: American Hertage Publishing Co., 1966. Reproduced in color from the collection at the New-York Historical Society.

Peterson, Roger Tory. *Birds East of the Rockies.* Boston: Houghton Mifflin Co., 1980.

———. *Western Birds.* Boston: Houghton Mifflin Co., 1961.

Robbins, Chandler, et al. *Birds of North America: A Guide to Field Identification.* Racine, Wis.: Western Publishing Co., Golden Press, 1983.

Sotheby Parke Bernet. *John James Audubon, "The Birds of America."* Catalogue of the sale of plates from the Sotheby Parke Bernet copy of *The Birds of America.* Sotheby's, New York; sale number 5054, June 16–17, 1983.

Trevelyan, Julian. *Etching.* New York: Watson-Guptill Publications, 1963.

Williams, Benjamin R. "Audubon's 'The Birds of America' and the Remarkable History of the Field Museum's Copy." *Field Museum of Natural History Bulletin* (June 1986): 7–21.

Acknowledgments

The author's debt of gratitude to Mrs. Mary LeCroy, Senior Scientific Assistant in the Department of Ornithology of the American Museum of Natural History, is inestimable. Her wise advice, guidance, editorial pencil, and generosity of time were unceasing from the conception of this work to its completion. Truly this work would not have been possible without her.

The author is grateful for the encouragement and support of Dr. Thomas D. Nicholson, Director of the American Museum of Natural History, and of Dr. Wesley E. Lanyon, the museum's Lamont Curator of Birds.

The Library of the American Museum of Natural History was most cooperative in making available their copy of *Birds of America.*

Miss Carole Ann Slatkin of the New-York Historical Society made the society's collection of Audubon's original paintings available and gave enthusiastic support for which the author is most appreciative.

Mr. J. G. Studholme, Chairman of Editions Alecto, Ltd., London, was most generous with his knowledge especially in the matter of Havell's technique and escorted the author through Edward Egerton-Williams's studio where prints were being pulled and colored from Havell's plates just as in Audubon's day.

Mr. Douglas Preston, also of Alecto, provided encouragement and crucial help through the years of writing, putting the author greatly in his debt.

Mr. Gerold Wunderlich of Wunderlich and Co. joined the author in a close inspection of variants of the first ten plates, where his expertise uncovered new information contrary to long-held beliefs. Mr. Rudolph Wunderlich gave good and welcome advice as the book got under way.

Mr. Benjamin W. Williams, Librarian for Special Collections of the Field Museum of Natural History, Chicago, generously gave permission to use the results of his scholarly research into the composite plates.

Mr. Gary Esposito proved himself a master of the computer. His sense of design, helpful suggestions, and willingness to do endless revisions were a great help and eased the author's path considerably.

Dr. Richard Zweiful, Curator in the Department of Herpetology in the American Museum of Natural History, supplied the information about the Timber Rattlesnake in Plate XXI. The staff of the Talbot County Free Library, Easton, Maryland, was ever ready with help. Professor Clare Romano of the Pratt Institute and Professor John Ross of the New School for Social Research supplied some of the technical knowledge necessary to understand how the copperplates were engraved and aquatinted. Helena Wright, Curator of the Division of

Graphic Arts, the National Museum of American History of the Smithsonian Institution, provided a letter from their archives describing the history of the copperplates after they were sent to the United States. Judy Blakely of the Old Print Gallery in Washington, D.C., added an interesting observation about the quality of the Whatman paper. Professor Cathleen Baker of the State University College at Buffalo, New York, kindly made her research into the Syracuse University copy of *Birds of America* available. Mr. and Mrs. William Loscomb expertly produced the final printout of the manuscript. Last, but most important, Mr. Walton Rawls, Senior Editor at Abbeville Press, together with his able staff patiently guided the author through the intricacies of getting the book ready for publication.

To all of them and to countless others who helped in so many ways, the author gives heartfelt thanks.